THE UNIVERSITY OF
WINCHESTER

Doing It Right ▶

The Best Criticism on Sam Peckinpah's
The Wild Bunch

Edited with an Introduction by
Michael Bliss

*Southern
Illinois
University
Press*

Carbondale
and
Edwardsville

Library of Congress Cataloging-in-Publication Data

Doing it right : the best criticism on Sam Peckinpah's
The Wild Bunch / edited with an introduction by
Michael Bliss.
p. cm.
Includes bibliographical references.
1. *Wild Bunch, The* (Motion picture). 2. Peckinpah,
Sam, 1925–1984—Criticism and interpretation.
I. Bliss, Michael, 1947–.
PN1997.W536133D6   1994
791.43'72—dc20   93-14502
ISBN 0-8093-1863-6   CIP

For Paul Seydor

What *Citizen Kane* was to movie lovers in 1941, *The Wild Bunch* was to cinéastes in 1969. Its adrenaline rush of revelations seemed to explode the parameters of the screen. The director and cowriter, Sam Peckinpah, turned the last stand of the Hole-in-the-Wall Gang into a wrenching piece of early-twentieth-century mythology. His filmmaking both evinced and catalyzed complex feelings about the outlaws' freedom, brotherhood, and professionalism, their manliness and childishness, and the way they experienced the closing of the West as Purgatory and used Latin America as an escape hatch. The movie remains the most extraordinary summation of Peckinpah's tender-torturous personality. He rips himself open and, against all odds, puts himself back together frame by bloody frame.

The actors include William Holden as Pike Bishop, the Bunch's leader; Robert Ryan as Deke Thornton, his ex-partner and reluctant nemesis; Ernest Borgnine as Dutch, Pike's right-hand gun; and Ben Johnson, Warren Oates, Edmond O'Brien, Strother Martin, Bo Hopkins, Jaime Sanchez, and Emilio Fernandez. The script, cowritten with Walon Green, puts the cast through tests of individual strength and loyalty that dramatize Peckinpah's preoccupations with the bandits' appetites and anarchy, and with the codes and social pressures that rein them in. These trials release the group energy of the most quirkily expressive ensemble ever assembled for an action movie. Holden's forceful, gnarly performance gains from the recent restoration of flashbacks that were cut from the original American-release prints. These scenes depict Pike as a man who screwed up in the past and is now determined to pull off his last job—and "do it right." Peckinpah did it right in *The Wild Bunch*; he produced an American movie that equals or surpasses the best of Kurosawa. *The Wild Bunch* is the Götterdämmerung of Westerns.

—Michael Sragow, *The New Yorker*, 19 August 1991

Contents

CONTENTS

PART 3. *Epilogue*

Illustrations

Acknowledgments

What is remarkable about the scholarship on *The Wild Bunch* is how little of it there is. Although there are many reviews of the film, insightful critical writing, especially writing that runs longer than a page or two, is relatively scarce. In this respect, at least, the editor's job is easy. The difficulty enters in when you try to secure the rights to articles. I must confess that if the proper credit for securing rights were given, much of it would go to Paul Seydor, who afforded me direct access to such commentators on the film as Paul Schrader, Michael Sragow, Aljean Harmetz, and Robert Culp.

Yet I would be remiss if I didn't also point out the astounding generosity of the writers represented in this volume, most of whom gave me permission to reprint their articles without regard for remuneration. As Robert Culp put it when I spoke to him about including his wonderful piece on the film, "Just reprint it accurately." I have followed this credo with regard to all of the articles in this book.

My usual feeling is that an editor's inclusion of his own writing in a casebook is unjustifiable. I have done so in this book only because this extract from a chapter of my recently published book *Justified Lives: Morality and Narrative in the Films of Sam Peckinpah* draws attention to fine elements in Peckinpah's narrative technique in *The Wild Bunch* that are not fully discussed by the other writers represented here.

My thanks to Southern Illinois University Press's James Simmons, who encouraged me in this project; to Christina Banks, who rescued me by helping me edit the manuscript; to Jeff Slater, who provided some wonderful stills for the book; and to the community of Peckinpah scholars who, united in their love and admiration for Peckinpah's greatest film, helped to make this book a reality.

Introduction

Both praised and condemned, *The Wild Bunch* incites agreement on at least one point: it is one of the most influential motion pictures ever made. Directed and cowritten by Sam Peckinpah after his four-year forced hiatus due to having been blacklisted, the film is the director's masterpiece. Nowhere else in Peckinpah's work does there exist such a powerful and effective meeting of form and content, stylistics and theme, casting and character. When he finished editing the film, Peckinpah pronounced himself 94 to 96 percent satisfied with the results;[1] for those of us who have been studying and admiring the film ever since, the degree of satisfaction is even higher.

Initially, one should realize that, predominantly, *The Wild Bunch* is a love story. The film expresses a love for the Old West (which was virtually dead at the time period during which *The Wild Bunch* takes place), a love for the camaraderie of men on a shared mission. But above all, love is embodied in the respect—ironically sullied by alienation and regret—between two men, Pike and Thornton, the film's principals. These former friends find themselves in the classic antipathetic psychological situation to which Peckinpah was firmly devoted throughout his feature film career. Every Peckinpah film, from *The Deadly Companions*, his first feature, through *The Osterman Weekend*, his last, showcases a pair of characters, usually men, whose redemption is dependent upon one another (an ironic situation given the alienation between these individuals) and who are, sometimes reluctantly, placed in alarming proximity. In *The Wild Bunch*, this melancholy paradigm assumes tragic proportions, since Pike is aware that his abandonment of Thornton years before set in motion the chain of events that now causes his best friend to pursue him. In essence, Pike is really being pursued by his own guilty conscience in the person of Thornton.

Another antecedent for the film's story of paired individuals can be found in the literary theme of the doppelgänger, which goes back at least as far as Samuel Taylor Coleridge's "The Rime of the Ancient Mariner" and continues through Edgar Allan Poe's "William Wilson," Fyodor Dostoyevsky's *The Double*, and the writings of Jorge Luis Borges, with each new work developing an analogue for classic neurotic anxiety by deepening the psychological poignancy underlying the romantic notion that one personality may be represented as two. In the films of Sam Peckinpah, we see the pathology of anxiety reach new levels of sophistication. Peckinpah's characters, especially those in *The Wild Bunch*, are caught in a nether realm; like the classic Western hero, they're men who know that they've either already lived beyond their time or are about to see the decay of a time when their values really meant something. The Bunch's desperate, often wrongheaded attempts to do the right thing, to stick together, form the basis for one of the richest psychological tapestries ever put on film.

In *The Wild Bunch*, Peckinpah appropriates this schema of anxiety and points us toward a cure through a resolution of his film's contrarieties, but not without first taking us on a journey through various hells: the battlefield of Starbuck; the compromised deal with Mapache; and the final bloodbath of Agua Verde (the latter a purgative hell, though, since it is in the service of a moral ideal: Angel's reclamation). All of these events make it clear that what the film ultimately suggests is a schema of religious redemption. A feeling of melancholy only emerges when we realize that the Bunch come to understand almost too late—just before they return to reclaim Angel—what they could have done with their lives had they been a bit more ethical, a little more thoughtful.

Yet *The Wild Bunch*'s conclusion doesn't leave us without a proposed cure. After the Agua Verde massacre, when Thornton picks up that talismanic object, Pike's gun, we know from classical tales of redemption that an important resolution of conflicting desires will take place and that a new tradition will emerge. When Thornton subsequently joins Pike's successor (and one of the old Bunch), Sykes, and the revolutionary Mexicans to form a new Bunch, we see what Peckinpah intends for us to understand: that moral and political progress have finally been united; that indeed, if they are to be effective at all, the two realms must be inseparable.

Peckinpah repeatedly demonstrates through his films how much of an idealist and sentimentalist he really is. Witness *The Wild Bunch*'s ending, which never fails to make us feel that we have risen above the world's pettiness and passed into a realm in which there is joy and hope and, above all, forgiveness. The emotional milieu in which we experience these feelings cannot be called anything other than religious—and a religious feeling is evoked every time you see the film. *The Wild Bunch's* finale isn't just the film's high point; it's the high point in Peckinpah's career, the one time that he achieved a supremely total union of thematic intention and expression.

Two of the film's most striking characteristics are its plethora of conceptual doublings (two friends alienated from each other, two collections of associates, two major shootouts, two robberies, two debates about what to do about Angel) and its circular structure (the film begins and ends with a massacre). The doublings are analogues of the Pike/Thornton story, while the circular structure reminds us that no matter what we do or how far we roam, we must always return to a confrontation with the need to establish a set of values to live by. These strategies lead to questions about identity, especially the necessity of recognizing who one is and remaining true to one's self. Sören Kierkegaard says in *The Sickness Unto Death*, "To have a self, to be a self, is the greatest concession made to man, but at the same time it is eternity's demand upon him."[2] In *The Wild Bunch*, the universe demands that Pike and the Bunch ultimately act with integrity. Flawed though these men be, they finally, triumphantly, meet this demand at the film's end.

While it is not necessary here to discuss the evolution and history of the Western in American films, we should have some general idea of how *The Wild Bunch* fits into this genre. I believe it is sufficient if we understand that the most important attribute of the Western that *The Wild Bunch* appropriates is the need for a set of values by which one lives. As Jack Nachbar points out, the classic Western hero "is civilized in that usually his life is patterned after a gentlemanly code."[3] Even a "dirty Western" (the term is Richard Schickel's)[4] like *The Wild Bunch* seems to have remained true to this requirement. Nachbar asserts that "underneath their natural brutality . . . the members of the [Wild] Bunch have their own strong code of honor based on personal loyalty."[5] The Bunch's code has less to do with acting morally in relation to people outside the group than it does with simply remaining true to one's associates, at least those who are either still alive or capable of continuing to perform (thus the interesting bit of dialogue when Dutch makes it plain that sentimentality about the dead, even a dead group member, is a waste of time, although it's interesting that Dutch reacts with glee when the Bunch decide to return to the center of Agua Verde for Angel, who is nearly dead). Yet this aspect in no way diminishes the code's value: "We're gonna stick together, just like it used to be," says Pike. Unwittingly and ultimately, the Bunch find their redemption in precisely this way.

But *The Wild Bunch* is more than just an action/pursuit drama or a redemption story; these aspects are merely the frame on which Peckinpah hangs his theme about the nature of commitment, the effects of memory and regret, and the nagging desire to act in an ethical way. What makes this last desire all the more difficult to achieve is that the Bunch have to operate in a postlapsarian universe. Surely the film's interlude in Angel's village, the only time during *The Wild Bunch* in which the Bunch enter into the Shakespearean green world of placidity, fertility, and realized desires, quite obviously represents a return to the Garden of Eden. Yet this is a garden that has been severely compromised, one in which Satan, in the form of Mapache and the other soldiers working for Huerta, has raped and pillaged the pastoral village. Indeed, in the midst of the festival in the village, the Bunch's main innocent, Angel, who represents that state of moral and political commitment that the Bunch have been unable to either accept or achieve, learns that his idealized woman, Teresa (whom he revered as "a goddess," chaste and untouchable), has run off with Mapache.

Peckinpah continues to shuttle us back and forth between corruption and innocence in this scene, showing us the corrupt Gorches innocently playing cat's cradle with a young woman while making sure that the game, with its piece of string moving through a gap, suggests sexuality; having Angel cry out Mapache's name in the midst of the diverting revelry. Ironically, it is in Angel's village that the Bunch decide to visit Mapache in Agua Verde (ostensibly to sell their extra horses, although the Bunch's reasoning on this issue has always struck me as a bit weak). Yet despite what turns out to be a bad decision, resulting in the Bunch robbing a munitions train and then losing Angel to Mapache, there nonetheless seems to be a divine plan at work: had the Bunch never gone to Agua Verde, they never would have lost Angel and then, through that happy fault, would never have redeemed themselves by going back to retrieve Angel and, in decimating Agua Verde, inadvertently pushing the revolutionary dialectic forward. Ironically, the actions of these bad men work to the common good.

Since much commentary on the film has focused on its violence, it might be profitable to look at one of its most notable examples, the Starbuck massacre at the beginning of the film, to see just how the scene works and what Peckinpah appears to be trying to accomplish in it. I believe we'll see that there is a morality operating within this representative sequence which counteracts the charges of self-indulgence and nihilism leveled against the film in general and Peckinpah in particular.[6]

The Starbuck massacre is without doubt one of the most brilliantly constructed, and violent, set pieces in motion pictures. By my count, there are 191 shots from the time that the railroad company clerk is pushed out of the building until Thornton tells his group to quit firing because the Bunch have "cleared out"; these shots take up three minutes and forty-five seconds of screen time. This count includes the passages within the shootout during which Crazy Lee is talking to the three people whom he is holding hostage, sequences that provide necessary breathing space in the midst of extremely chaotic action.

Despite the massacre's accelerated pace, Peckinpah wasn't aiming solely for a sense of speeded-up action in this scene; he also wanted to communicate the feeling of confusion being experienced by the three groups involved in the shootout: the two rival gangs and the bystanders caught in the middle of the action, whose point of view is the one that predominates. The film's use of this vantage point does more than highlight the massacre's chaotic nature: it also makes it plain that despite Harrigan's reference to the town of Starbuck (and, by implication, its inhabitants) as "manure," Peckinpah wanted to show how terrible violence can be, especially from the perspective of innocent people caught in the middle of it.

While one remembers the Starbuck massacre for its large number of shootings and dead, what is most striking about the scene is the manner in which Peckinpah breaks up individual pieces of action. A man's fall off the roof where Thornton's men are positioned is fragmented into three separate shots. The sequence involving a Bunch member who is shot off his horse and lands in a dressmaker's store window is broken into four different shots. With Peckinpah cutting back and forth from these actions to others, this technique does more than simply communicate a simultaneity of events; it also gives us a chance to ponder what the slow-motion photography suggests to us: that the manner in which abrupt or violent actions arc across time in the film is an approximation of the way that, when we are caught in the midst of striking events, these events seem to be taking place in slow motion. The fact that the massacre's slow-motion shots also unlock the balletic grace in violence (I'm thinking in particular of the shot in which a Starbuck resident is wounded three times and falls back, his leg at a right angle to his body, then lands softly, almost gracefully, bounding up slightly off the street before coming to rest) only adds a further critical dimension (and an additional moral dilemma, since the violent images are so attractive) to the scene. The editing and slow-motion techniques create in us a bifurcated reaction that is characteristic of Peckinpah's work. Simultaneously, the violence aesthetically entrances and intellectually repels us. This contradictory response is so striking that Peckinpah could not have been unaware of it; the director was very possibly enthralled by the beauty in violence that was unlocked by his filmmaking technique at the same time that he wanted to produce a film that stressed ethics. The fact that Peckinpah doesn't seem to be troubled by this contradiction (there's no evidence in *The Wild Bunch* that any character sees violence as wrong) suggests that he recognizes that the conflict between violence and morality is incapable of being resolved, and that, ideally, what we must do is to unquestioningly accept them both as part of a continuum of experience. As in *The Ballad of Cable Hogue* and so many of his other films, Peckinpah implies in *The Wild Bunch* that horror and beauty coexist—almost suggesting, as in *Bring Me the Head of Alfredo Garcia*, that the two realms are virtually equal.

The Wild Bunch expresses both Peckinpah's despair regarding human beings' bestial nature and ability to enjoy violence (present in the forms of the cruelties perpetrated by Mapache) and his hope that people's higher nature, their moral sensibility, may somehow prevail. The slippage between the two realms forms the basis for the tragic poetry of Peckinpah's best films (Steve Judd's death at the end of *Ride the High Country* comes to mind here). Peckinpah doesn't flinch from depicting brutality, nor does he romanticize it, as some critics have implicitly claimed.[7] Indeed, these critics could only have missed Peckinpah's critique of violence by ignoring the moral context involving responsibility within which Peckinpah situates his film's excessive actions. *The Wild Bunch* isn't predominantly about death and killing; it's about life and love, about loyalty, about the sadness devolving from having made bad choices in one's life and the potential for happiness accruing from the good choices that one can always still make. Just think about the way that the Bunch reclaim Angel three times, each time placing their own safety in peril. These aren't the actions of selfish individuals, and while the killings may be the actions of misguided men, they are not the actions of bad men. The Bunch are outlaws looking for a law they can respect and live by; in the end, thanks to the act of grace that Peckinpah perpetrates at the film's conclusion in having the

Bunch return for Angel, they find such a law, thereby attaining their reward.

The film's moral sensibility encourages us to respond on an unconscious level to the fact that the Bunch is made up of three generations of men: Sykes, Pike, and Dutch as the elders; the Gorches as the mid-adult generation; and Angel as the child/idealist. This generational aspect suggests the classic trope of wisdom being passed on to a youthful member who represents an altruistic morality (albeit here somewhat bruised) that the group's older members have apparently foregone. At the end of the film, Peckinpah closes the generational circle by uniting the spirit of the Bunch's youngest member, Angel, with that of its eldest, Sykes, by having Sykes join the Mexican revolutionaries. In so doing, Peckinpah shows us how idealistic his vision really is, for what do we have here but the spirit of revolution rising out of what only seems to have been pointless violence?

The Wild Bunch affects us so strongly because we see ourselves in it. All of Peckinpah's films have universal elements: the sense of a great, lost epoch (*Ride the High Country*); the need to fight against the incursions of time (*Junior Bonner*); the heavy sense of foreboding and regret that comes with old age (*Pat Garrett and Billy the Kid*). But no Peckinpah film is simultaneously as lighthearted and solemn as *The Wild Bunch*. Perhaps a great deal of the film's impact has to do with the fact that we've all made mistakes and we'd all like to be able to start over. The film's schema, then, is universal, touching the most basic elements in existence. How, the film asks, does one earn forgiveness? Peckinpah suggests that one does it by remaining true to one's friends, which is the same thing as remaining true to one's self. The payoff is resurrection accompanied by laughter, surely as joyous an apotheosis as one could possibly wish for.

The Wild Bunch didn't immediately achieve a critical prominence of place. Many reviewers condemned the film outright; some filmgoers walked out on the film's violent sequences or strongly protested against them, thereby overlooking the fact that *The Wild Bunch* was just as unabashedly shameless in its depiction of more tender moments, as when Angel plays guitar and sings in the adobe or, during the fiesta, when Sykes playfully cuts in on Dutch's dancing. Throughout the film, Peckinpah seems powerfully dependent on our indulgent understanding; he wants us to be shocked by the film's violence, engaged by its humor, entertained by its action sequences, and touched by its deep emotions. In other words, he wants us to respond, in the words of Don José, as though we were "child[ren] again," with laughter and tears, pleasure and terror.

The film is also manifestly fair in dealing with its protagonists. *The Wild Bunch* does for the Bunch what Cable Hogue wanted Josh to do for him in his funeral peroration. To appropriate Cable's words about what he wants in his eulogy, it neither "make[s] [them] out saint[s]" nor "put[s] [them] down too deep." In other words, the film deals justly with Pike and his associates; it's honest but merciful. By the film's end, we miss the Bunch. Judging by their strong reactions to the film, a large number of critics miss them too. When Peckinpah's camera magically rises over the walls of Agua Verde at the film's conclusion and Pike's Bunch reappears, superimposed over what is now the new Bunch, we know that the old Bunch's final dawning realization of devotion reigns over this new group—and we, too, in spite of all the horrors we've seen, feel uplifted, deliriously so, in a wild achievement of paradox resolved.

I have attempted in this casebook to gather together a sampling of essays that represents a range of critical responses as varied as the emotional reactions that the film itself calls forth. Robert Culp's piece establishes the mythological links between Peckinpah's film and classic trends in storytelling. Paul Schrader highlights the director's attitude toward that special Peckinpah region, Mexico. Stephen Farber not only catalogs many of *The Wild Bunch*'s important features but also provides us with Peckinpah's comments on the film. The first of Paul Seydor's essays definitively charts the textual transmission aspects of *The Wild Bunch*'s versions, while his second examines the film's epic qualities. Jim Kitses at once distills and expands on much of what makes *The Wild Bunch* so appealing, while Cordell Strug brings up questions of the film's morality, which is a large part of its appeal.

John Simons balances the masculine-oriented approach of much of *Wild Bunch* scholarship with a demonstration of how the film brings out the feminine point of view. Leavening the book are my piece on the film, which highlights the virtually wordless aspect of its conclusion, and Aljean Harmetz's touching portrait of Peckinpah. Together, these selections represent *Wild Bunch* criticism at its best, at once incisive and appreciative, critical and sincere.

The essays in this book all tend to perform the same miracle: to bring *The Wild Bunch* back to us in almost as vibrant a form as the actual film itself. In tranquility, we recollect *The Wild Bunch* and celebrate it, faults and all. I've ended the book with a somewhat different kind of celebration: Michael Sragow's eulogistic piece on

Sam Peckinpah, with the hope that the reader will come away from it with the feeling that now, ten years after his death, Peckinpah too—along with Pike and the rest of the Bunch—deserves to be counted among the immortals.

Notes

1. Richard Whitehall, "Talking with Peckinpah," *Sight and Sound* 38, no. 4 (Autumn 1969), p. 175.

2. Sören Kierkegaard, *The Sickness Unto Death*, in *"Fear and Trembling" and "The Sickness Unto Death,"* trans. Walter Lowrie (New York: Doubleday, 1954), p. 154.

3. Jack Nachbar, "Riding Shotgun: The Scattered Formula in Contemporary Western Movies," in *Focus on the Western*, ed. Jack Nachbar (Englewood Cliffs, N.J.: Prentice-Hall, 1974), p. 102.

4. Richard Schickel, "Mastery of the 'Dirty Western,'" in *Film 69/70: An Anthology by the National Society of Film Critics*, ed. Joseph Morgenstern and Stefan Kanfer (New York: Simon and Schuster, 1970), p. 150.

5. Nachbar, p. 106.

6. See, for example, Judith Crist, review of *The Wild Bunch*, *New York Magazine*, 30 June 1969, p. 43; and 14 July 1969, p. 57; Arthur Knight, review of *The Wild Bunch*, *Saturday Review*, 5 July 1969, p. 21; Joseph Morgenstern, review of *The Wild Bunch*, *Newsweek*, 14 July 1969, p. 85.

7. See Crist, Knight, and Morgenstern.

PART 1

Prologue

1 ▶

Sam Peckinpah, the Storyteller and *The Wild Bunch:* An Appreciation

ROBERT CULP

The world's oldest profession is not Whoring. It is storytelling. Of course, there's a certain amount of overlapping . . . or so it has always seemed to the Storytellers.

My first twenty years in the Theatre I was always vaguely ashamed of my profession. It seemed all narcissism. Vanity of vanities, rendered quite literally. Then someone told me a story about Lionel Barrymore. Near the end of his life, he was wrathfully explaining to some young and foolish actors that theirs was a profession antedating any other, *an answer to man's first communal need; to understand about killing, the nature of it.* Which then leads to the only conundrum, death itself. All the recent speculative blockbusters in Anthropology and Zoology regarding instinctual behavior versus learned ritual would seem to bear out Mr. Barrymore.

No moment in an actor's lifetime ever again will equal his first entrance onto the stage. It is a splendid and terrible happening, outweighing first love and last, and the younger the actor the more indelible the moment. I had just turned fourteen. The next morning there were no more of those awful questions: I had become a Storyteller, though I did not know it yet.

Looking back from here, there can't be any doubt that it was a moment possessed of the magic without which we would all wither, atrophy in numbed withdrawal.

Thank God and Eve and The Divine Serpent for our magic. The Eve whom we all love best, and look for all our lives, listened to the

"Sam Peckinpah, the Storyteller and *The Wild Bunch:* An Appreciation" by Robert Culp originally appeared in *Entertainment World* 2, no. 2 (January 1970): pp. 8–12. Reprinted by permission of Robert Culp.

first story and believed it: she bit the apple and learned about herself. She listened to the first Storyteller and learned about death. It was the only thing she and Adam didn't know. It wasn't sex at all, of course; it was death the Serpent talked of. That's what the idea of sin is: a child's primer on death. And like most child's primers, it is not simply foolish nonsense. The idea that the wages of sin is death is such a patent truism that it becomes dangerously untrue, misleading for children's minds. The implosion of which un-truism we are just now approaching for the first time.

When Eve took the apple it was the first moment of magic; the Storyteller gives us magic tricks that transform literally and before our eyes one thing into another, unexplained and unexplainable.

That is what Storytelling is about: tricks; having to do with death.

For a moment in the day the Theatre tries to do what the Church promises to do over a lifetime of training: to take away fear (hence anger, anguish) by linking us to death in great intimacy and then explaining it away self-righteously (Melodrama) . . . by making love to death (Tragedy) . . . or by scoffing at death (Comedy). Each of these forms suggests that if you have the will, the courage to believe in it, in man, in yourself, you are superior to/in control of all things, even death. That's what Storytelling was invented to do for us.

By the time I was twenty-one and very wise now in the ways of the Theatre, with many plays and much applause behind me as a writer and an actor, the magic part of it was pretty much gone. It had become difficult to believe. Tragedy, for example, could no longer be written, could not be played except by children in college; a quaint antique form, casualty of Grape-Nuts and IBM. Nobody proved me wrong.

At thirty-eight, after two marriages and stumbling through a third, with a blurred professional life of savage effort and little reward except money, only the old, stoic commitments to craft and children still untarnished, and, finally having lived through the year of the locust, 1968, in the United States of America . . . I wanted out. Out of my responsibilities, out of my physically and spiritually betrayed, utterly mindless country, out of my silly, truncated profession (where, finally now, even comedy is no longer relevant), where everyone I grew up with in the Theatre and in Film is fixed, slack-jawed in endless repetition of patterns that have lost their individual lives, have lost the magic ability to rise Phoenix-like: all of my beautiful America is in the hands of used car salesmen on television . . . .

Sam Peckinpah, the Storyteller and *The Wild Bunch*

(. . . In our beautiful America, where we are now in our hand-wrought chains, one after another gleefully forged for profit, the screaming prisoners of man's noblest communal experiment, in such a short time by the mind made mindless, unbearably ugly, all our blazing beauty ravaged, bottled and canned on the counter for sale; all our brave feats and visions like our Great Grandmothers' buffalo-hair pillows for sale; going, going, gone), and then a man named Sam Peckinpah told his story, called *The Wild Bunch.*

Great and ruthless artists change the world, make it more habitable. They cannot directly change the life of nations anymore. The images we perceive are all superseded too quickly now. In the case of *The Wild Bunch* that is a very lucky break; if this film were to be considered more than just another remarkably good flick on the periphery of our vision, we would all be driven quite mad with its anguish. Among other things it says the only good American is a dead American (". . . the Americans who are now all lost and gone were much better than we are, and what we have lost in them we will never get back"). All of which we have long suspected. In 1968 we proved it.

Mr. Peckinpah, like Malraux, is very deeply into Ecclesiastes (". . . Vanity of vanities, saith the preacher, all is vanity. And a striving after wind").

In *The Wild Bunch* the story he uses is so simple that it doesn't matter whether it hangs together or separately. It can be told without any words (and has been). It is almost the only story there is about men as a group that always works. On four occasions that I can think of it was called, in English, something with *Magnificent Seven* in the title. The Mirisch Company has made it into a sort of conglomerate unto itself. It's a serviceable story. I wrote it several times for "I Spy." Everybody does.

I read the screenplay of *The Wild Bunch* on a gray, empty morning two years ago in Peckinpah's house on the beach above Malibu. I groaned with each foolish page, to think he had to go and do this nonsense for all those bleak months in Mexico.

And sure enough, he went. With the script I read. While all the rest of us passionately dedicated people were at work in Chicago and New York and Washington and Resurrection City, putting the country back in shape, back on its feet intellectually and spiritually, this cop-out artist was down in Mexico, didn't know who was getting killed at home, didn't want to hear about it because he was doing his dumb Western Flick.

Nineteen sixty-nine rolls around and the rest of us, the dedicated intellectuals, having put the nation back on its feet and Mr. Nixon into office, are now staring dully at the walls, turning slowly again to work on our endless string of identical paper dolls, as Mr. Peckinpah quietly finishes his Western Flick that he's made and an utterly bewildered Warner Bros. Sales Department releases it.

Rather than making fools of us all he has touched us firmly with the touch that heals, the one that gives faith, strength to go on. We didn't kill all the divine madmen in '68. One was hiding in Mexico, just working.

Mr. Peckinpah has created a tragedy and put it up on the screen, which is perhaps as important in its way, in its very rude, empirical way as any single work by Sophocles. And the odds were greater against its being created. Of course the comparison is odious; it is apples and oranges. But as a spiritual point of departure (for that's just what *The Wild Bunch* is), it is terribly important for us to know that the creation of an artificial (Theatrical) Tragic Event is still possible. They don't all have to be on the six o'clock news.

All of us who worry about such things have presumed for a very long time now that there was no new metaphor in which to couch enough believability to permit the mounting of a tragedy. Mr. Peckinpah is possessed of an extremely devious instinct, however. He has taken the oldest form of pure cinematic Storytelling (The Great Train Robbery, i.e., the Western) and injected into it the men he knows and the women he loves (all of whom we have forgotten), and couched the whole in the only absolutely relevant, unmined metaphor, genuine anger. And genuine (as opposed to "realistic") anger as a tool in the hands of Mr. Peckinpah mounts very swiftly into a towering rage of passion, which, in turn, is the only emotional state in which the elements of Tragedy can penetrate an audience in a theatre. It is a state so long missing in the Theatre as to be presently almost unrecognizable. Which has been at the heart of the confused state enveloping the film's critics. What is even more annoying, Mr. Peckinpah is wise enough to know he must make us come to him, those that are capable: the material seems *too* lean, *too* oblique (even for film), deliberately mysterious, careless or clumsy. But that is the nature of Mr. Peckinpah's new "behavioral Tragedy" and why he is its only master. Behavior is behavior; you cannot explain it or you don't mean it. That is called lying. It is also called Melodrama.

Using the shorthand of behavior, Mr. Peckinpah has made a film only about the hardest honesty: life is bitter and cruel and very hard to get through, and men and women, the best of them, are endlessly foolish. And the absolutely imperative need to be Right is nearly always rendered corrupt. Maybe *once* it redeems, but you will have to be ready to die for it. And practically nobody is. Except the Wild Bunch.

As the odds against them steadily mount, their implacable enemies are everywhere before them. Each maneuver becomes an appointment in Samara: Pike Bishop (William Holden) says it low and clear, "I wouldn't have it any other way." With equally grim, simplistic purity, Dutch (Ernest Borgnine) echoes him later, "I wouldn't have it any other way either": a banal exchange between witless, simple men . . . but *that* is the gesture of will that is man's only salvation when faced finally with himself.

The Wild Bunch is about the discovery by these witless, limited men (which means all of us) of the difference between Right and Wrong, in this case by a process of elimination: if year after year for a lifetime you do everything wrong, you will wind up having done it all wrong, and nothing can change it. Since there is nothing else to do wrong, and something must be done, ergo you will finally do something Right . . . almost by accident. And it will cost you everything. This is exactly what happens to the Wild Bunch: it is called the human condition, and it is a definition of the terrible path toward tragedy. Mr. Peckinpah, to clarify further, states unequivocally that Good and Bad (resulting in any moralistic judgments, as in Melodrama) have absolutely nothing to do with it. Good and Bad are easy concepts for children and women, says Mr. Peckinpah; Right and Wrong are awfully damned hard to tell apart . . . and between them, after a given point of no return, grown men *may not vacillate*.

Near the end, after it has all gone wrong, Bishop (Holden) is putting on his shirt in the dark adobe room, sitting on the bed. He looks again and again from the unbearably young whore-camp-follower at the washbasin to the tiny baby wrapped in filthy rags on the dirt floor in the corner of the room. He begins to get terribly angry, and we, if we watch carefully, understand the silent, stoic question in the young whore's eyes ("I don't understand; how did I fail you?"). Bishop picks up a whiskey bottle, drains the last few precious drops . . . and just at the instant the bottle is empty, just then and with blinding clarity his life is over . . . forever. My God, what a terrible moment! All four of them that are left of the old Bunch, all of their lives are forever ended in that instant: they have it all now, the gold, the stake to go on with, but it's no good because they let the kid down. They let their partner, the boy, Angel (Jaime Fernandez), take the fall alone for being Right and made no move to stop it, since they were outnumbered hopelessly by an entire army. Bishop stares at the whiskey bottle. He shakes it. It doesn't come any clearer. It doesn't get any better. It's all over. (They might as well do one thing right.) He goes to the doorway to the next room where the Gorch brothers (Warren Oates and Ben Johnson) interrupt their mean, bitter little argument over payment to another (naked, weeping) whore to stare at Bishop. Finally, in one of surely the great moments of all time on film, Bishop says, flat as a mashed snake, "Let's go." The brothers, Lyle and Tector, look at each other and instantly make Bishop's discovery in themselves. And the moment holds: The Bunch is together again for one last go-round. The whole book of Peckinpah's Ecclesiastes burns in Lyle's (Warren Oates's) eyes as he turns back to Bishop and croaks, "Why not!?" No more words are necessary, just those. And it begins to open for us then, the tragic feeling, the knowledge and hating it of what they are about to do. They are going to hopeless war against a whole army, just literally throwing their lives away, not to do something noble or selfless as in the case of *The Seven Samurai* (though they *do* "save the village" by decimating General Mapache's army, it is completely an irrelevant side issue), but to pay off a mistake, to obliterate their error as Oedipus obliterated his vision . . . ("It's not your word that counts, it's who you give it to," yells Dutch at Bishop earlier) . . . and because that was the price of it anyway. That was always the price of it.

In the midst of all this (several minutes of running time) a woman near me in the dark kept saying, "Now, what's that supposed to mean? This is the silliest trash I've ever seen. They must be crazy." And she was right. She paid for a ticket, so she's right.

All of the divine madmen (Buddha, Christ, Gandhi) have known that to be right and to say so is a very expensive proposition. But we learn from *The Wild Bunch* that being wrong costs more, costs everything. And ends up the same.

That is all we know about The Bunch and all we need to know: just their *collective* behavior, just that. In 1969 it is supremely valuable to see once more in our fiction men who are only men make a decision (neither Good nor Bad . . . simply a *Right* decision, balanced on a hair)—and back it with their lives.

Finally, in the least creature on this earth, only the quality of his behavior is important to survival, to establish intrinsic value. That's all there is. The rest is literally only talk. And talk is a trick of the mind, not very reliable: The Bunch spits in death's eye (for us), embraces the final knowledge of every man (for us), that he must at the end go down alone and must do it well. They don't talk about it, they just do it. For us. The passionate rage that forces the issue is stone-real and this work's touchstone of genius. It is Peckinpah, his special, secret metaphor, and the reason why *The Wild Bunch* is so terribly alone as a work of stunning art and commitment. No other motion picture in history stands beside it at this level. All that Sartre and Camus have done from their massive, agonized intelligence, Peckinpah attempts empirically from his guts. He makes hard, unyielding, unequivocal, utterly committed love to Death herself on her own ground. He does it not through choice. And of course he will not get away with it.

The Wild Bunch is more quintessentially and bitterly American than any film since World War II. Before that there are only *Citizen Kane*, two or three by John Ford and a couple by Frank Capra.

The similarities in character between Peckinpah and Ford are not exactly lost on those who know of them. He *is* Ford, come again just as mean, a little more mad, a little angrier, a little more vulnerable, perhaps a little more valuable to the people around him now, since he is absolutely the last of the breed. With him the line runs out. He is not the technical master of the form that Ford was, but his vision is greater and he is bolder, infinitely more reckless and self-destructive, and as a consequence very precious since he will be with us only a short time. And the body of his work will be smaller. It is very difficult for him to, in his incessant phrase, "just get it on!" It costs him more to get the job done than any of the rest of us, and there's only so much currency, only so many feet and inches of entrail. Mr. Peckinpah is all alone just like the rest of us. Except that he knows it. He knows how terribly cold it is out there and he cannot come in. But he sends messages.

Truly Mr. Peckinpah has done the flatly impossible. He has made a genuinely passionate film, the first one ever made. The first Passion Film. Passion is real. Because it is also frightening we have attempted to deny it progressively in the twentieth century. But it will not be denied: it has come home to us every year with mounting lunacy. In Film, thus far, from Griffith to De Mille to Kubrick, acts of aggression, war, etc., have lacked reality because they have lacked *personalized* anger, which is quite necessary (even in symbolic amounts) before man or any other animal can kill with deliberate purpose.

When I first saw *The Wild Bunch* the screening room was filled to bursting with young film students in L.A. who had all heard of Peckinpah and were eagerly awaiting his film. They were fascinated; there was a little squirming, a couple of feminine moans of protest, some were perhaps horrified. These are children of considerable sensibility, if nothing else. At the end the applause was loud, respectful and devoid of emotion. Alas, in screening rooms one comes as an individual, to test oneself against the material. We are not there just to enjoy it, which is the way it works out.

I wondered about these children. I wondered if any of it were true, the idea that fictional violence begets real violence. I wondered about madness.

A month later in New York I saw the film again, this time in a theatre. It certainly was different: after The Bunch is ambushed and decimated by Bishop's old running mate, Deke Thornton (Robert Ryan), in the first of the now-famous battle sequences, a man five rows in front of me in the darkened theatre jumped up shouting and attacked another man *eight seats away from him, in another row*. Of course, the "instant" paranoid response I observed in the theatre may have been a coincidence. But I do not believe in coincidence, any more than I think Peckinpah made one frame of this picture by accident.

It has been suggested that this film should be censored or not shown at all. Mr. Peckinpah (on Canadian television) has counter-suggested that a little judicious censorship is like a little syphilis. Both points of view have validity relative to each other. Citizens must try to censor the Storyteller; it is that natural resistance of sovereign personality that continues to give the Storyteller a job to do. He would have none without it; it is a balance, a demonstration of Storyteller-Audience symbiosis. If it were not there the Storyteller would run away with people's minds much too quickly; it would be madness. Senator John Pastore is not so trivial a man as he obviously feels he is. The idea that he is a mindless Pygmy, dressing up mice as elephants and attacking them savagely with sharpened toothpicks, is quite beside the point. It must be remembered that he will get around to the rest of us in time. If not him, somebody else. They are not welcome but they are necessary. They have a necessary job to do. And it is necessary that they not accomplish it.

Dangerously sick people are just plain dangerous. Any personalized experience, no matter how obliquely symbolic, can trigger a sick personality: a stalled elevator, anonymous laughter in the street. Or a movie. And *The Wild Bunch* is a very personalized film: its metaphor is genuinely desperate anger. What's more, for the Paranoid as well as for the Ordinary Garden Variety Halfwit, it appears to suggest violent aggression as the logical solution to a pressing problem, and to glorify that solution.

Most madness in males is rooted in a damaged masculinity, in the overwhelming need to be sure where we are unsure, to assert ourselves precisely where we feel the most vulnerable. But these are the needs of all "sane" people, too. And it is to those needs in all of us that the Theatre addresses its abilities, momentarily, to heal and to restore. If the communication is misread by some "madder" people, who misinterpret all communication, the fault would seem not to lie in the Theatre. The very notion of a THEATRE says, " . . . there is no danger in this place, . . . in you, maybe."

All folks of substance in the Theatre are quite arbitrary on this point, but it does no good to frame it so; it simply sounds arrogant. Still, and quite flatly, the job of the Theatre is to make people think, feel, and to give them strength. If "crazy" people get stirred up with unfortunate results, then that's what happens in that situation. Women and children get killed in wars. It is not an accident, yet it is not deliberate.

The final proof of *The Wild Bunch* is in its utter lack of actors. You cannot find one anywhere among the Americans. Among the Mexican performers, even when that old ego pops out in little flashes, it is curiously just right for the character. There has surely never been such ensemble playing in an action piece before. There is nothing in the world more offensive than "good" actors in a good story. It's one or the other. Either we have fun in the company of some good actors, glancing at our watches, or we are permitted to enter into a story that's being told. We cannot do both. It's like making love with the television on, it works but not really. No one but another actor can know what it cost experienced and powerful and ego-driven men like William Holden, Ernest Borgnine, Robert Ryan and Edmond O'Brien for their ego-less performances in this film. The price, I promise you, is high, unknown to almost everyone, largely even to themselves until later. But it was worth it and I for one thank them from the bottom of my heart.

For Warren Oates, Ben Johnson, Strother Martin and L. Q. Jones I have little thanks. In fact, they should thank me for watching their film. For indeed it is theirs, just as much as it is Mr. Peckinpah's. They are the iron nails that hold together Mr. Peckinpah's platform. He could not make any pictures at all if they were not there someplace (shades of John Ford), perhaps not always on the screen; maybe just in the bar at night when the company gets back to the motel. Even there, he could not ever pay them enough money for their help. It is a rare case of genuine ecological balance in the Theatre. For these particular actors, their performances are the only meat they can eat and the only water they can get down. To act for Mr. Peckinpah is, for dedicated actors, nothing less than several weeks of survival.

Sam Peckinpah tells a story about meeting David Lean, whom he holds in very high esteem indeed. Lean, it appears, feels that the younger picture makers very likely hold him in contempt as old-fashioned, a linear Storyteller. It is a depressing thought. Near the end of their time together Lean walked Peckinpah through the exterior sets he had built for *Zhivago*. Looking around, he said quietly, "This is my hometown." And pointing to his Rolls-Royce he said, "This is my house. I live in there." He suggested to Peckinpah that the picture maker (as opposed in common parlance to the motion-picture director) is the last vagabond. Such men are not supposed to be happy men, the heartbreaking efforts of their women to the contrary notwithstanding. These men are supposed to keep a flame for us, and to pay everything for it, to keep it burning so we can sleep at night; they keep our dreams. The Storyteller survives; we had him before we had Priests and now we will have him afterward.

We are all rapidly becoming empiricists on this earth (rejecting everything we do not just feel) in terrible desperation. It is not the world that is growing smaller, it's us. And we are strangling on it, each breath a gasp. We can't hold it anymore, can no longer encompass its enormity in our little dreams. There are no more lonely men. There is only loneliness: poor fellows on the moon, they came too late.

Of all the permanent jobs, and there are only four (Priest, Doctor, Storyteller, Attorney), only the Storyteller may still be considered among the lonely, angry flame-keepers of old. The job of the Doctor is limitless, as is that of the Attorney, if only the Storyteller can keep our fainting spirits afloat, fight off our madness. We must be cupped, and held, and rocked and told that we may believe, that our wounds may with stoic effort again be bound. Powerful, unbending, empirical Storytellers can do this.

Mr. Peckinpah is surely the foremost empiricist in the Theatre today. I know this man, and I know that he has spent forty-four years holding himself together with barbed wire and a staple gun to make this picture. No other man anywhere can do what he has done. He is a relic, a hundred years out of his time. Like Pike

Bishop and Dutch and Deke Thornton, yes, and like the Gorch brothers, he is lost and falling through space, as anyone who knows him can tell you, but by God, he makes a light! He is utterly mad, and I wouldn't have him any other way.

PART 2

Dialogue

2 ▶

Sam Peckinpah Going to Mexico

PAUL SCHRADER

"*The Wild Bunch* is simply," says director Sam Peckinpah, "what happens when killers go to Mexico." And in the beleaguered career of Sam Peckinpah, Mexico has become increasingly the place to go. It is a land perhaps more savage, simple, or desolate, but definitely more expressive. Sam Peckinpah's Mexico is a spiritual country similar to Ernest Hemingway's Spain, Jack London's Alaska, and Robert Louis Stevenson's South Seas. It is a place where you go "to get yourself straightened out."

The Wild Bunch is Peckinpah's first unhampered directorial effort since *Ride the High Country* in 1962. The intervening seven years had brought personal bickerings, thwarted projects, black-listing—and belated critical acclaim. Critics called *Ride the High Country* an "American classic," and Peckinpah wrangled for television writing assignments. When Peckinpah finally regained his voice, he found it had changed. The violence had lost its code, becoming instead something deeper and more deadly. The new violence responded to the years fresh in Peckinpah's memory, the new mood of the country, but more importantly, to a feature of his personality which had previously worn more polite guises.

After working for director Don Siegel and on "The Westerner" television series, Peckinpah's first film was a small-budget Western, *Deadly Companions* (later called *Trigger Happy*), which he now describes as "unmanageable" and a "failure." But it did catch the attention of Richard Lyons, who brought Peckinpah to MGM and produced *High Country* that same year. A year later, in the 1963 winter issue of *Film Quarterly*, editor Ernest Callenbach wrote

"Sam Peckinpah Going to Mexico" by Paul Schrader originally appeared in *Cinema* 5, no. 3 (1969): pp. 18–25. Reprinted by permission of Paul Schrader.

17

PAUL SCHRADER

about *High Country*: "When it appeared, no one took it terribly seriously. But as time wore on, its unobtrusive virtues began to seem more appealing, and by now it is hard to see what American picture of 1962 could be rated above it." But in 1962 MGM, like the daily reviewers, was unprepared for this leisurely moral fable; *High Country* filled out the second half of double bills in neighborhood theaters and drive-ins.

Ride the High Country was painfully an old man's picture, all the more painful because its director was only thirty-seven years old. Two old gunfighters, Joel McCrea and Randolph Scott, are reduced to guarding a $20,000 gold shipment from a small mining town. In an extension of their earlier roles, McCrea extols the virtues of the classic Western code of honor and Scott tempts him to run off with the gold they both admit they well deserve for their selfless past of gunfights and wound mending. After a scuffle, Scott becomes reconciled to McCrea's code, not because the code is particularly appropriate, but simply because they are old Westerners. Together they stand off three coarse, half-crazed brothers. In the fusillade, McCrea is killed and dies a hero's death, saying, "I want to go it alone," as his bullet-ridden corpse sinks to the bottom of the frame. *Ride the High Country* had it both ways: it presented old Westerners caught up in their own outdated myth, and also justified their existence in terms of that myth. British critic Richard Whitehall wrote that *High Country* "is not only a celebration of the myth, it is also a requiem." Sam Peckinpah's film more acutely captured the Western's old-age pangs than did two films of the same period by old Westerners about old Westerners, John Ford's *The Man Who Shot Liberty Valance* and Howard Hawks's *Rio Bravo*. Like McCrea and Scott, Ford and Hawks could close their careers with honor and dignity; Peckinpah had to look beyond the myth and situate it in time. In retrospect, the Sam Peckinpah of *High Country* seems to be playing the game of Western directors like Ford, Hawks, George Sherman, Delmer Daves, and Budd Boetticher. In many ways he was playing the game better, but it still wasn't Peckinpah's game. *Ride the High Country* was a prologue, not an epilogue.

Ride the High Country and Peckinpah's television programs demonstrate certain values which, prior to *The Wild Bunch*, have invariably been associated with the director. In 1963, he told *Film Quarterly*, "My work has been concerned with outsiders, losers, loners, misfits, rounders—individuals looking for something besides security." These heroes, often old in body as well as mind, fall back on certain virtues: Biblical stoicism, practicality, primitivism, and honor. When a Peckinpah character makes the effort to verbalize his desires, which is rare, they are often banal. In Peckinpah's "Dick Powell Theater" episode "The Losers" (1963), Lee Marvin tells Keenan Wynn, "Peace of mind and an understanding heart. That's all we need." This is not obvious satire, but pure Peckinpah hokum; the insidious parody comes in when his characters, in rare moments, can actually come near to obtaining such a goal.

The crucial line in *Ride the High Country*, a line by which Peckinpah has often been characterized, was a simple profession by Joel McCrea, "I want to enter my own house justified." The line originally came from Peckinpah's father, a superior court judge of Fresno County, California, and before that it came from the Gospel of Saint Luke, the parable of the pharisee and the publican. Some of Peckinpah's most vivid memories of his Madera County, California, childhood were his family's dinner table discussions about justice, law, and order. "I always felt like an outsider," he says. It was in the strong Biblical sense of the publican that Peckinpah sought to justify his characters—and himself—and it has been his desire to justify himself in his own way that has informed his early work. In *High Country*, McCrea, Scott, and a fanatically religious farmer swap Biblical texts, each trying to make his point. McCrea loses the battle of the text, but wins justification in the battle of honor. The farmer deprives his daughter of a full life; McCrea returns it to her by sacrificing himself meaningfully. Both the farmer and the gunslinger die, but only one goes to his home justified. Peckinpah has no qualms about adding the second half of the Biblical injunction regarding justification: "Whom he justified, them he also glorified." McCrea's glorification is explicit, unsubtle, and shattering.

Honesty and purity of intent (and thereby justification) no longer come naturally to the Westerner (as they did to the Virginian); they must be fought for and defended. Peckinpah's characters are ruthlessly cynical about ways to protect the Westerner's code against the corrosive influence of "civilization." The code is not a game, but must be defended in every way possible, even unsportly ways. In "Jeff," Peckinpah's favorite episode of "The Westerner" series, a bare-knuckled boxer-pimp complains that the Peckinpah hero, David Blassingame (Brian Keith), isn't being a good sportsman. "You're a bad loser, Mr. Blassingame," the heavy says. "I sure am," replies Blassingame. "This isn't a game."

As in all Westerns, the gun is immediately behind the code. Sooner or later it comes down to killing. Like the code, the gun is

PAUL SCHRADER

not a plaything. In another "Westerner" episode, "Hand on the Gun," Blassingame tells a cocky Easterner, "A gun ain't to play with. It's to kill people. And you don't touch it unless you plan to shoot, and you don't shoot unless you plan to kill." Implied in that logical progression are the tenets that you don't kill unless you have to, or you don't kill without a purpose. In his early work Peckinpah clung tenaciously to the Western code. *Ride the High Country* was great as a Western—at heart it functioned the way Westerns were supposed to function. But there was also a strong sense of expectation. Sam Peckinpah was young and strong; the code was old and weak. Something had to give.

But nothing had a chance to give. After *High Country* came Sam Peckinpah's seven lean years. Peckinpah underwent a series of reputation-damaging producer clashes. And as Orson Welles learned so well, once a filmmaker's reputation is damaged in Hollywood, nothing short of a miracle can retrieve it. No longer is the bum script, the meddling producer, the restrictive budget to blame, but the fault always falls on "that" director: the kiss of death.

Major Dundee was Charlton Heston's idea. He had seen *High Country*, loved it, and proposed Harry Julian Fink's script to Peckinpah. *Major Dundee* was Peckinpah's first big-budget film (costing $2.5 million compared with $813,000 for *High Country*). Producer Jerry Bresler (*The Vikings*, *Diamond Head*, *Love Has Many Faces*) was described by a member of the cast as "wall-to-wall worry." In a power play with the studio, Columbia Pictures, Heston and Peckinpah won the right to shoot the entire film on location in Mexico, and also, supposedly, final-cut privileges. But after the film was shot, Heston and Peckinpah's influence began to wane. Peckinpah's final cut ran three hours. Columbia wanted it shortened, and Peckinpah cut it to two hours and forty minutes, suggesting that ten minutes should go back in. But Bresler got nervous, Peckinpah assumes, and cut the film to under two hours. Peckinpah asked that his name be left off the credits, contending that the film was neither the long powerful film he intended nor the short action film it could have been. Peckinpah still regards his two-hour-forty-minute version as an excellent film, but there are few to verify his opinion. Against contractual obligations, neither of Peckinpah's cuts was ever previewed. Heston was one of the few who saw it, and liked it so much that he offered to turn back his salary if the picture were left untouched. Peckinpah also offered to defer most of his salary, but Columbia won the day and *Major*

Dundee premiered as a double-bill feature in multiple situations. The anonymous *Newsweek* reviewer knew where to set the blame for the *Major Dundee* fiasco. His review began, "Think of Yosemite Falls, or suicides from the top of the Empire State Building, or the streaking of meteorites downward toward the earth, and you get some idea of the decline in the career of Sam Peckinpah." Like Welles after the *Journey Into Fear* debacle, Peckinpah saw his reputation plummet without being able to do a thing about it.

Another Hollywood producer played the next part in the decline of Peckinpah's career. He accused Peckinpah of being a "perfectionist," adding that Peckinpah wanted to make a dirty movie (sex is a remarkably minor factor in Peckinpah's films, and whatever there is, is far from titillating). Peckinpah found himself on the street. A projected film for MGM and another for Heston failed to materialize. "I got angry and named names," Peckinpah says. "Then I spent three-and-a-half years without shooting a camera. That's what you call blacklisting," Peckinpah says. "I made a living, but for a director there can be nothing but making a film. It was a slow death." During those three-and-a-half years he wrote a Western called *The Glory Guys*, which was filmed by Arnold Laven in 1965, and *Villa Rides!*, which was rewritten by Robert Towne and directed by Buzz Kulik. Peckinpah's only minor triumph during this period came when he filmed Katherine Anne Porter's *Noon Wine* for ABC's "Stage 67" program. Peckinpah's adaptation starred Jason Robards, Olivia de Havilland, Per Oscarsson, and Theodore Bikel, and won the praise of critics as well as Miss Porter. That year the Screen Director's Guild ironically selected Peckinpah one of the ten best television directors.

In late 1967, producer Phil Feldman selected Sam Peckinpah to direct *The Wild Bunch*, Feldman's second producing effort (the first was Francis Ford Coppola's *You're a Big Boy Now*). "It was nice to get picked off the street and given a $5 million picture," Peckinpah reflects. "This picture came about only because of two wonderful reasons: Phil Feldman and Ken Hyman." Although Peckinpah didn't have final-cut rights, *The Wild Bunch* was shot and edited the way he desired. "A good picture is usually 70 percent of your intentions. *Ride the High Country* was 80 percent for me. I'd say *The Wild Bunch* was about 96 percent. I'm very satisfied."

Peckinpah's original cut of *The Wild Bunch* ran over three hours. Warner Bros. was understandably queasy about many of the graphic scenes of killing. Two disastrous previews (one in Kansas City and the other in Hollywood) had indicated some degree of audience revulsion. "I hope you drown in a pool of Max Factor Technicolor blood," one UCLA graduate film student told Peckinpah. Warner Bros. stuck with Peckinpah, however, letting him cut the film down to its present two hours and twenty-three minutes. "There was never danger of an X rating for violence," Peckinpah says, "We had an R right from the beginning. I actually cut out more than Warners requested. There were certain things Warners wanted cut, but I went farther. I had to make it play better." To make the film play better, Peckinpah excised much of the explicit violence in the initial fight scene, particularly the disembowelings, letting the violence come at the audience more gradually. Included in the 4 percent Peckinpah regretted losing was a flashback of William Holden (in addition to the present two flashbacks of Robert Ryan and Holden). The flashback, which is curiously included in the international print, revealed how Holden had received a leg wound.[1]

At one point in the prerelease intrigue of *The Wild Bunch*, Peckinpah feared that it would receive the inadequate distribution of his earlier films. "It was a funny thing," he says. "The European distributor saw it and said, 'Roadshow.' The domestic distributor saw it and said, 'Double-bill.'" This time Peckinpah won the battle, and *The Wild Bunch* came to be regarded as Warner Bros.'s "picture of the summer" and received a massive publicity campaign.

The Wild Bunch is again about old Westerners and killing. Like McCrea and Scott, the Wild Bunch actors are battle-weary veterans of many movie Westerns: William Holden (8 Westerns), Robert Ryan (14), Ernest Borgnine (10), Edmond O'Brien (10), Ben Johnson (16), and Warren Oates (8). Warner Bros. wanted to cast a "young leading man" in the role of Holden's sidekick, but Peckinpah balked. "Someone said what about old Ernie Borgnine, and I said, 'Go to it.'" The year is 1914, the pickings are slim, and the killers are tired. "This is about what Bill Holden is today," Peckinpah says, "fifty, middle-aged, wrinkled, no longer the glamor boy." Holden talks wistfully about giving up the Bunch's outlaw existence: "We're getting old. We've got to think beyond our guns." "I'd like to make one good score and back off," he tells Borgnine. "Back off to what?" Borgnine replies.

On the action level, *The Wild Bunch* is the most entertaining American picture in several years. The scenes flow evenly and quickly, and the high points seem to pile on top of each other. The editing (by Lou Lombardo, assisted by Peckinpah) is superb, if only for its unostentatiousness. Although *The Wild Bunch* has more cuts than any other picture in Technicolor, 3,643, it flows naturally and smoothly. Lombardo skillfully intercuts slow-motion shots (taken at 25, 28, 42, 48, and 64 frames per second) with normal action, demonstrating Eisenstein's theory of collision montage even better than the master himself, whose assemblages always seemed more didactic than natural. Someone suggested to Peckinpah that the editing of *The Wild Bunch* was as good as any in the Kurosawa samurai epics. "I think it's better," he replied.

"*The Wild Bunch* is a very commercial picture, thank God," Peckinpah says. "I just happened to put some of myself into it." It is important to Peckinpah that *The Wild Bunch* be a "commercial" picture and play to large audiences, and not only to retrieve its large budget (approaching, by common estimate, $8 million). Peckinpah's film speaks in common, proletarian themes and is effective for even the most unsophisticated audiences. Its first appeal is to the vulgar sensibility: callous killings, bawdy jokes, boyish horseplay. *The Wild Bunch* flaunts the vulgar exhilaration of killing. Like the best of American films of violence, *The Wild Bunch* has it both ways: it uses violence to excite and then applies more violence to comment on the excitement. And like such indigenous, murderous American masterpieces as *Underworld, Scarface, The Killing, Bonnie and Clyde, The Wild Bunch* puts the stinger in the butterfly: the violence moves beyond itself, becoming something much more virulent—artifice.

Peckinpah carefully manages his violence, bargaining between the violence the audience wants and the violence he is prepared to give. Peckinpah uses violence the way every dramatist has, to make the plot turn. Then he applies vicarious violence to the plot mechanism. We don't really care whether it's logical if so-and-so is killed; we need more blood to satiate our appetite. Most "serious" war films do not progress beyond vicariousness; we simply want to be better war heroes. At the final level, the most difficult, Peckinpah goes beyond vicariousness to superfluity. We no longer want the violence, but it's still coming. Violence then can either become gratuitous or transcend itself. Peckinpah enjoys walking the thin line between destructive and constructive violence. For much of the film he allows the violence to verge on gratuity until, at one moment, it shifts gears and moves beyond itself. For Peckinpah, this moment occurs during the literal Mexican standoff at Mapache's Agua Verde encampment. Holden shoots the general as two hundred soldiers watch on. A silence falls; no one moves. A few soldiers tentatively raise their hands; the Wild Bunchers look at each other and begin to laugh. This is what their lives have led to, one brief moment between life and death. And into death they plunge, the gore and bodies mounting higher and higher.

Robert Warshow wrote that the Western was popular because it created a milieu in which violence was acceptable. After years of simplistic Westerns, Peckinpah wants to more precisely define that milieu. Violence, Peckinpah seems to say, is acceptable and edifiable primarily for the spectator. It may also be edifiable for the participant, but only to the extent that it is suicidal. Like the Western code, it succeeds most when it is self-destructive. To be of any value, violence must move from vicariousness to artifice. The spectator must be left "disinterested" in the Arnoldian sense, evaluating what he had previously reveled in.

In the postslaughter epilogue of *The Wild Bunch*, Peckinpah rubs the spectator's nose in the killing he had so recently enjoyed. New killers arrive to replace the old. A way of life has died, but the dying continues. In a departing gesture of shocking perversity, Peckinpah brings back the fade-in, fade-out laughing faces of each of the Wild Bunch killers to the stirring chorus of "La Golondrina." This is Sam Peckinpah's Mount Rushmore: four worn-out frontiersmen who ran out of land to conquer and went to Mexico to kill and be killed. It is a blatant parody of Ford's *Long Grey Line* and the petulant perversity of it, like the final gunning down of Bonnie and Clyde, throws the viewer out of the movie and into the realm of art. It is one of the strongest emotional kickbacks of any film. The viewer leaves the theater alone, shattered, trying to sort out the muddle Peckinpah has made of his emotions. A friend after seeing *The Wild Bunch* for the first time remarked, "I feel dirty all the way through." Peckinpah wouldn't have it any other way.

The Westerners of *The Wild Bunch* have only the remnants of the code. They mouth many of the familiar platitudes but the honor and the purpose are absent. The cynicism has hardened; it no longer protects another set of values but is a way of life in itself. When Angel, the only Mexican Wild Buncher, grieves over his recently murdered father, Holden perfunctorily admonishes him, "Either you learn to live with it or we leave you here." As Holden explains later, "Ten thousand dollars cuts an awful lot of family ties." The Wild Bunch do have their particular code, which they like to think separates them from the others. Concerning Mapache, Borgnine remarks, "We ain't nothing like him. We don't kill nobody." When Ben Johnson threatens to leave the Bunch, Holden warns him, "I either lead this Bunch or end it right now"; and later,

"When you side with a man you stay with him. If you can't do that, you're no better than [an] animal. You're finished. We're finished." But the irony of the Wild Bunch is that they are finished, and that they are little more than animals. The Bunch has taken on the characteristics which McCrea repudiated in *High Country*. Warren Oates, playing one of the vulgarized, psychopathic Hammond brothers in *High Country*, explodes in frustrated anger during the final shoot-out, wildly shooting at some nearby chickens. In *The Wild Bunch* there is a similar scene when Ben Johnson, after he and Oates have refused to pay a young whore an honest wage, plays with a baby sparrow, killing it. Unlike Blassingame in "The Westerner," the Wild Bunch draw their guns often, with little purpose and obvious delight. McCrea and Scott have died, the Hammond brothers have firmed up and headed for Mexico. It could be said that the Bunch represents "better" Westerners, in contrast to the broad comedy bounty hunters, but this was not Peckinpah's primary intent. "I wanted to show that each group was no better than the next," he says. The only thing that distinguishes the Wild Bunch is their ability to die appropriately.

The Wild Bunch is not a Western in the sense of *Ride the High Country*. (Peckinpah claims that neither is a Western. Although he doesn't mind being labeled a "Western director," he states, "I have never made a 'Western.' I have made a lot of films about men on horseback.") The film is not about an antiquated Western code, but about Westerners bereft of the code. The Bunch are not Westerners who kill, but are killers in the West. *Ride the High Country* gave a perspective on why the code was valuable; *The Wild Bunch* gives a perspective on the age that could believe the Western code was valuable.

The metaphor for the old men of *The Wild Bunch* becomes, ironically, children. Peckinpah does not emphasize their honor, but their infantility. The film begins with the frame of the naively cruel village children. After Mapache's disastrous defeat at the hands of Villa, a young messenger boy proudly struts with the general away from the bloody Las Trancas battle scene. It is a child who, in the final battle, terminates the massacre by killing Holden. At Angel's village (a scene which Peckinpah considers the most important in the film), an old villager and peasant revolutionary, Chano Urueta, characterizes the Bunch in a conversation with Holden and O'Brien. "We all dream of being children," he says, "even the worst of us. Perhaps the worst more than others." "You know what we are then?" Holden asks. "Yes, both of you," Urueta replies. "All three of us!" Holden laughs. Peckinpah conceived of his characters as children and made object lessons of them the way we do of children. "They are all children," Peckinpah says. "We are all children."

In *The Wild Bunch* Peckinpah comes to terms with the most violent aspects of his personality. A longtime acquaintance of Peckinpah recently said of him, "I think he is the best director in America, but I also think he is a fascist." He was using the term "fascist" personally rather than politically. Peckinpah has a violent, domineering streak. There is in Peckinpah the belief that the ultimate test of manhood is the suppression of others. He maintains an impressive collection of guns, and his California home is kept up by "Spanish domestics," householders who do not speak English. Peckinpah is, in a sense, a colonial in his own home. A good friend of Peckinpah recalled that once he came into the director's office and found him intently watching a cage on his desk. In the cage was a resting rattlesnake and a petrified white mouse. The rattler had already eaten one mouse, probably the survivor's mate, and was now contentedly digesting the large bulge in its stomach. "Who do you think will win?" Peckinpah asked his friend. "You will, Sam," the friend replied.

The fascist edge of Peckinpah's personality does not make him particularly unique. It is a trait he shares with directors like Don Siegel, Howard Hawks, Samuel Fuller, Anthony Mann and all the rest of us who have always wanted to believe that those horseriding killers were really making the West safe for the womenfolk. What makes Peckinpah unique is his ability to come face-to-face with the fascist quality of his personality, American films, and America, and turn it into art. (I realize that "fascist" is a particularly vicious epithet. But its viciousness implies pain—and pain is the cathartic emotion Peckinpah experiences as he moves away from the old West of youth.)

In *The Wild Bunch* Sam Peckinpah stares into the heart of his own fascism. What had been formerly protected by the code is laid bare. The Western genre is ideally suited to such an examination; Jean-Luc Godard has noted that the Western is the only surviving popular fascist art form. In the past, the Western had been able to perpetuate the myth of its own altruism, but for Peckinpah, that myth had died its honorable death in *High Country*. The Westerners of *The Wild Bunch* have lost their code—only the fascism remains. The power of *The Wild Bunch* lies in the fact that this fascism is not peculiar to Peckinpah but is American at heart. The

America that created the Western (and the Communist Conspiracy) is the America Peckinpah determined to evaluate in his own life.

Like America's former macho-in-residence, Ernest Hemingway, Sam Peckinpah fights his private battles in public, both in life and art, but unlike Hemingway, Peckinpah comes increasingly to terms with his own persona as he ages. As Hemingway approached death he relied increasingly on his code; as Peckinpah grows older he progressively discards his, preferring to confront death head-on. *The Wild Bunch* is *The Old Man and the Sea* without a boat, a great fish, or a native boy. The great anguish of *The Wild Bunch* is the anguish of a fascist personality coming to terms with itself: recognizing its love of domination and killing and attempting to evaluate it.

The new psychopaths in the best of recent American films—*Bonnie and Clyde, Point Blank, Pretty Poison*—have had a strong environmental context in which to make their killings plausible, whether it be the rural Texas of the Depression era, garish new Los Angeles, or the polluted Massachusetts countryside. Codeless, Sam Peckinpah goes to the land he loves best to re-create and understand his violence: Mexico. Peckinpah has lived in Mexico off and on during the past few years (a refuge from the Hollywood ordeal) and is a student of Mexican customs and history. "Mexico is the greatest place," Peckinpah says. "You have to go there, just to sit back and rest. You have to go there to get yourself straightened out."

Peckinpah thinks of *The Wild Bunch* as a Mexican film: "It is what really happens when killers go to Mexico. It is my comment on Richard Brooks and *The Professionals*." Brooks's 1966 south-of-the-border adventure story treated Mexico as facilely as it did the Americans who went there; John Huston's 1948 *The Treasure of the Sierra Madre* is much more to Peckinpah's liking: "*Treasure of Sierra Madre* is one of my favorite films. In fact, *The Wild Bunch* is sort of early Huston. Ever since I saw that film I've been chasing Huston." It was not so much Huston's moralistic story that impressed Peckinpah but his expressive use of the Mexican milieu (of *Treasure* the late James Agee wrote, "I doubt we shall ever see a finer portrait of Mexico and Mexicans"). Mexico had lent a depth to *Treasure*, a depth Peckinpah wanted to pursue in *The Wild Bunch*.

Agee to the contrary, Huston's characterization of Mexicans was not so much incisive as it was stereotypic—a fault which Peckinpah unfortunately shares. Mexicans fit into preexisting categories: *federalistas, rurales, caudillos*. Like Huston's Mexican bandits, Peckinpah's *bandoleros* speak broken English, have bad breath, and

possess a charming sense of humor. Alfonso Bedoya's Gold Hat in
Treasure ("Badges? We don't need no stinking badges") is the
prototype of Jorge Russek's Lieutenant Zamorra in *The Wild Bunch*
("I want to congratulate you on the great bravery you have done").
Peckinpah wanted to show that the Mexicans (all varieties) were no
less psychopathic than the Americans, but compared to the Bunch,
the Mexicans (with a few notable exceptions, like Angel's girl,
Teresa, and the old Urueta) seem colonial subjects.

But *The Wild Bunch* is only secondarily about the individual
psychology of the Mexicans; it is primarily concerned with the
mood of their country. Peckinpah's film is not about Mexicans, but
murderous Americans who go to Mexico. Peckinpah's Mexico is
much more powerfully drawn than Huston's and more accurately
resembles the Mexico of Luis Buñuel's films. Although Peckinpah
does not achieve the individual Mexican psychology of films like
Los Olvidados, Subida al Cielo, Ensayo de un Crimen, Nazarin, he is
able to capture the irrationally savage mood of Buñuel's Mexico.
The comparison would please Peckinpah. "I loved *Los Olvidados*,"
he says. "I know that territory well. I've lived there. I would like to
make *Children of Sanchez* one day. *The Wild Bunch* is only a beginning." The opening shot of the taunted scorpion in *The Wild Bunch*
is almost identical to the opening shot of Buñuel's 1930 *L'Age d'Or*,
although Peckinpah says he has never seen the Buñuel film (the
idea for the ant-scorpion battle in *The Wild Bunch* originated with
actor-director Emilio Fernandez, who plays Mapache). Peckinpah's
Mexico, like Buñuel's, is a place where violence is not only plausible
but inescapable.

Peckinpah was recently asked which films stood out best in his
memory. He started to reply, "*Breaking Point, Rashomon, My Darling
Clementine, Ace in the Hole*," and then he abruptly added, "If you
really want to know about *The Wild Bunch* you should read a book
by Camilo José Cela called *La Familia de Pascual Duarte*." It is from
the sensibility of *Pascual Duarte*, a seminal book in modern Spanish literature, that Peckinpah draws the frame in which to make the
violence of *The Wild Bunch* meaningful. On the most immediate
level, there is an instant meeting of the minds between Cela and
Peckinpah. Cela's dedication to *Pascual Duarte* could serve as the
frontpiece for *The Wild Bunch*: "I dedicate this thirteenth and
definitive edition of my *Pascual Duarte* to my enemies who have
been of such help to me in my career." *The Wild Bunch* shares
themes and sentiments with *Pascual Duarte* which do not figure in
Peckinpah's earlier films. "I'm not made to philosophize," Pascual

writes in his diary, "I don't have the heart for it. My heart is more like a machine for making blood to be spilt in a knife fight." McCrea and Scott were philosophers first, killers second; Holden and Borgnine are laconic psychopaths like Duarte. Pascual's wife says to him, "Blood seems a kind of fertilizer in your life." Pascual dedicates his diary to "the memory of the distinguished patrician Don Jesús Gonzalez de la Riva, Count of Torremejia, who, at the moment when the author of this chronicle came to kill him, called him Pascualillo, and smiled." Peckinpah tells a similar story: "I once lived with a wonderful man in Mexico. He was the most trustworthy man I have ever met. I would have done anything for him; I would have put my family in his care. He took me for every cent. A true friend is one who is really able to screw you."

Like Pascual, the Wild Bunch disguise their barbarity in boyish innocence. Whenever Pascual mentions hogs or his behind, he adds "begging your pardon" and then goes on to describe the most savage acts. Just before the initial massacre in *The Wild Bunch* the Bunch stroll insouciantly down the main street, helping an old woman across the street. Like the scorpion-torturing children of *The Wild Bunch*, the children of *Pascual Duarte* tease injured dogs, sheep, and drown kittens in the watering trough, lifting them out of the water from time to time "to prevent their getting out of their misery too quickly." Like Pascual, the Wild Bunch are picaros, men who roam the country in a never-ending war, spawning a rich heritage of death and suffering. It is into this tradition of Spanish suffering, the tradition of Cela, that Peckinpah thrusts his battle-weary Westerners.

Mexico represents an older, more primitive culture, a place where violence can still have meaning on the functional level. As the works of Oscar Lewis indicate, the Mexican peasant still regards the *macho*—the Mexican Westerner—as a practical proto-type, and not just a mythological figure. Mexico is the ideal place for an old Westerner to go to give his violence meaning. The American frontier has been superseded by the more sophisticated mayhem of the city, but in Mexico there is an ongoing tradition of significant violence. There you can fill a hero's grave, even if it is a shallow one. In Mexico you can extend the external frontier and postpone the conquest of the internal frontier. The Mexico of 1914 was the Wild Bunch's Vietnam, a place where the wolf of fascism goes to wear the sheepskin of purpose.

Mexico cannot justify the Westerner's fascism, but it can bring the Westerner to an honorable end. If Holden, Borgnine, Oates, and Johnson do enter their homes justified, it is not because of any intrinsic virtue, but because of their enthusiastic demise. Deprived of both the mythical and functional qualities of his character, Peckinpah dies the only way he knows how—with his boots on. But Peckinpah has the sensitivity, self-awareness, and feeling for America and Mexico to give his death poignancy and art.

The Wild Bunch is a powerful film because it comes from the gut of America, and from a man who is trying to get America out of his gut. The trauma of expatriotism is a common theme in American art, but nowhere is the pain quite so evident as in the life of Sam Peckinpah. *The Wild Bunch* is the agony of a Westerner who stayed too long, and it is the agony of America.

Note

1. On July 18, Warner Bros. cut five minutes from the domestic print of *The Wild Bunch*. The original idea was, Peckinpah says, to cut out the flash-backs in two theaters. Instead three scenes were excised in four hundred theaters. The flashback of Ryan's capture and Holden's escape in a brothel was cut out, as was the flashback to the death of Sykes's nephew Crazy Lee (Bo Hopkins, who says, "I'll hold 'em here till Hell freezes over or you say different, Mr. Pike"). Particularly damaging was the deletion of the entire Las Trancas battle scene, mentioned later in this article. The battle sequence revealed the other side of Mapache's character, the machismo in battle and defeat. Without the sequence, Mapache is only comic relief, a drunken sot. The reason for the July 18 cut, the *New York Times* News Service reported, was to shorten the picture, thereby allowing the distributors more screening times per day. One theater, however, the Pacific Pix in Hollywood, used the extra time to insert a "Tom and Jerry" cartoon. Peckinpah is no longer "very satisfied."

3 ▶

Peckinpah's Return

Stephen Farber

I hate that word "comeback." It's a return.
— Gloria Swanson in *Sunset Boulevard*

The Wild Bunch is Sam Peckinpah's first film after more than four years of forced inactivity, and it is gratifying, in a way, that the most recent outcast from Hollywood has directed, for his "comeback," not just a good movie but a commercially successful one, too. Nothing makes the industry forget its grudges quicker than the sound of money. The critics have responded as Peckinpah hoped they would, with either ecstatic raves or angry denunciations; almost no one is neutral on this film. *Ride the High Country* was a sensitive, modest film, but Peckinpah has aimed much higher this time. *The Wild Bunch* is not a minor film; it's a sprawling, spectacular, ambitious, willfully controversial picture, an assault on an audience's senses and emotions, an aggressive bid for the spotlight. Fortunately, the film deserves the spotlight. Its first impression is literally overpowering. *The Wild Bunch* is much more dazzling than *Ride the High Country*, but it loses some of the reflective qualities that made Peckinpah's early film so quietly memorable. There were stark images of violence in *Ride the High Country* too, but violence is the subject and the controlling passion of *The Wild Bunch*. Let me say right away that the violence does not offend me, even though this is the goriest film I have ever seen. But the gore is not gratuitous; the film is intelligent about the significance of violence in America, and in addition, the images of violence are quite simply beautiful. I don't believe that the violence in this movie (or in any other movie) will send children out on the streets to murder, nor do I feel that Peckinpah's obvious fascination, even obsession, with violence is more degenerate than other filmmakers' obsessions with religion or sex or decor.

I do object to some of the film's equivocations, and its tendency to sacrifice characterization to action and spectacle. The individual characters are just distinct enough to be believable, but none of them are really very interesting. The only way to accept the characters at all is to see them as one conglomerate character, the Wild Bunch. Peckinpah is interested in these men as a *group*, and he uses them to epitomize a major generic character, the Outlaw. But even granting this, the film, particularly on a second viewing, seems flat and underwritten.

The characters in *The Wild Bunch* are not complex, though the film's attitudes toward what they represent, toward violence, and toward the Western myth in general are very complex; but complexity is very close to confusion, and the film often seems out of control (which is a corollary of its high emotional charge). But I respect even the film's confusions, for they always seem to grow out of Peckinpah's most profound doubts and uncertainties, a very rich, intense self-questioning; they never seem concessions to the audience.

One first notices these confusions in the visual style of the film. The material is straightforward and conventional in many ways, and there are several elegant panoramic shots that are a staple of Westerns; but there are also some very contemporary tricks of filmmaking—slow motion, subliminal cutting—that testify to Peckinpah's dissatisfaction with the Western form, his desire to break it open and reconceive it. The sophistication of his technique does not always match the simplicity of the plotting and characterizations, and audiences encouraged by Peckinpah's mastery of the medium to expect a more subtle film are probably bewildered by the crude humor and old-fashioned melodrama of many scenes. The middle sections particularly lack dimension—effectively photographed but protracted, essentially hollow action scenes. And even the technique can turn surprisingly old-fashioned, as in some turgid flashback dissolves (just recently cut out of the film) or the sentimental superimposition of the laughing faces of the Bunch over the final scene. At these moments the film recalls vintage John Ford, while in the editing of the gun battles Peckinpah shows that he is a contemporary of Kurosawa, Truffaut, and Arthur Penn.

The Wild Bunch, like the traditional Western, is concerned with

honor among men. There are exuberant scenes of masculine camaraderie on the order of Ford or Hawks—the Bunch laughing over
the abortive results of a robbery attempt, drinking and whoring
and taking baths together, nostalgically reminiscing about old
times over the campfire. The grittiness and ribald humor of these
scenes should not blind us to their familiarity and robust sentimentality. The film sometimes bathes the Wild Bunch in a soft
golden haze, particularly during the lyrical scene of their exit from
the Mexican village where Angel (Jaime Sanchez) lives, serenaded
by the peasants, handed roses by the women. But at other moments the film sees them with a harshness that *is* unconventional
and bracing—as limited, slow-witted, mercenary opportunists
ruled by an unnatural blood lust. *The Wild Bunch* has been compared to *Bonnie and Clyde* because of its sympathy for the outlaw
and its mockery of all forms of "law and order"—whether it be the
temperance union and railroad men in South Texas, Pershing's
incompetent army along the border, or the coldblooded *federales*
fighting Villa's revolutionaries in Mexico. But in one respect the
film is sharper and more honest than *Bonnie and Clyde*—it does not
flinch from showing the brutality of its heroes. One thing that has
always bothered me about Penn's film is its uneasy unwillingness
to acknowledge the same sadism in Bonnie and Clyde that looks so
appalling in the police. Bonnie and Clyde kill only in self-defense,
and the camera almost never puts us into the position of their
victims; we always identify with *them*, suffer with the violence
inflicted on them, but never with the violence that they inflict.
Even in the scene in which the Texas Ranger spits in Bonnie's face,
Clyde's reaction is surprisingly mild and gentle—he gets angry
and throws the man into the water, but he doesn't really hurt him.
The Wild Bunch is more hardheaded because it admits the heroes'
attraction to violence. We can't delude ourselves that the Bunch are
innocent; they're clearly depraved and vicious—savages who love
the thrill of slaughter.

And yet they do retain our sympathy. Perhaps one reason is that
in a world where the "respectable" people seem equally sadistic,
where, indeed, violence seems the primary fact of human nature
(as Peckinpah emphasizes by his repeated shots of children responding enthusiastically to torture), the qualities of candor and
resilience that distinguish the Bunch seem especially precious.
They are at a disadvantage in comparison with the respectable
people, not just because they are outlaws but because they are old
men trying to find their way in a land that is beginning to change

beyond recognition. There is one striking shot of the Bunch leader, Pike (William Holden), stumbling to get onto his horse and then riding off, weary, beaten, hunched over, and still unafraid, that crystallizes the film's admiration of these men for their refusal to submit to time and inevitable decay. They are outsiders, failures, with nowhere to turn and no place to go, but they have not been defeated. They have the strength to endure.

To give a better idea of the richness of the film's attitude toward the Bunch, I'd like to consider the conclusion of the film in some detail—a series of sequences with a quite remarkable gradation of moods. Angel has been taken prisoner by Mapache's *federales* for giving a carton of stolen guns to the revolutionaries, and the Bunch, though regretful, casually decide to leave him to his death—the first twist on the Western myth of loyalty. But they return to Mapache's village to take refuge from the bounty hunters who are pursuing them. When they see Angel being dragged along the ground by the German general's automobile, they are disgusted, but not disgusted enough to try to save him, and they accept Mapache's offer of whores for the evening. But the next morning—in an unusually sensitive and understated sequence— Pike is haunted by feelings of remorse and embarrassment that he cannot quite interpret. As he watches his woman wash her body, the delicacy of her movements as well as her humiliation when he offers her money make it clear that she is not really a whore, and he is troubled because of his insensitivity to her and his obliviousness to the torture of his friend. So when he calls the others to help him retrieve Angel, the decision grows convincingly out of a sense of guilt and self-revulsion.

As the Bunch begin their walk into town, Peckinpah changes mood, swells the music, and films the march with the classical rhythm and dramatic flair of all archetypal Western showdowns. The Bunch look imposing and heroic, but this vision is shaded by irony if we remember to place it against the uncomfortable pre- ceding scene and the horrifying one that is to follow. Mapache cuts Angel's throat before their eyes, and they respond with rage, turning their guns against him and the rest of the village, massa- cring the Mexicans who are too drunk to make much of a stand against them. Eventually they get hold of a machine gun that is mounted in the center of town, and with that, they are able to take a toll of hundreds of lives. Peckinpah films this battle with great urgency and passion, drawing it out with almost hallucinatory, surreal relentlessness, yet punctuating it with jagged, electric-shock cutting. (Lou Lombardo's editing is the finest editing of an American film since *Bonnie and Clyde*.) When Warren Oates takes hold of the machine gun and shrieks like a maniac as he fires in a fit of orgasmic release, it is one of the most appalling images of human bestiality ever filmed—an echo of a primeval war cry. The Bunch may go into the slaughter in search of honor and retribution, but the blood quickly washes away their noble sentiments. There is a fine moment when Pike, shot in the back by a woman, turns and without flinching fires directly at her breast, that economically conveys the Bunch's mindless, automatic instinct for brutality—an instinct that overwhelms their moral aspirations. When the massacre is over, and the town is littered with bodies, including those of the Bunch, Deke Thornton (Robert Ryan), their former partner and tireless pursuer, rides in, and the bounty hunters under his command, a vile pack of gutter scavengers who make the Wild Bunch look saintly, begin stripping the bodies of boots, watches, gold fillings. Peckinpah has daringly shifted mood again, from a shattering vision of apocalyptic horror to the grotesque black comedy that has always been one of his specialties as a director; the comedy seems an effective way of underscoring the senselessness and absurdity of the massacre—a bitter, nihilistic laugh at the Bunch's pretensions of virtue.

But the film does not end quite there. There are some sere, mournful images of peasant women in black moving among the bodies, then gathering their belongings and leaving the village in desolate, silent exile. Thornton sits at the gates to the town, revolted by what he has seen, exhausted by the effort of life itself. But when the old man who is the last survivor of the Wild Bunch rides in and asks Thornton to join him again, Thornton comes to life, and the two of them laugh together as they ride off in search of adventures. "It won't be like the old times," the old man tells him, "but it's something." And it is over this affirmative conclusion that the laughing faces of the dead members of the Bunch are superimposed. The final image is a reprise of the Bunch's resounding farewell to Angel's village, their one moment of grace and glory.

During these last twenty minutes of his film Peckinpah so disturbs our emotions that we are literally drained by the conclusion. Just as we are convinced of the meaninglessness of the Bunch's life and death, Peckinpah once again twists our response and forces us to pay a final tribute to their irreverence and their resilience. It may be because of the tremendous complexity of the film's evaluation of the Bunch that many critics have been so

STEPHEN FARBER

outraged. What *is* Peckinpah trying to say? If he means to repel us by the life of violence, why that strangely sentimental finale? And if he means the film as a celebration of the outlaw, why must he so immerse us in the outlaw's brutality? There are no easy interpretations of *The Wild Bunch*. Peckinpah is feeling out his own responses to his characters' way of life, and he is asking us to struggle with him to make sense of the experiences on the screen. For all of its technical assurance, this is an unfinished, open-ended film, a tentative exploration of a peculiar, vanishing way of life, rather than a clearly formulated thesis film. Peckinpah has not resolved his own feelings about the masculine code of honor of the Westerner or about the violence of the outlaw, and *The Wild Bunch* reflects his confusions. We rightly demand more clarity from an artist, but at the same time, the genuinely agonized temper of *The Wild Bunch* makes it a searching, unsettling film.

The film opens on a group of children "playing" by placing a couple of scorpions in a container filled with red ants, then setting fire to both, and at the very end it is a child who murders Pike; the film's vision of children is perhaps most revealing of its ambivalence. After the massacre in the Texas town near the beginning, a group of children run among the corpses in the street firing make-believe pistols and imitating the gunfighters with admiration and delight; later, even more devastatingly, as Angel is dragged around Mapache's village, children chase after him laughing and shouting. With these images, Peckinpah clearly means to say that violence is an inherent part of human nature, but it is interesting that the faces of the children almost always contain expressions of innocence and wonder that are not quite accounted for by the philosophical statement about their intuitive cruelty. When the children in Angel's village look at the Wild Bunch, with shy curiosity and admiration, we cannot help but be touched by their responsiveness to these lost men. One of the Mexicans says to Pike shortly afterwards, as they observe the playfulness of the Gorch brothers, "We all dream of being a child again. Even the worst of us." For the faces of the children are still unformed, open to possibilities, and it is that sense of possibility that makes us dream. Children may be instinctively violent, but the freshness of their faces teases us to believe that they are capable of *something more* than violence. It is this something more that Peckinpah searches for in the Wild Bunch, too—call it an inchoate sense of honor or loyalty or commitment—and just as often as he is wryly skeptical about the Bunch, he asks us to believe that they are redeemable. The children in the film embody innocence and evil, beauty and corruption, gentleness and brutality, and the film as a whole wavers between a harsh, very contemporary cynicism and an older, mellower belief in grand human possibilities that has always been the most sentimental affirmation of the Western. Traditional Westerns wallowed in this sentimentality and became rosy parables of virtue triumphant, while some very recent Westerns have gone to the other extreme and opted for a cynical stance that is often just as hysterical and glib. It is Peckinpah's effort to play these two attitudes against each other that makes his Westerns seem so rich; his mixture of realism and romanticism (a mixture that was already recognizable, on a much smaller scale, in *Ride the High Country*), even if not yet quite rationally proportioned, illuminates the Western myths so that they seem relevant, not remote.

I spoke with Peckinpah about *The Wild Bunch* and about his career generally several months ago, while he was still completing the editing of the film and simultaneously making preparations for the shooting of his next film, *The Ballad of Cable Hogue*. During the afternoon that I spent with him, he was running down to the editing room, testing girls for a secondary role in *Cable Hogue*, looking at the art director's drawings, making arrangements for rehearsals, ordering horses. His ability to keep in command of everything was impressive, an ability that shows through the following conversation. But what is most interesting about this interview is that it reveals many of the same uncertainties that can be "read" in more disguised form in the film itself. Peckinpah is an instinctive director, not an intellectual one, and his instinct for cinema is unquestionably masterful. But I would say that if he is to continue to grow as an artist, he needs to strive for more intellectual clarity; he needs to order and question his hidden assumptions even more ruthlessly, so that he can go on testing himself instead of simply repeating and reworking the themes of *The Wild Bunch*. I hope that his next film is not a Western.

It's well known that you had a lot of trouble before you started working here at Warners, and I wanted to ask about your working relationships here. Apparently they're very satisfying.

Very satisfying. Delightful. I work very closely with my executive producer, Philip Feldman, and very closely with Ken Hyman, who is the president of Warner Brothers-Seven Arts. I find them to be very creative, tough, stimulating, and damn fine people to work with.

And you find that you have all the freedom that you want?

I think Ken Hyman described it as limited total carte blanche. And I find I work very well under these circumstances. I wouldn't want to change a damn thing. I like it.

How did you get involved with them?

Both Ken Hyman and Phil Feldman had seen *Ride the High Country* and *Major Dundee* and knew the circumstances behind the mutilation of *Dundee*, and they knew some of my television work also, and both wanted me to make pictures for them and with them. I was *delighted* in their trust and their encouragement, because I literally hadn't worked for four years because of the fiasco with Jerry Bresler on *Dundee* and Martin Ransohoff on *The Cincinnati Kid*. To some degree I have to take the blame, because I was an idiot to start to make a picture with those two people in the first place; their approach to films was so completely different from mine.

During the interim you did some television?

Some television and a screenplay or two, and wrote and directed "Noon Wine" for "Stage 67," which was a *joy* to do. That was with Jason Robards, Per Oscarsson, Olivia de Havilland. Dan Melnick of Talent Associates produced it. I worked very well with Dan. We were all very pleased with the way the show turned out. I received two nominations on it actually, one from the Writers Guild, one from the Screen Directors Guild.

But you didn't have any opportunity to work on films during that period?

No. I was known as a troublemaker—I think for all the wrong reasons actually. When you set out to make a certain type of picture, it's very difficult to change in the middle, particularly if you don't respect the people who are suggesting the changes, and if the changes are bloody fucking awful. Ransohoff talked one kind of picture on *The Cincinnati Kid* to me, but he didn't really want the kind of picture that I wanted to make; he wanted the kind of picture he got, which I thought was very, very dull.

Yes, I did too. What was the original intention?

The intention was to give a fairly honest look at life in the thirties, in a Depression area, and what happens to a man who plays stud for a living, how it affects his life and those around him. I thought the picture came out just like a story in an old *Cosmopolitan* or something, although I enjoyed the color. But I was dead set against casting Ann-Margret in that picture. I had a feeling I would never do the picture, but I didn't really expect to be fired after I got started. But that was just Marty's way. I found out later that no matter what I'd shot—and I thought it was some astonishingly good footage—I was going to be fired, or shall we say sandbagged. But he has his way of making films, and I have mine.

What about Major Dundee? *Did you have a lot of trouble while you were making that, or was it mostly in the cutting?*

A great deal of trouble all the way through. *Unbelievable* situation.

Was that also a case of starting out to do one kind of film and then being pressured to do something else?

Absolutely. It was a very tight script, intricately intertwined; you know, if you removed a part of it, something else would fall out fifteen pages later. Bresler wanted to cut after we started shooting, and we tried, but it didn't work.

And it was this bad reputation that kept you from working?

Yes. I know several people who wanted me for pictures, and the studios wouldn't touch me in any way, shape, or form. I couldn't even get on the lot at Columbia.

That's one of the frightening things about the whole industry.

I think it's changing. I hope it is.

Do you think you'd have less trouble now?

Well, I *am* less trouble now, let's put it that way. Maybe I've learned a lot. I will not start a picture until we know the ground rules, how we're going to work. And thank God, I don't have to. I can more or less pick and choose the properties I want to do, and who I'm going to do them with. It's a very good feeling.

With Mr. Feldman and Mr. Hyman, is it that they don't interfere as much, or is it that you feel that their attitudes are very close to yours?

They're enormously creative people, and I feel we work together very well. I respect them, and they respect me. They let me do my thing, so to speak, and whenever they can, they highlight it, and give me all the help that I could possibly need. They're *damn* good, they're tough, they've got good ideas. And I either have to get a better one, or I use theirs. You don't mind working with people like that; it's a delight.

I was listening to what you said earlier about the unions and guilds. Do you have trouble with them?

You always have problems with them. They make it very, very hard to make a picture, particularly the kind we're doing now on *Cable Hogue*, which is a low-budget picture. We are right on the line of not being able to make it. But it doesn't make any difference to the unions whether you only have a limited budget, or whether you're making a multimillion-dollar picture; the same rules go into effect. And I think that's detrimental to the industry. I think they should encourage low-budget pictures, and a lot more pictures would be made. I think they ought to have two rates. I *believe* in the unions, but I think they're hurting themselves, and they're hurting a lot of us who want to make particular stories that we have to do out of price. We should be *encouraged* by the unions to do these stories rather than being penalized—perhaps something like deferred payment if the picture makes money.

Was The Wild Bunch *an expensive film?*

That was a $4 million picture. But if we'd tried to do it here, it would have been impossible to bring it in for 6 or 7 million because of the extra problem and the sets, which are all Mexican. It was a difficult picture because of its size. We had a large cast and an enormous amount of action.

Are you more comfortable working on a smaller, more intimate film?

No, the amount of concentration is about the same. Both are challenging.

I ask because I've noticed that in your films the interplay of characters is something you are always very interested in and handle very well. So I was curious whether the epic scope of Wild Bunch *gets in the way of that concern with character.*

Well, I wasn't trying to make an epic; I was trying to tell a simple story about bad men in changing times. I was trying to make a few comments on violence and the people who live by violence. It's not a means to something; violence is an end in itself to these people. I enjoyed making it. We all worked very hard. I was talking to Bill Holden and Ernest Borgnine and some other members of the cast, and they all want to do another one. I guess we all knew we were making a serious picture when we were down there; there's a certain delight in that.

Everybody is so concerned right now about violence in films. What was your attitude about the violence?

Actually, it's an antiviolence film, because I use violence as it *is*. It's ugly, brutalizing, and bloody fucking awful. It's not fun and games and cowboys and Indians; it's a terrible, ugly thing. And yet there's a certain response that you get from it, an excitement, because we're all violent people; we have violence within us. I don't know if you can legislate against it. It's in children, as I bring out in the film. I don't know about violence on television. I object to it because I think it's usually so goddamned dull. They just have a lot of violence for its own sake; it's not motivated. Violence is a part of life, and I don't think we can bury our heads in the sand and ignore it. It's important to understand it and the reason people seem to need violence vicariously. We had five million years, you know, of surviving, and I don't see how the species is going to survive without violence.

You say that the film is really antiviolence, because it shows how ugly violence is. But as you also say, obviously a lot of people who watch it won't respond to it in that way.

I think they will, because there's enough of it.

You don't think some people will just get a kick out of it?

I don't think so. I think everybody will be a little sickened by it, at least I hope so, or a little dismayed, at least dismayed—which is the effect that I'm trying for. On *Dundee* they cut 80 percent of the violence out and made it very attractive and exciting; but the really bloody, awful things that happen to men in war were cut out of the picture, which I thought was *unforgivable*—along with most of the story and all the character interplay and the rest of it.

Did you face any sort of pressures to tone down the violence in this film because of all the uproar about it last summer?

No. We discussed it, but we had a particular story to make, and we thought that we had a point to make about violence—that it's awful, this *kind* of violence. Other kinds of violence may be very necessary; the violence in a pro football game is certainly fascinating to millions, and I thoroughly enjoy it. But I don't think we should say it doesn't exist and we should *destroy* violence—by what means? You can't legislate against it. On the one hand, you have the violent protests of these kids today, which I believe in. Some of the racial problems have only been brought to the public attention through violence. Then you can deal with the *horror* of President Kennedy's assassination and his brother's death. But a political assassination has very little to do with film violence. I don't think television had too much to do with training either Oswald or Sirhan.

Yes, I agree that people are really much too willing to jump to the con-

clusion that just because there have been violent acts, television and films must be the cause.

You know, that's *bullshit*; that's absolute bullshit.

Well, that's why I wondered whether you had been affected in any way by this talk.

No way whatsoever. I think war is a hideous thing, and we show a small part of a war; we show what kind of people get into the situation, and how they end. We try to make them human beings, and not all black, but there's certainly very little white in them.

One thing I felt in the early parts of the film was that the "good guys," the people on the side of the law, are really more ruthless and more brutal, even, than the criminals.

This was shot before the Chicago incidents, but I think they more or less prove the point I was trying to make, that power corrupts just as much as lawlessness.

Is Cable Hogue *a contemporary film?*

No, 1908, 1909—about people in the West, but it's not a Western.

That general period seems to be one that you're interested in.

No, I'm just trying to get out of the 1870 period. Right now I'm up to 1913, 1914. The next one is going to be even later.

In Wild Bunch, *why did you want to do a film about a group of criminals?*

The outlaws of the West have always fascinated me. They had a certain notoriety; they were supposed to have a Robin Hood quality about them, which was not really the truth, but they were strong individuals; in a land for all intents and purposes without law, they made their own. I suppose I'm something of an outlaw myself. I identify with them. But our characters in *The Wild Bunch* are limited and adolescent; they're not too bright. They're fascinating characters. I've always wondered what happened to the outlaw leaders of the Old West when it changed. It's been a fascinating subject to me, and I thought this story by Walon Green dramatized it, set it up well. So I wrote the screenplay with him and made the picture. It's a very uncompromising film—the language, the action, the details, the lives of these people are as I imagine they were. We tried to re-create an environment, an era, and I think we were reasonably successful with it. It's a disturbing film; people who've seen it call it a *shattering* film. The strange thing is that you feel a great sense of loss when these killers reach the end of the line.

Did you write Cable Hogue, *too?*

No, Warren Oates gave me a script that he'd read and liked, and I liked it enough to buy it. Gordon Dawson did the rewrite on it. John Crawford and Edmund Penney did the script, and I think it's a *lovely* script; I'm very happy to be doing it. It's got a lot of warmth. It's a love story really, but again it deals with some degree of morality.

Going back to what you said earlier about having a reputation as a troublemaker—I know this is an industry where people get labeled very easily. Does that reputation still affect you in any way?

I make trouble with shoddy workmanship, and with shoddy, shabby people—people who don't do their job—and the whiners, and complainers, and the bitchers, and the sore-asses who talk a good piece of work and never produce. I don't know why the hell they went into motion pictures in the first place. It's certainly not to make pictures; it's just a sort of masturbation or something, and I don't like to be around them. I was very lucky. I started in television with Dick Powell—an extraordinary man, who always encouraged you to do your best, and was creative and had good ideas, and with him I was able to do "The Westerner," which turned out to be quite an extraordinary little series. So he spoiled me, you might say—that dedication and enthusiasm and talent that he brought to the organization where I more or less grew up; and I was appalled to find out that there were so many self-centered idiots floating around who have other interests than making a good film. Again, it's my fault that I didn't understand this. I understand it better now.

Have you found a lot of sloppy work among studio people and technicians?

Well, I've found enough of it. I think Mr. Feldman and I fired twenty-two people off *The Wild Bunch.* That's not all studio people, of course. Some of them were independent; some of them were from the Mexico City Syndicato. But we work very hard. The days are certainly not eight-hour days for all the people concerned. There's actually a very fine staff here at Warner Brothers.

Do you plan to go on working with Phil Feldman?

We've got two other projects that we're preparing. And I'm up for two other pictures off the lot, and it depends on which one is going to be put together first. As I said, I like working with Phil very much. I expect to be working with him in the future.

STEPHEN FARBER

It's interesting to know what kind of relationship between a director and a producer works best. Very few filmmakers are able to find a producer whom they can work with congenially.

You have to be very careful with Phil, because if I would casually say, I would like to shoot past the top of a mountain, that night he would have the top of the mountain gone. He's beautiful. And he will do it at a cost that is hardly anything. He's a miracle man. He's interested in making good pictures.

And you feel that you and he have the same interests?

Absolutely. Absolutely. We have *enormous* differences sometimes, thank God. It keeps me stimulated. And sometimes he's very right indeed. Phil is executive producer on *Cable Hogue*. We're forming, I think, a fine staff here, and we have some great plans.

Was The Wild Bunch *almost all shot on location?*

Every bit of it.

And how about this new film?

Every bit of it is on location. And then I think I will take a couple of months off. By June, it'll be two years I've been working on *Wild Bunch*. I will have completed two pictures in two years, which is a lot of work when you're involved in writing and directing and producing. But I don't like to work any other way.

Did you have difficulty working in Mexico?

Not really. The staff of the Syndicato is difficult to work with. The workers, the crews, the technicians are marvelous; they're as good as they are here, very enthusiastic. But their unions present problems as unions do here. But I like Mexico very much. I have an ex-wife there, many good friends.

Did you do a lot of reconstruction work, or did you find that you could use the locations as they existed?

No, we did some reconstruction work in the town of Paras. It's an old town, built in the 1600s, so we reconstructed some of the buildings to give it a little more of an Anglo look, like a Texas border town, and it came out very well. The film looks exactly like the newsreels of 1916 of the Revolution. I got a lot of old newsreels from the Mexican government. And actually I wanted to make the picture in black and white. We have no choice. I think black and white evokes a different kind of feeling. We have scratched prints in negative of some of the film, but I'm using it, I'm scratching other prints to give it a newsreel quality. I think it'll play.

How much actual visual planning do you do? Do you try to conceive all of the shots very carefully before you get to the set?

Every one. I'm up at four o'clock in the morning, looking at my day's work, which I've already sketched in before, and I go over it again and again. Light changes, action; something may come up, so I try to know every single possible approach, and then I pick the one I want. I always prepare. That's why I lose fifteen to twenty pounds on every picture; it's like an endurance race or something. No, I don't like to go on the set and start "creating." We do that before in rehearsal. But we know our work so well that if some new idea does come up, we've gone through everything else, and we know exactly where to go. For example, the exit from the village in *Wild Bunch* was not in the script. I shot that in less than a day, and it's one of the high points in the picture. All of a sudden we knew the picture needed it. But that couldn't have happened unless we'd been so well prepared.

Saw *Red Desert* the other night. Jesus, it's a beautiful film, extraordinary; I loved it. A little self-indulgent here and there. That thin line of doing something right and then getting carried away. I've only seen two Antonioni films—that and *Blow-Up*. I thought *Blow-Up* was flawless. And I think that's the only film outside of *Bonnie and Clyde* that I've seen in the last two years. I ran *Bonnie and Clyde* when I got back from *The Wild Bunch*.

What did you think of it?

Loved it, *loved* it—they did all my shtick. I thought everything about it was great. Although our picture is completely different in many ways, there are strange similarities. I don't know *how* they are similar, except they both deal with violence and the people involved in violence. Our people are not as attractive as Faye and Warren, but yet they are attractive.

Again, it's that sympathy for the outlaw.

I just tried to make them honest. Yet they come off as human beings, which possibly is a frightening thing.

They're going to really get disturbed about this, I'll tell you. I'm exhausted when I see it, I'm literally exhausted for hours, and all it is really is a simple adventure story.

4 ▶

The Versions of *The Wild Bunch*

PAUL SEYDOR

There is nothing more futile under the sun than a mere adventurer. He might have loved at one time—which would have been a saving grace. I mean loved adventure for itself. But if so, he was bound to lose this grace very soon. Adventure by itself is but a phantom, a dubious shape without a heart.

—Joseph Conrad

I

"I read the screenplay of *The Wild Bunch*," Robert Culp said in late 1969, "on a gray, empty morning two years ago in Peckinpah's home on the beach above Malibu. I groaned with each foolish page, to think he had to go and do this nonsense for all those bleak months in Mexico."[1] When he saw the completed film, Culp, in one of the most intelligent and perceptive commentaries yet published on *The Wild Bunch*, radically reversed his judgment. Nevertheless, it is ironic that the actor, himself on occasion both scriptwriter and director, should have made the common mistake when assessing a script by itself: failing to realize that the director may see possibilities that others don't. At the time, Culp was not alone. Lee Marvin first told Peckinpah about the script when, in the director's words, it existed only as "an outline of some thirty-two pages" by Walon Green and Roy Sickner and as a "rough screenplay, including some of the dialogue that was used in the picture."[2] Peckinpah eventually did a rewrite, polishing a lot of the dialogue, adding some incidents, changing others, before submitting it to Warner

"The Versions of *The Wild Bunch*" by Paul Seydor is a revision of a portion of chapter 3 of *Peckinpah: The Western Films* by Paul Seydor (Champaign: University of Illinois Press, 1980). Reprinted by permission of Paul Seydor.

Brothers, whereupon Ken Hyman, the studio's head of production, bought it. Marvin, in the meantime, was not interested in playing in the film; and several more of Peckinpah's friends couldn't understand why, after all those years of being out of work, he would want to make *another* Western, and one with a story apparently this simple.

In fact, *The Wild Bunch* was not the first project Peckinpah turned to when he was called by Warner Brothers. Hyman had a property of his own, called *The Diamond Story*, for which he wanted Peckinpah's services, and the director himself had at least two other projects. Sometime in 1967, Warren Oates had shown him an original script by John Crawford and Edmund Penney entitled *The Ballad of Cable Hogue*, which Peckinpah had liked so much he had purchased it, set to revising, and thought about casting. He was also talking about directing James Gould Cozzens's *The Castaway*, a script for which he had already prepared. When casting problems forced *The Diamond Story* to be postponed indefinitely (and eventually abandoned altogether), Hyman gave Peckinpah the go-ahead on *The Wild Bunch*, which by then was beginning to exert a strong claim upon the director's attentions.

Once he was committed to the project, his involvement was total. In addition to the extensive work he had already done on the script, he personally supervised every aspect of production from cinematography to editing to special effects to wardrobe. By the conservative estimate of several crew members, he worked fifteen to eighteen hours a day and cared about only one thing: what was "going to be finally realized on the screen."[3] One of the reasons he worked this hard is that he wanted to be as absolutely free from studio interference as possible while shooting the picture. To this end, he polished a few self-contained sequences while shooting the rest. According to his assistant, Joel Reisner, Peckinpah "outguessed the studio. They did ask to see film and the ten reels they saw were the ten reels Peckinpah wanted them to see." Peckinpah was as a consequence left unhassled during production and editing. It wasn't until after the picture opened that the betrayal came. The upshot was that within the first month of its release there were three different "official" versions of *The Wild Bunch*—one European, two American—and any of several individual prints that were different from any other mostly because of haste and carelessness.

The first filmgoers to see *The Wild Bunch* were an audience in a Kansas City theatre, where the film was sneak-previewed at a length of about 151 minutes.[4] It was this version that started the controversy about the violence: over thirty persons walked out, and a few actually became physically ill in the alley outside the theatre. Peckinpah returned to Hollywood to resume work on the editing. He deleted several repetitive scenes and in general tightened the narrative line. "I had to make the film play better," he said.[5] He also excised several moments of violence, despite the studio's wish for more rather than less bloodshed. As the producer, Phil Feldman, has pointed out, "Some people have accused Sam of wanting to make it more bloody. Actually he toned down the violence that I wanted, especially in the first fight."[6]

Peckinpah's reasons were several. He felt that some of the violence was "excessive to the points I wanted to make," and he didn't "want the violence, per se, to dominate what is happening to the people," adding, "I have a story to tell, too."[7] He also wanted the violence to enter and accumulate more gradually, to which end he heightened the contrast between the opening and closing gunfights. The point of view in the opening gunfight, which is an ambush of the Bunch by bounty hunters and railroad men, is generally that of innocent bystanders caught in a crossfire that suddenly erupts through the fabric of everyday life in a quiet, middle-class Texas border town. The violence is therefore more elliptical and oblique. The point of view in the closing gunfight is generally that of the Bunch themselves, who, in returning for a friend, are making their one last-ditch stab at glory; the carnage is, therefore, far more explicit, escalating past horror into exultation. There can be little doubt, moreover, that the response of that preview audience influenced Peckinpah's decisions profoundly, and that he came away having learned something about the dynamics of film violence. "If I'm so bloody that I drive people out of the theatre," he once remarked after he had made *Straw Dogs*, "then I've failed."[8] It is after all easy enough to disgust people (as Godard demonstrated in *Weekend* by having a pig's throat cut on screen). But the real artistic achievement consists in treading that thin line between meaningful excess and mere exploitation, and the first problem in winning an audience's assent to a vision in which violence is part of the very essence is to get audiences to watch the film. All things considered, Peckinpah was probably right when he speculated that the reason some people hate his films is that they want to walk out "but they can't. They can't turn their faces away. They watch, and that makes them mad."[9] It also tends to corroborate one of the things he is trying to say about the seductive power of violence. For all its intensity and ferocity, Peckinpah's has never been, by any stretch of the imagination, the goriest or even the most "realistic" violence to be found in films. It is quite unlike any other filmmaker's, and much of its distinction lies in his fusion of beauty and ugliness, of excitement and terror, the point being simultaneously to entice and revulse, to attract and appall. It is precisely that ambiguity which makes his violence so artistically complex, emotionally disturbing, and psychologically sophisticated. We *don't* look away, and therein consists equally his argument and his achievement.

Peckinpah's final cut ran 145 minutes. Around this time there arose a disagreement as to how to market the film. According to the director, "The European distributor saw it and said, 'Roadshow.' The domestic distributor saw it and said 'Double-bill,'"—meaning second-run theatres and the drive-in circuit, paired with another film, preferably a Western—and also wanted it shorter.[10] As a conciliatory gesture Peckinpah agreed to remove part of one scene for the American version only, and the studio supported him and made *The Wild Bunch* its feature summer attraction. In Europe, meanwhile, the film received full prestige treatment with limited bookings, hard-ticket sales, intermission complete with entr'acte overture, and first-run prints in 70-mm CinemaScope with six-track stereophonic sound. In America it was shown in 35-mm Panavision. In either case, *The Wild Bunch* was previewed to critics and shown to audiences in a form that Peckinpah was happy to pronounce himself 94 to 96 percent satisfied with.[11]

From here on the tale becomes rather involved. If a filmgoer had gone to see *The Wild Bunch* in early July 1969, he would have seen a two-hour, twenty-three-minute film; if he had gone in mid-July, he would have seen a two-hour, fifteen-minute film, as Vincent Canby, the reviewer for the *New York Times*, discovered when he went to see the film for a second time. The missing footage, which will be described in detail later on, consists principally of flashbacks that fill in the past of the Bunch's leader, Pike Bishop, and an attack by Villa's rebels on the army of Mapache. Canby immediately telephoned Feldman, who said that the studio had been contemplating the cuts for a good while and would have made them before the premiere had there been time.[12] If this had been done, Feldman continued, arguing with curious reasoning, Canby would not have been bothered by the missing scenes because he would never have seen them in the first place. This was not, of course, the issue, which concerns on the one hand the director's wishes and on the other the artistic integrity of the film. Feldman was misleading as regards the one and simply wrong as regards the other.[13] Assuring Canby that the cuts had been made with the good of the film in mind, Feldman said that filmmaking is a cooperative enterprise and strongly implied that the cuts were carried out with Peckinpah's full awareness and approval. Here are Peckinpah's comments on the subject: "I do not agree with that in any way, shape, or form"; "all I can say is that these cuts are a disaster."[14] Canby wasn't aware of Peckinpah's feelings at the time, for when he tried to verify Feldman's statements he discovered that the director, exhausted from having made two films back-to-back, had gone to Hawaii for a short period of rest and recuperation and could not be reached by telephone. As it happened, Feldman *had* managed to reach Peckinpah in Hawaii to consult him about the cuts, but told the director only that he would like to remove two of the flashbacks as an experiment in a couple of theatres. "I okayed it," Peckinpah said, "on an *experimental* basis in two theatres *only*." What happened instead, and the next thing Peckinpah knew, was that two whole scenes and parts of four other scenes had been removed from prints in three hundred theatres.

Feldman has been made to shoulder much of the blame for the postrelease cuts in *The Wild Bunch*, but any of several memos indicate that he was in fact working very hard to protect the film and to persuade the studio to let it find its audience. From the beginning, he and Peckinpah wanted the same marketing strategy Warners had used on *Bonnie and Clyde* the year before: few theatres, select cities, letting the word of mouth build, then widening the release after several weeks. Instead, having decided to make the film its feature summer attraction, the studio proceeded to launch it out the back door. An expensive summer Western with big Hollywood stars, *The Wild Bunch* was marketed according to the standard John Wayne picture strategy: it was first opened in about twenty theatres in Texas during June. Given the richness, depth, and complexity of Peckinpah's vision, the returns in this market were terrible, to no one's surprise but that of the studio executives, who immediately panicked and demanded a shorter picture with a wider release. By July the film was playing in over three hundred theatres across the country, a small figure by nineties' standards, but large in 1969.[15]

What happened next was almost predictable. With the film in so many theatres, yet without benefit of adequate word of mouth, ticket sales per theatre were relatively low. This did lead some exhibitors, as Feldman told Canby, to ask that the film be short-ened, not to "accelerate the pace" or "improve the aesthetics" but simply to try to generate more box office by squeezing in another showing each day.

It seems clear in retrospect that the director and the producer understood how their picture should be marketed much better than the studio did. *The Wild Bunch* became the most talked about, commented upon, and argued over film of the summer. Although predictably controversial, well over half of the first round of reviews was favorable, many of them quite enthusiastic and from publications that mattered, like *The New Republic*, *The New Yorker*, the *New York Times*, the *Los Angeles Times*, *Life*, and *Time*. Word of mouth is exactly what *The Wild Bunch* needed and exactly what it was starting to get. And though it doesn't work quickly, it was working, as the excellent returns in New York, Los Angeles, San Francisco, and a few other big cities were already demonstrating. Unfortunately, it wasn't working fast enough for an impatient studio desperate to take some action, any action, to bolster ticket sales.

To make matters worse, Ken Hyman, the Seven Arts half of Warner Brothers-Seven Arts, had pulled out of the partnership, thus leaving the film without its staunchest advocate and protector at the studio and leaving Feldman to fight on alone. Once the new management was in place, Feldman was issued through channels an ultimatum from the office of the studio head Ted Ashley ordering fifteen to twenty minutes cut from *The Wild Bunch*. It is curious to know why at a juncture like this the producer did not alert the director, who was still in Hawaii, as to exactly what was going on, choosing instead to withhold some things and simply lie about others. Had Peckinpah been told of the studio's plans, he could have returned, and together he and Feldman stood a good chance of prevailing. One explanation is that in addition to feeling beleaguered, Feldman also found himself in an increasingly com-promised position. It was no secret that throughout the months of editing he had argued continually for the removal of the flashbacks and a couple of other scenes. Suddenly he was being presented with an opportunity to do something creative that he sincerely believed was for the good of the film and with the justification that the studio was ordering him to do it anyway. Nor was he alone in thinking the scenes in question problematic. The first national magazine to review *The Wild Bunch* was *Time*, which in its 20 June 1969 issue published an extraordinarily laudatory review that had just one critical comment. "Peckinpah is sometimes guilty of overkill himself," the reviewer wrote. "Action sequences—like an attack by the Villa forces on Mapache—occasionally destroy the continuity of the elaborate story, and flashbacks are introduced with surprising clumsiness."

What clinched Feldman's decision was a bit of professional jealousy. Once the film was released, he was, perhaps understandably, resentful that all the talk, and credit, went to the director, little or none to himself as producer. He went so far as to write Peckinpah a long letter complaining of how little attention the press was paying him. What he couldn't have known is that earlier in the spring, before postproduction was even completed, Peckinpah had *already* praised both Feldman and Hyman in the most enthusiastic terms in interviews that would not see the light of publication until later that summer or fall. All the same, the director responded to the letter by personally taking out a full-page ad in *Variety* thanking Feldman and indicating in no uncertain terms his great creative contribution to the project. Ironically, the *Variety* ad appeared in the 14 July 1969 issue, just about the time that, unbeknownst to the director, the last of the cuts in the last of the prints was being completed.[16]

As things turned out, the decision was questionable in economic, logistical, *and* aesthetic terms. The studio had to lift six scenes in whole or in part from over three hundred prints that by then were all over the country. As recalling them was impossible, the job had to be done at the various distribution centers, either with counts—i.e., beginning and ending footages of the scenes to be removed in their respective reels—or with a template print provided by the postproduction facility back in Los Angeles. In other words, those who physically made the cuts did not even look at their work when they were finished. (Had they even been motivated, there were too many prints, not enough time.) This explains why during its first run, several "versions" of *The Wild Bunch* were playing, including prints in which some of the scenes were removed but not others, and prints in which *pieces* of some scenes were removed while the rest of the scene was left in. And several prints, mostly those playing in small towns, were left untouched entirely. This was also a sloppy way to execute the lifts, especially egregious to a film of the supreme stylistic unity and technical finish of *The Wild Bunch*. When a cut is made in a composite print (i.e., a print with the optical sound-stripe), it leaves a visible tape splice on the film and, worse, an audible "pop" sometimes preceded by a dropout. As most of the transitions between scenes consist in lap dissolves, the effect of the cuts on the soundtrack is brutal. Still, barbaric as the whole procedure was, it had one unexpected benefit: the master negative was left untouched, so that when new prints were struck in subsequent years, they were at least of the version Peckinpah approved for domestic release.

In the end, the cuts had no material effect on the film's box office. Nor did most of the exhibitors bother to rearrange their schedules to get in another showing. Many of them just added the extra time between showings to sell more refreshments, and one theatre is known to have filled up the spare time with a "Tom and Jerry" cartoon.[17]

What is so sad about this story, quite apart from any damage done to the film, is the effect upon Peckinpah himself. When he embarked upon *The Wild Bunch*, he was so happy to be making films once more that he couldn't praise Feldman and Hyman highly enough. By the time he was into postproduction work, his generosity was positively lavish. He spoke of "the courage and wisdom of one man—Kenny Hyman" as having made it possible for him to be directing again, and he referred to Feldman as "a miracle man."[18] In the spring of 1969, he said of both of them: "They're enormously creative people, and I feel we work together very well. I respect them, and they respect me. They let me do my thing, so to speak, and whenever they can, they highlight it, and give me all the help that I could possibly need. They're *damn* good, they're tough, they've got good ideas. And I either have to get a better one, or I use theirs. You don't mind working with people like that; it's a delight."[19] He couldn't have known then that the "high-lighting" would take the form of surgery, and when he did know it, he tried his best to suppress his anger, frustration, and disappoint-ment, as he remained grateful that he could get *The Wild Bunch* made at all. But he continued to be especially hurt that after all they had been through together making the film, Feldman had still deceived him. Nor were matters made much better by a letter Feldman wrote him shortly after the prints had been cut saying that if he had known Peckinpah cared so much about this material he wouldn't have let it be removed. It must be reported, however, that Feldman, perhaps by way of atonement, tried the rest of the summer and into the fall to get Warners to strike prints of the European version for release in selected theatres in New York and Los Angeles. He was not successful, but he must be credited with efforts that were authentic and sincere. Meanwhile, as time wore on and the full extent of the damage sank in, the hurt Peckinpah felt over what he believed was betrayal became anger, and the anger became a rage less and less susceptible of suppression. Once, in Feldman's presence, a reporter asked Peckinpah to detail exactly what was cut from the film. The director deferred to the producer, who "began ticking off the shots and sequences one by one. Suddenly a crash came, the dishes on the table rattled. Peckinpah had slammed his fist against the table, and he looked livid with anger. 'You mean *that's* out,' he squeezed out through his apoplexy. 'Yes, Sam,' Feldman said pacifyingly, 'I thought I told you.'"[20]

By the spring of 1970, when it became abundantly clear that Warner Brothers had withdrawn all support from *The Wild Bunch* at the Academy Awards and was planning to dump *The Ballad of Cable Hogue* on the market with no advance publicity, Peckinpah was already looking for new associates. Two years after his association with Feldman had dissolved, Peckinpah told a reporter: "I've had my share of headaches with producers. Phil Feldman was another one. I had great difficulties bringing in *The Wild Bunch*—it took eighty-one days of shooting—and then Feldman let those rotten sons of bitches at Warners chop out twenty minutes so they could hustle more popcorn."[21] Those who wish to know why Sam Peckinpah became an angry, rather hard-bitten, somewhat cynical man have only to meditate upon how it happened that this film, which Robert Culp has accurately called "more quintessentially and bitterly American than any film since World War II,"[22] cannot readily be seen in America in the form its maker conceived.[23]

II

Arnold Schönberg once warned opera-house managers and conductors about the dangers of trying to reduce, however judiciously, the length of Wagner's music dramas: when you attempt to shorten a long work by removing sections, he told them, you do not make it into a shorter work, merely into a long work that happens to be short in places. What exactly was removed from *The Wild Bunch*, and how does its elimination affect the film? To place things in perspective, it should be stated immediately that even in its truncated version the film remains a great achievement, the mutilation in no way approaching what was done to *Major Dundee* (or what, later, would be done to *Pat Garrett and Billy the Kid*). The three great action sequences—the opening and closing gunfights and the Bunch's assault on the train—are untouched, and the continuity in general does not suffer. If the film were nothing more than what *Variety* is fond of calling an "action-oater," the cuts could even be said to constitute an improvement. However, as there was nothing wrong with the narrative flow before they were made and as the film depends upon more than just its action sequences, the net effect of the cuts is to diminish the epic scope slightly, reduce some of the ironies moderately, and lessen the complexity of characters and character motivations considerably. In all, three flashbacks with related dialogue, two whole scenes, and part of another scene were removed. The first flashback reveals how Pike's best friend, Deke Thornton, was captured; the second is of Crazy Lee in the opening robbery; and the third shows how Pike was wounded in the leg.[24] The two scenes lifted are the long one of Villa's raid on Mapache's forces at the telegraph station and a short one set in Mapache's village showing the aftermath of the raid. Finally, part of the festivities at Angel's village was excised. Involving little dialogue and about a minute's worth of screen time, this last is hardly damaging at all. However, the film as a whole is richer for its inclusion, as it shows the Bunch relaxing and establishes more clearly their status as guests of honor in Angel's village. It thereby serves as preparation for the big scene the following morning when the entire village turns out to bid the Bunch farewell, and it helps to account for why these people view the Bunch as liberators—all of which is crucial to the reprise of this farewell at the end of the film.

This elision contains, moreover, one bit of business—Dutch dancing with a Mexican woman, and Old Sykes cutting in—that, if back in, would mercifully eliminate a nonexistent ambiguity some viewers have claimed to find. Near the end, Dutch does not accompany Pike and the Gorch brothers into the brothel, which led one interviewer to ask Peckinpah if Dutch is homosexual. The director laughed and replied: "In the first place, I didn't know where to put him. In the second place, he had the closest ties with Angel, so he was more preoccupied with things, right? It was on his mind—all he wanted to do was get him out. . . . Angel saved his life on the train, and, you see, in many ways Dutch . . . was the conscience of the Wild Bunch."[25] The favored interpretation of the interrelationships within the Bunch pegs Angel as the group's conscience. But in this case, the artist—not his critics—is correct. Angel is victim both to the Bunch's readiness to renege upon their code of honor and to his own revolutionary ideals; but it is Dutch who, at two moments, draws some vital distinctions. "We ain't nothing like him," he says, when Pike compares the Bunch to Mapache. "We don't *hang* nobody." And sometime later, it is Dutch who reminds Pike that Angel, by keeping his mouth shut about the Bunch's complicity in the theft of the rifles, "played his string right out to the end."

The longest cut has Mapache awaiting a telegram that will inform him whether the Bunch have successfully looted the U.S. munitions train, for which he is paying them ten thousand dollars in gold. As there is no telegraph in Agua Verde, the village in which his army is headquartered, Mapache and his retinue have taken a train to a nearby station where, awaiting the message, they are attacked by Villa's forces. While most of his men scurry for cover, urging him to join them, Mapache refuses to budge and, soldiers dropping around him, holds his ground until he receives the telegram. The point made is that for all his loathsomeness he is a genuinely fearless man, which Peckinpah reinforces by having a small boy, dressed in military clothes, deliver the telegram and watch, wide-eyed with admiration and even envy, as Mapache reads it. Although it has been shown that Mapache is little more than a bandit and a killer, a dupe whom Huerta has put in charge of a regiment, clearly for this boy the general is a hero, someone to be emulated. The boy puffs out his chest, salutes, and together he and the general walk calmly under fire toward the train as the scene ends. Moreover, the attack by Villa's forces, their sole appearance in the film, is vital; without it, the only revolutionaries seen are the Indians of Angel's village, for whom Angel has traded his share of the gold to provide them with weapons. Yet in the absence of a *dramatic* demonstration of Villa's military power, there is no longer any urgency behind the advice of Mapache's German advisors to steal arms from a neutral country by employing men who are fugitives from that country. A whole dimension of the international- al implications of the story is thus lost, and with it an important character revelation and several shades of irony.

In *Major Dundee*, Peckinpah said he was trying to tell the story of a man who repeatedly fails in what he sets out to do. The director himself failed in that telling, but he told it in *The Wild Bunch*, and the remainder of the missing scenes deals directly with that aspect of the story. Pike Bishop is an aging outlaw distinguished or notorious (depending on one's point of view) for robbing trains in the Southwest. By 1913, the pickings have become pretty lean, the available territory more and more crowded. Most of the companions of his youth and middle age are dead or imprisoned (for instance, Deke Thornton); the older companions of those days are by now so old as to be infirm and a nuisance (such as Old Sykes); and the younger members of the Bunch (the Gorch brothers, Angel) all have other interests and are fast becoming impatient with the older members. Pike and the Bunch, dressed in regulation army uniforms and riding army horses, enter San Rafael to rob the train office only to discover they've walked into a trap laid by Pat Harrigan—a railroad official who is Pike's old nemesis—with the help of Deke Thornton, Pike's former partner. The Bunch have to fight their way back out of town, through bounty hunters who fire from the surrounding rooftops with manic abandon and through dozens of citizens, including several children and a group of temperance marchers, mostly women. In one horrifying moment of confusion, Pike, wheeling his horse to flee, accidentally knocks down and tramples a woman before he can get the terrified animal under control. (On the outskirts of town, as the Bunch regroup, Pike untangles her shawl from his stirrup.) When the remaining members of the Bunch go to divide the take, they find washers, not coins, in the payroll sacks. "Silver rings!" exclaims a disbelieving Tector Gorch, while his brother Lyle shouts at Pike, "All your fancy planning and talking damn near got us shot to pieces over a few lousy bags of washers!" Pike ignores the charge, and mutters, half to himself, "We've got to start thinking beyond our guns. Those days are closing fast."

The theme of entrapment is thus quickly established, and it comes from all directions: advancing age, diminishing space, changing times, and, for Pike himself, a loss of self-respect owing to a series of blunders, mistakes, and failures of which the botched train office robbery, in which the Bunch's number was reduced by half, is only the first to be shown. The second occurs in the first flashback that is no longer in the film. Thornton and his bounty hunters sit around a campfire as one of them asks what kind of man Pike is. "The best," Thornton answers, "he never got caught." In the revised version, this cuts to Pike's camp, where he and Dutch talk about the next job, which might involve looting an army payroll train. Dutch warns, "They'll be waiting for us," and Pike answers, "I wouldn't have it any other way." As the film now stands, this sounds like empty, macho bravado, and Dutch's repetition, "Pike, I wouldn't have it any other way either," which closes the scene, sounds maudlin. In the original version, when Pike first speaks the line it is followed by a flashback which has Pike and Thornton hiding out in a bordello in a town where they've just pulled a job. Thornton, visibly apprehensive, urges they leave, while Pike orders him to relax, assuring him this is the last place the law will think to look. "How can you be so damn sure?" Thornton asks. Pike, with excruciating pomposity, replies, "Being sure is my business!" At that moment, the door bursts open to reveal a Pinkerton agent drawing a bead on Thornton. He fires and hits Thornton, while Pike uses the momentary diversion to escape out the back way. The flashback is not presented continuously, but is repeatedly interrupted by dissolves back to the present, to closeups first of Pike, then of Thornton, the editing itself establishing a structural arc that binds the two men—formerly partners, now on opposite sides of the law—by way of a common memory.

Unfortunately, when the flashback was removed, it took with it several lines of dialogue. "Damn," Dutch says, "you sure must have hurt that railroad. They spent a lot of money setting up that ambush." Pike replies, "I caught up with them. Two or three times. There was a man named Harrigan, used to have a way of doing things. I made him change his ways. There's a hell of a lot of people, Dutch, that just can't stand to be wrong. They can't forget it, that pride, being wrong, or learn by it." These remarks allude to his longstanding duel with Harrigan; and when Dutch asks if the Bunch learned anything from being wrong that morning, Pike answers, "I sure hope to God we did." The exchange is both revealing and curiously touching. It suggests the pride Pike himself feels in his accomplishments as an outlaw over the years, and it identifies Pike's own flaw, that very pride which doesn't want to admit to mistakes. At the same time, the quickness with which Pike informs Dutch that he got even with the railroad finds an immediate explanation in his recollection of Thornton's capture, and the whole scene establishes the twin components in Pike's motivation: his past failures and his desire for success, for another good score, to prove himself. When we see that it was essentially his fault that Thornton was captured, we realize why Pike talks so much about the old days, and why he is so insistent that the next job the Bunch pull not be an easy one: he has a terrible need right then for reassurance that he is worth anything at all. We also realize why throughout the film he is so obstinately disinclined to judge Thornton for teaming up with the railroad: it was because of Pike's carelessness that Thornton wound up facing the alternative of remaining in prison to be whipped day after day or joining the posse. (In an early argument between Thornton and Harrigan,

The Versions of *The Wild Bunch*

Peckinpah rapidly fades in and out a flashback of one of those whippings, the strong implication being that Harrigan used his wealth and influence to have Thornton beaten as a way of forcing him to join up.) Finally, when Dutch echoes Pike by saying, "I wouldn't have it any other way either," the effect, far from maudlin, is to provide an undercurrent of pathos, Dutch's refrain becoming a sympathetic response to the need he senses in his friend for reassurance.

The next flashback to be removed reinforces the motif of desertion. During the opening robbery, Pike had ordered Crazy Lee, the youngest member of the Bunch, to hold some customers hostage "as long as you can until after the shooting starts." C. L. replies, "I'll hold them here until hell freezes over or you say different." The order is initially puzzling, as it has no strategic value for the Bunch's escape (the customers are unarmed). It is not until the kid is shown to be a near psychopath that we realize the reason for Pike's order: C. L. is obviously too reckless to be reliable, too dangerous even for a "wild" Bunch, and Pike was using this opportunity to get rid of him. The following day, Pike discovers that C. L. was Old Sykes's grandson. Sykes hadn't told Pike because he figured Pike had enough to worry about, and anyhow he didn't want the kid getting any special treatment. All the same, Sykes wants to know how his boy handled himself when things got hot, wants to be sure the kid didn't run out on anybody. Before Pike can answer, Peckinpah rapidly dissolves in a flashback of C. L. in which we hear Pike's "Hold 'em here" reverberate a few times, much as his earlier "Being sure is my business" echoed and re-echoed throughout the whole flashback of Thornton's capture. Pike simply mutters that the kid did "fine, just fine." The scene also has some ironies of its own—for example, Pike's readiness to lie about the kid's actual performance to preserve his friend's illusions: C. L. didn't run when things got hot, but neither was he very reliable beyond the simple expedient of following orders. Moreover, the scene is so placed that it creates another irony, for together with the flashback of Thornton's capture it frames the big scene in which Pike declares his code. Earlier that same day, Tector had threatened to get rid of Sykes, but Pike had intervened: "You're not getting rid of anybody. We're going to stick together, just like it used to be. When you side with a man you stay with him, and if you can't do that you're like some animal. You're finished. *We're* finished! All of us." The point here is not so much that Pike is a hypocrite as that he fails to live up to his own standards of behavior from time to time and becomes, according to those standards, like an animal. However limited we may find his code, what is significant in the context of the story is that the code is quite important to him, and it is the disparity between word and deed in his past which eats at him throughout the film.

The third and last flashback that was cut shows how Pike was wounded. He was courting a woman named Aurora whom he wanted to marry. Late one night her husband returned, caught them in the bedroom, and shot at them, killing her but only wounding Pike in the leg. The staging and details of the set are significant and will reverberate later in the film. The room is dark, lighted only by an oil lamp that Aurora extinguishes. Behind her there is an armoire with a mirrored door. When her husband bursts in, we see it first as a reflection in the mirror behind her. As Pike tells it, the husband was supposedly gone for good—"He's never coming back," Aurora had said—and Pike had gotten careless and dropped his guard. As with the other flashbacks, this one is structurally significant, because it is placed immediately before the assault on the train. When Dutch asks if he ever caught up with the husband, Pike says, "No, but there's not a day or an hour goes by that I don't think about it." Then he adds, "This is our last go-round, Dutch; this time we do it right." As before, it is the triggering of a painful memory that makes us aware of how desperately Pike needs to have something in his life go right, and it is in this particular memory that the line "Being sure is my business" finds its saddest resonance. Being sure is Pike's business, yet he got careless, and the woman he loved was killed as a consequence.

Another resonance lost when this flashback was removed occurs in that moment in the final battle when Pike backs into a room for cover. On one side there is a woman, reflected in a mirrored door on the other. Noticing a slight movement, Pike fires, shattering the reflection and killing an officer hiding behind the door. But Pike does not shoot the woman. When he turns from her, she raises a pistol and shoots him in the back. Almost reflexively, he wheels, shouts "Bitch!," and blasts her with his shotgun. The moment is deliberately, intentionally shocking, but it is not gratuitous. The small room, the mirrored door, the triangle of one woman, two men, only Pike now the intruder, the double killing, the single wounding (this time near the heart)—all these are clearly meant to invoke the earlier scene and to play off it themes of buried rage and retribution. As always with this artist when he is working at the peak of his capacity, nothing exists by itself alone, nothing is without both immediate and long-range effect.

This flashback also serves to contravene a general objection often lodged against *The Wild Bunch* to the effect that all the women characters are unsympathetic. This is, even with the flashback missing, a specious objection. For one thing, Peckinpah is being true to his materials, and part of that truth requires that he deal with the kind of women—whores, for example—men like these would probably be associated with. For another thing, some reviewers even got the plot garbled. It is not Angel's own mother but the mother of the girl (Teresa) he kills who turns him in. The point is thus not that all women are treacherous or even that this particular woman is treacherous; the point is that the mother is grief-stricken, and telling on Angel becomes the only way she has of getting justice for the murder of her daughter. (Peckinpah even has the girl's funeral cortege pass through one scene.) Most of the same reviewers were also insensitive to many of the nuances in the exchange between Angel and Teresa prior to the killing. Presented entirely in Spanish and thus a remarkable demonstration of Peckinpah's ability to suggest much with filmic means alone, the exchange makes it clear enough that there was more to their relationship than the simple matter of her betrayal of him, that Mapache had become for her a way of getting out of her village and also a way of surviving. But when she flaunts this, Angel, enraged, shoots her. Yet Peckinpah's command of the emotional dynamics that underlie so much masculine honor, especially during moments of tension, is so astute that Angel's action becomes at least as much a response to the ridicule by the Gorch brothers, who, insensitive to his mounting rage and frustration, make wisecracks like, "She sure ain't your woman no more" and "Look at her licking inside that general's ear." This killing is also obviously meant to be placed against the flashback which shows Aurora's death, only there it is not a matter of any betrayal—her husband had, for all practical purposes, abandoned her—merely the man's sick thirst to salve his pride by getting even. In both cases, however, women wind up dead.

There are also several other instances in the film of women as victims—the woman Pike accidentally tramples, the woman he deliberately shoots during the closing gunfight after she has shot him in the back, the women that Dutch and the other members of the Bunch use as shields against bullets, the women killed and mangled during the opening gunfight—which are not offered for our delectation or presented in such a way as to invite approbation. And although the story does not permit the introduction of any major women characters, it is not true that there are no sympathetic women or women who act admirably. In addition to Pike's lover and the woman he is with in the bordello, consider how often, when the shooting starts, the women think first of protecting not themselves but their children or their husbands. Consider, too, that a good many of the men, including the main characters, are shown to be less than admirable and often pretty treacherous, greedy, and bloodthirsty themselves. Peckinpah dwells on none of this, and he doesn't preach. He doesn't have to, because he is able to *show* so well. It may be a sad footnote to contemporary evaluations of his films that many polemical reviewers respond primarily to preaching and only secondarily, if at all, to drama.

Peckinpah once said that *Major Dundee* had "a very tight script, intricately intertwined," so that "if you removed a part of it, something else would fall out fifteen pages later."[26] The same is obviously true of *The Wild Bunch*, and it is nowhere better illustrated than in the now-missing flashbacks. We have already noted how in *Ride the High Country* Peckinpah used the convention of the young lovers to reflect the issues at stake in the conflict between the two heroes. In an analogous way, the flashbacks here give a private urgency to Pike's dilemmas, for it is in them that Peckinpah crosses and thus fuses the personal and professional aspects of Pike's life. Each of the flashbacks is marked by a personal loss that is the direct result of a professional mistake, miscalculation, or equivocation. In the first, his best friend is captured while he runs out; in the second, he opportunistically violates his code and consigns another friend's grandson to death; and in the third, he loses the woman he loves. Collectively, the flashbacks thus serve to ironize Thornton's description of Pike as "the best": he's the best, it seems, merely because he never got caught, being sly, deceitful, or heedless enough to let others get caught or killed in his stead. That the flashbacks are therefore to the point is beyond dispute; what has been disputed, as old-fashioned and clumsy, is the manner of their introduction. It is true that the technique is hardly new, especially for the first flashback, where the image becomes wavy as if seen under water.[27] But Peckinpah has rarely been interested in style for its own sake; he wants style to serve meaning, technique to convey the *right* feeling. The image does not so much dissolve as appear to quiver momentarily before deliquescing, and the effect is as if the present tense of the film were struggling to suppress the past tense, which nevertheless fights its way to the surface. Inasmuch as the flashbacks are from Pike's point of view, what is this but an exact objective correlative to the way these painful memories intrude themselves upon his consciousness? He would like to forget them, as they remind him of failure, and he tries to suppress them, because the recollection of them humiliates him. He can do neither. The very *look* of the flashbacks—the settings dark, flat, claustrophobic, the decor and furnishings carefully chosen for their dated, antique character, the lighting an alternately harsh and muted chiaroscuro that contrasts distinctly with the dust and desert sand and the blue, sunlit sky in the rest of the film— suggests the weight of suppressed guilt and hidden shame. The cumulative effect of both their style and the manner of their presentation—including the artificially reverberant acoustic in which Peckinpah records the sounds of the past, and the way each flashback is never run continuously but is faded in and out of the present—is to suggest the existence of a past reality, living still in memory, that runs parallel to and never far beneath the surface of the present reality and that bursts through at key moments to remind Pike how, when, and with whom he has failed to live up to his reputation as "the best" and what the consequences were.

It is perhaps the oppressiveness of this sense of the past that has led several critics mistakenly to align Pike too closely with Steve Judd. "I'd like to make one good score and back off," Pike says, and Dutch asks, "Back off to what?" This much-quoted exchange is usually taken to indicate that Pike's problem, like Steve's, is that he is so far into his life that he is incapable of doing anything else. Yet whatever these two may have in common, resistance to changing times isn't part of it. To be sure, they share some characteristics: both are well past their prime, with established reputations they care very much about and are proud of, while William Holden, as Pike, bears an unsuspected resemblance to Joel McCrea (unsuspected perhaps by everyone except Peckinpah, who took care to attire them similarly in austere black and white and to set up and photograph identically the close-ups in which they declare their codes—tight, slightly low-angle, with just enough blue sky to outline the faces). Both men are as well equally aware of the distance they've traveled and the self-respect they've lost along the way. And we see both men make a lot of mistakes in their work, mistakes which have less to do with getting old (which would explain physical infirmity but not the lapses in judgment) than with how much they have on their minds: Steve, the betrayal by Gil and the dilemma of what to do with him; Pike, all his shame and guilt (in this context the manner of the flashbacks' introduction— in particular the way they overwhelm and obliterate the present for Pike—is especially telling). But Steve has no plans to retire; indeed, his whole concern is to find means of employment that will restore his dignity and allow him to remain the man he was. Pike, no less in love with the life he used to enjoy, is nevertheless considerably more tired than Steve, and when we meet him, he is not only ready for a change, he wants one. In this respect, he is quite unlike the rest of the Bunch, the sense of his alienation subtly heightened by groupings and compositions that leave him isolated from the others at precisely those moments when he must insist most strenuously on their solidarity, lest their petty gripes, mean hostilities, and personal animosities flare into violence.

After one especially volatile dispute in which he narrowly prevents Tector from killing Sykes, Pike lifts himself part way to the saddle only to come crashing back down on his weak leg when the stirrup breaks. As he lies there in pain, the Gorches trade abusive wisecracks: "It appears Brother Pike needs help, Brother Lyle" and "Riding with Brother Pike and old man Sykes makes a man wonder if it ain't time to pick up his chips and find another game." Pike mounts up without saying a word, quietly turns his horse, and rides slowly away. The camera follows with a very slow zoom, a telephoto lens conferring upon the solitary figure a stature that magnifies as he recedes in the distance. When the horse and rider fill the screen from top to bottom—in what is surely the film's most beautiful single image—Peckinpah fades in the next shot underneath, a long view of the Bunch strung out across an expanse of desert, and leaves the two shots overlapped just long enough for Pike's immense figure to dwarf the others and tower above the sandy terrain. The composition is simplicity itself, built out of primary forms and materials reduced to an absolute minimum: man and animal, earth and sky. Yet they are made to open onto depths of feeling, areas of experience, and extremes of loss we have only begun to suspect exist in this lonely man. The steady gait of his horse climbing the dune, the slight hunch of one shoulder as he winces in pain striving to straighten himself against the ridicule, and the seemingly infinite space stretching back and beyond both horse and rider suggest the weight of responsibilities stoically assumed, the burden of a reputation recklessly made and now courageously sustained, and the weariness of trying to live up to it even as he longs to be rid of it. Above all, the image foreshadows

Pike's destiny—which is to fulfill his reputation in spite of himself—in the very reluctance with which the shot yields to its successor, the gradual disappearance of the stalwart figure so subtly photographed that it seems to have become indelibly impressed upon the environing wilderness, lingering ghostlike in the mind's eye long after the horse and rider have faded from view.

Even though it is placed later in the film, the flashback showing Aurora's death is most to the point here, for it is in it that Peckinpah makes manifest the full extent to which Pike keeps his deepest feelings to himself. This is the only flashback accompanied by voice-over—Pike, as we have seen, affecting a toughness of attitude, telling Dutch all he thinks about is getting even with Aurora's husband. The images, however, focus chiefly on Pike's own sometimes careless treatment of Aurora (he arrives two days late for a rendezvous, offering neither explanation nor apology) and on their last few moments of tenderness together before she is killed. The point, then, is the contrast—between what Pike says and how he says it, and what is actually on his mind, the latter revealed to us by the images. It is clear that what he thinks most about is not getting even; rather, it is about having lost her. This flashback has, as a consequence, two retroactive effects. First, it confers a poignance on Pike's earlier remark to Angel about Teresa—"Either you learn to live with it or we'll leave you here"—as that is exactly what Pike has had to do about Aurora, and not at all easily. Second, it helps fill in the shot of Pike riding over the dune, suggesting that the greatest burden he shoulders is his guilt over losing her, his deepest loss the loss of her.

It is this unflinching assumption of responsibility for the life Pike has made for himself and his resoluteness despite (perhaps because of) his failings and his losses that Peckinpah may want to acknowledge. It finds a more or less explicit expression when Thornton's exasperation with the inept bounty hunters reaches the point of outburst: "You think Pike and Old Sykes haven't been watching us all the way down here? They know what this is all about, and what have I got? Nothing but you egg-sucking, chicken-stealing gutter trash, with not even sixty rounds between you. We're after men, and I wish to God I was with them. If you make one more mistake, I'm going to ride off and leave you to die." No banal machismo is being trotted out here; rather, Peckinpah is trying to suggest an outlook neither childish nor cynical but simply realistic and therefore adult, to indicate the necessities of such attitudes and modes of thought in a world as dangerous as the world the film contains. It is perhaps difficult to appreciate the full measure of his achievement in this respect until the film is placed against the many shopworn movies and novels in which these subjects—professionalism and professional discipline—have been poorly handled because of inadequate observation or insufficient characterization. But Peckinpah knows this milieu, feels it keenly, and obviously believes in it deeply; and, thanks to his attention to detail, he has managed to revitalize these subjects and restore them to the realm of serious art simply by tying them securely to character and in turn locating character in an appropriate filmic world fully visualized. As a consequence, *The Wild Bunch* became the best film since *The Seven Samurai* about men whose lives and work involve violence and killing. Not the least of Peckinpah's achievements consists in getting from his actors performances of unselfconscious ease and naturalness, utterly free from the kind of pomp and display that in more overtly "stylized" action films signals the actor's awareness of the onlooking camera. The men we see here are the men we would see if there were no camera present; there is no empty gesturing or hollow striking of poses, because their validity is made to inhere not in their claims but in their very physical being, and it finds expression in the way each of them sits or stands or rides in this hostile setting. Or in the way Pike enters a new place. In one especially revealing moment, Peckinpah makes the cinematic tissue of the narrative convey what it is like to be on guard every waking hour. Pike passes through an enclosed walkway that leads to the main square of Agua Verde. He pauses at the threshold, while Peckinpah cuts in three successive pans that sweep the area, taking note of the places that provide cover, the high walls with sentries positioned on them, the open arches on the far side that permit egress or entry. It is things like this—or the way that Pike, without raising his head, surveys the surrounding rooftops when he dismounts at the beginning, or the piece of hide that is wrapped around his binoculars to prevent telltale reflections from the sun—that give force to Thornton's description of Pike as the best. But then that applies almost equally to the others, as in a tense moment that has the Gorch brothers, without any word from Pike, put down their glasses and turn from the whores they've been eagerly awaiting to prepare themselves for trouble when an unexpected dispute arises, or in an earlier scene that has Sykes soundlessly cock the triggers of his rifle when the Gorch brothers demand a larger share of the take than is rightfully theirs. Even the few self-conscious displays of bravado originate in necessity, as when Pike, tipping his hat, offers himself as a target, buying just enough time for the spark to touch the dynamite.

Of course each of the Bunch achieves a personal style, which Peckinpah exploits to magnificent effect in the great image of the four remaining members of the Bunch going off to confront Mapache. As they stride past the camera, Peckinpah cuts to a reverse angle. When they reach middle distance he has the telephoto lens once again initiate a slow, subtle zoom-in that creates the illusion of figures growing in size while receding in space until it stops just as, their backs still toward us, they fill the screen shoulder to shoulder, marching and marching like ancient mythic soldiers. These are men whose every movement tells us they've lived lives close to the edge, largely on the run, and have thereby acquired lethal skills which have long since become second nature to them. "The clothes seem to smell of the people who wear them," Stanley Kauffmann observed.[28] But the scent is the scent of danger, a quality to which Peckinpah is continually alluding in the recurring scenes where the slightest provocation is enough to call their skills into play. Indeed, it is an irony he inflects throughout that the Bunch seem able to forget their internal differences and bring their skills under full control only when they are forced to close ranks against encroachers or are involved in daring and violent exploits. This is a group of men for whom fighting really is the easiest solution to all problems, a position Pike himself is forced to assume when, during one rift, he says, "I don't know a damn thing except that I either lead this Bunch or end it right now." It is significant that the first time we see the Bunch function as a group is during their assault on the munitions train, which becomes in this context not only a superbly crafted action sequence (the virtuosity of the filmmaking expressing the expert operation of the caper), but also an ironic vision of brotherhood, each man performing his appointed task to perfection as Pike's perseverance is at last rewarded with that good score.

If it is in moments like this, or when the Bunch celebrate their success by breaking out the whiskey, that Pike finds a provisional justification, there are nevertheless many other moments where his craftiness, his equivocations, and his opportunism suggest stronger parallels with Gil Westrum than with Steve Judd. Pike telling Angel, "Ten thousand cuts an awful lot of family ties," is not unlike Gil telling Heck, "The Lord's bounty may not be for sale, but the devil's is, if you're willing to pay the price"; and Pike's desire for one good score so he can retire is not unlike Gil's scheme to steal the gold so he can enjoy champagne and beautiful women in ease and comfort for the rest of his life. And late in the film, after Pike's good score is tainted by the capture of Angel and the ambush of Sykes, there is this exchange:

DUTCH: Damn that Deke Thornton to hell!
PIKE: What would you do? He gave his word.
DUTCH: Gave his word to a railroad.
PIKE: It's his *word*!
DUTCH: That's not what counts; it's who you give it to!

This, too, has been widely misinterpreted, perhaps because Peckinpah, with typical irony, allows Dutch the last word. But Pike knows that it is both simpler and more complex than that; and when Dutch suggests making a run for the border now that the posse is closing in, Pike answers, "They'd follow us every step of the way. I know Thornton. I'm tired of being hunted." Dutch may still be the conscience for the Bunch as a whole, but for Pike himself Thornton comes to occupy the same position as Steve Judd does for Gil Westrum, and Thornton's persistent disinclination to dishonor his word (if only to a railroad) recalls Steve's refusal to violate his contract (if only with a bank). Thornton becomes, therefore, both Pike's nemesis and the touchstone by which Pike's own failings and compromises are thrown into fuller relief ("It's his *word*!"); and inasmuch as Thornton's dogged pursuit symbolizes Pike's past, it is obvious that far from searching for that past, Pike has been trying all along to escape it.

Of course, escape is impossible, which is a realization that begins to close in on Pike like a vise. The Bunch return to Agua Verde and find Mapache and his soldiers celebrating their new weapons, part of the festivities being the spectacle of Angel tied behind the general's new motorcar and dragged through the dirt. Pike offers half his share of the gold in return for Angel, but the general, having too much fun, refuses to sell, instead offering the Bunch the pleasures of free women and whiskey. "Why not?" Pike says disgustedly, as the four of them ride off to a bordello. The next morning, after he has finished dressing, Pike sits on the bed watching the young prostitute wash herself at the table across the room, while, behind him, her baby lies on the dirt floor crying. Pike drinks the rest of his whiskey, throws the empty bottle aside, and walks to the adjoining room where the Gorch brothers haggle over prices with a whore they've just shared. "Let's go," Pike says; and, after one of the most expectant pauses in American films, comes the assent, paradoxically stated in the negative: "Why not?" Lyle answers.

This scene, the most delicately inflected in the film, is the pivot point, and not the least of its attractions is how little it says explicitly, how much it draws together and concentrates. Peckinpah had learned something in the years since *Major Dundee*, where he had planned to splice in a montage of Dundee's memories during the breakdown in Durango. What he learned was how to omit the most important things from a scene and make them conspicuous by their absence. For such a technique to work, however, what is missing in one place must be present in another, and this is why the flashbacks are so necessary in their appointed places elsewhere in the film. Peckinpah knew there was no need to reprise them here, for the past that Pike has been running from has finally caught up with and surrounded him, has become present by analogy and association. The prostitute and her baby are an ironic reminder of the family he might have enjoyed had he been, once in the past, just a little more careful. As he watches her and listens to the baby crying, he thinks as well of a member of the only family he has left, who lies broken and bleeding a short distance away. At this point, Angel is no longer just Angel; he is Thornton asking, "How can you be so damn sure?"; he is Crazy Lee saying, "I'll hold them here until hell freezes over or you say different"; he is Old Sykes wounded and left to die; and he is Angel after all, near death yet playing his string right out to the end.

Pike's decision has nothing in the final analysis to do with an inability or unwillingness to change. He has options left and a stake to pursue them with. It's just that they're no good in the face of a personal revelation, born of self-disgust and self-contempt, which shows him that no matter where he goes, what he does, or how far he backs off, he will never be free from these painful memories. He knows that if he were to leave now, he would only add another increment of shame to a load of guilt which has already become nearly intolerable and which all the gold, whiskey, and whores in the world will be insufficient to salve, lighten, or obliterate. The next woman will only remind him of the one killed beside him long ago; at the bottom of the next bottle he will find only the same desolation; and solitude will not bring him even the cold comfort of isolation, for he will always be haunted by the voices of the past that live in his heart, whispering of debts unpaid, words broken, and friends abandoned because all he cared about was saving his own skin and making another good score. It isn't

PAUL SEYDOR

enough, it cannot sustain, and so it places him in a situation as authentically tragic as any a man can know: walk away, his life's a fraud; stay and fight, his life is over. It defines not one string but two, each demanding to be played right out to the end; and either way—slow, mean, ignominious, or quick, violent, apocalyptic—it is the same end: death. Drawing the noose even tighter is an issue far more profound than the style of a man's passing or the manner of his dying. Pike himself identified it early on: when you side with a man you stay with him, and if you can't do that you're like some animal; you're finished. Pike is finished anyway, but his decision to reclaim Angel represents his decision to become a human being, and it is the full weight of what this choice means that confers upon the carnage to follow its terrifying dimension of tragic irony. For in that squalid room where a strange woman and her baby mock, by their very existence, every excuse and deceit by which he has tried to evade or justify his past, Pike makes a discovery which he is quite unprepared for and which comes too late for payment by any price less dear than his life: no matter how, a man alone ain't got no bloody fucking chance.

Notes

1. Robert Culp, "Sam Peckinpah, the Storyteller and *The Wild Bunch,*" *Entertainment World* 2, no. 2 (Jan. 1970), p. 8. [See this book, chap. 1, p. 5.—Ed.]

2. Sam Peckinpah to P. S., 8 Apr. 1977. Unless otherwise noted, all subsequent remarks by Peckinpah in this essay come from this source. For more detail on the differences between the Green and Peckinpah scripts, see Garner Simmons, *Peckinpah: A Portrait in Montage* (Austin: University of Texas Press, 1982), pp. 82–83, 99.

3. This and the next quotation from Joel Reisner and Bruce Kane, "Sam Peckinpah," *Action: Directors Guild of America* 2, no. 3 (May-June 1970), p. 25.

4. The figure has often erroneously been reported (in among other places, the first publication of this essay) as 190 minutes. That was, in fact, the length of the *first* cut of the film, finished shortly after completion of principal photography, before any fine cutting had begun, obviously much too long and in a form that nobody, the director included, ever planned to show. The only people who saw this and any of several intermediate versions on the way to that Kansas City preview of the fine cut were the director, his editors Lou Lombardo and Robert Wolfe and their crew, the producer Phil Feldman, and a few very close friends and working associates.

5. Quoted in Paul Schrader, "Sam Peckinpah Going to Mexico," *Cinema* 5, no. 3 (1969), p. 21. [See this book, chap. 2, p. 22.—Ed.]

6. Quoted in Vincent Canby, "Which Version Did *You* See?" *New York*

Times, sec. D, 20 July 1969, p. 7. Unless otherwise noted, all remarks by Feldman or Canby come from this source.

7. Richard Whitehall, "Talking with Peckinpah," *Sight and Sound* 38, no. 4 (Autumn 1969), p. 175.

8. Jay Cocks, rev. of *Straw Dogs* and profile on Sam Peckinpah, *Time*, 20 Dec. 1971, p. 87.

9. Quoted in Axel Madsen, "Peckinpah in Mexico," *Sight and Sound* 38, no. 4 (Spring 1974), p. 91.

10. Quoted in Schrader, p. 21. [See this book, chap. 2, p. 22.—Ed.]

11. Whitehall, p. 175.

12. Since Feldman is one of the two chief protagonists at this point in the history of *The Wild Bunch* (Peckinpah being the other), it should be noted that he either never answered or summarily refused repeated requests for an interview on the subject of his association with Peckinpah in general and with this film in particular. When, at last, he agreed to talk, it was only to say that he deems "Mr. Peckinpah and that whole period in my life as being too unimportant to comment upon" and that he stands behind every decision he made in his capacity as producer of the film (Phil Feldman to P. S., Oct. 1977). Since then Feldman has said that he considers *The Wild Bunch* unquestionably the best film he has ever produced (David Weddle to P. S., Oct. 1992).

13. Feldman's reasoning to the contrary, many filmgoers and critics familiar only with the shorter version *were* bothered by the cuts, faulting the film for weak and ill-motivated characters. When one of these critics finally did see the European version, he wrote, in a response that was typical of those who saw the uncut version only after they'd seen the cut version, "Many of the doubts about the motivations of the characters were alleviated" (F. Anthony Macklin, rev. of *Pat Garrett and Billy the Kid*, *Film Heritage* 10, no. 2 [Winter 1974–75], p. 35n).

14. "Sam Peckinpah Lets It All Hang Out," interview with Sam Peckinpah, *Take One* 2, no. 3 (Jan.–Feb. 1969), p. 19.

15. Much of the information throughout this portion of the essay was provided by David Weddle, who generously shared his research on the making of *The Wild Bunch* from his own forthcoming biography of Sam Peckinpah.

16. It is not always easy to appreciate how fragile the egos of powerful people can be. However much one may grant Feldman's contribution to the film—and by any reckoning it is immense—one's sympathies nevertheless remain a little strained, not just because of his opportunism. *The Wild Bunch* was made before the days when possessive credit above the title became standard for any director of Peckinpah's stature, which means that the first name one sees on the screen is not Peckinpah's, as in "A Sam Peckinpah Film," but Feldman's: "A Phil Feldman Production." Clearly, nobody regards *The Wild Bunch* as anybody's vision but Peckinpah's; still, one wonders how much more credit a producer could possibly need than to have his and *only* his name above the title of one of the greatest works of film art ever made.

17. *The Wild Bunch* cost about $6.5 million, including postproduction. Its grosses during its first twelve months have been variously reported as $7–12 million. The low end of this range must be questioned, as Hyman once told Peckinpah that the film kept the studio in business for over a year. And though

the higher figure, if accurate, in no way makes *The Wild Bunch* a hit, by any standards other than those of Hollywood bookkeeping it did respectable business, while its prestige value both at the time and since is literally beyond evaluation. There are those who estimate that if the marketing strategy favored by Peckinpah and Feldman had been adopted from the outset, the film would have grossed as much as 20 million its first year (David Weddle to P. S., 10 Oct. 1992).

18. John Cutts, "Shoot! Sam Peckinpah Talks to John Cutts," *Films and Filmmaking* 16, no. 1 (Oct. 1969), p. 8.

19. Stephen Farber, "Peckinpah's Return," rev. of *The Wild Bunch* and interview with Sam Peckinpah, *Film Quarterly* 23, no. 1 (Fall 1969), p. 8. [See this book, chap. 3, p. 39.—Ed.]

20. Winfred Blevins, "The Artistic Vision of Director Sam Peckinpah," *Show* 2, no. 1 (Mar. 1972), p. 38.

21. Grover Lewis, "Sam Peckinpah in Mexico," *Rolling Stone*, 12 Oct. 1972, p. 46.

22. Culp, p. 12. [See this book, chap. 1, p. 9.—Ed.]

23. As noted, since the negative was left untouched, all prints struck since the opening were of the original American version, close to the European version save for the latter's additional flashback, stereophonic soundtrack, and 70-mm CinemaScope prints (which were blown up from the 35-mm Panavision in which the film was shot). In the meantime, the first domestic prints, from which scenes were removed, have apparently all been destroyed, as the short version hasn't played in revival houses for years. The European version is available for domestic rental from Twyman Films (Dayton, Ohio) in the form of 16-mm CinemaScope prints struck in England and, since 1985, from Warner Home Video on Laserdisc and tape. (An *earlier* tape release, thankfully no longer available, was of some bastardized version between the long and short American versions).

None of these, however, is satisfactory. Twyman's English prints, preferable to the video because the image is projected on a screen of at least *some* size and in correct aspect ratio, are nevertheless technically deficient, as there is always a significant loss in definition, brightness, contrast, depth rendition, color quality, and especially sound reproduction when 35-mm is reduced to sixteen. As for the current video, even though it is frame complete, it still does not in a very real sense allow us to see the whole picture, because Warners did not "letterbox" the transfer, that is, preserve the proper widescreen aspect ratio. Nor is this a mere technical issue. *The Wild Bunch* isn't just a widescreen film: expressively, dramatically, and imagistically, it is one of the most masterly uses of the widescreen format ever made. When, as in the nonletterboxed video presentation, only about 60 percent of the image is available, it makes nonsense of the whole visual style of the film. Take, for example, those great shots of the Bunch filling the screen four abreast as they go to reclaim Angel: in the video they fill the screen one and a half abreast.

24. This last flashback is what Peckinpah with great reluctance pulled from the American version as a concession to the domestic distributors' pleas for a shorter film. There are two other differences between the European and American versions. As previously noted, in Europe the film played with an intermission, for which the composer Jerry Fielding wrote an additional piece

of music. The intermission comes just before the train robbery, so that the first half of the film ends with Pike's line, "This is our last go-round, Dutch; this time we do it right." It is also in this scene that the third flashback is placed.

The other difference is in the final battle. In an earlier cut of the film, before it opened, the associate editor, the late Robert Wolfe, had crosscut the moment when Lyle Gorch grabs the machine gun, firing wildly, with other parts of the fighting. Peckinpah asked Wolfe to simplify the editing so that once Lyle grabs the gun we hold on him in his mania without going back and forth to other action, and this is how it appears in the European version. However, the American version, which was locked slightly later, still has the original cross-cutting scheme. Both Peckinpah and Wolfe evidently forgot that the two versions differed slightly at this moment, as years afterward the director told the editor that he had always regretted asking him to make the change in the first place (Robert Wolfe to P. S., Nov. 1977). There are two possible explanations: either Peckinpah took advantage of the bit of extra time he had for the domestic version and had Wolfe restore the crosscutting, and then both of them forgot about it; or, more likely, the change was implemented first in the European version, owing to the demands of the schedule, but not in the American version (perhaps for lack of time). In either case, the actual amount of film involved is less than ten seconds of screen time. While both cutting schemes work, the European version, representing the director's second as opposed to third thoughts, is more effective. One of the film's most powerful moments is of Lyle taking possession of the machine gun and it of him. The crosscutting in the American version dilutes that power slightly but noticeably.

25. *Take One* interview, p. 19.

26. Farber, p. 7. [See this book, chap. 3, p. 39. —Ed.]

27. The specific name for this device is an "oil dissolve." According to the editor Lou Lombardo, the flashbacks were originally edited as straight cuts, but the studio "got cold feet because it had never been done that way before and they insisted on using oil dissolves (quoted in Simmons, p. 103). Actually, an oil dissolve is used for the first flashback only in the campfire scene; all the rest, including the back-and-forths in the first one, are introduced with lap dissolves. The point about confusion aside, it is doubtful that Peckinpah would have implemented a change he didn't like just because he was told to. For one thing, with Ken Hyman still the head of production at Warners, that was not the kind of relationship the director had with the studio at this time. For another, it is arguable that he would eventually have abandoned the straight cuts anyway given the overall narrative style of the film, which uses lap dissolves for nearly every scene-to-scene transition. And the pause that he *directed into* the campfire scene just before the flashback is introduced—Pike stops talking, turns away, and rubs the back of his head, his face clearly troubled—practically demands the more easeful, less abrupt transition that it finally got.

28. Stanley Kauffmann, rev. of *The Wild Bunch*, in *Figures of Light* (New York: Harper and Row, 1971), p. 181 (originally published in *New Republic*, 19 July 1969).

5 ▶

The Wild Bunch

JIM KITSES

The characteristic quality that stamps Peckinpah's work is its disturbing edge. This is clearly evident even in much of Peckinpah's early television direction, which deservedly has its own reputation. The surrealist jolt that so much of Peckinpah communicates flows from a particular way of seeing and experiencing the world. Luis Buñuel once observed that "neo-realist reality is incomplete, official and altogether reasonable; but the poetry, the mystery, everything which completes and enlarges tangible reality is completely missing." Different from Buñuel in many ways, Peckinpah nevertheless reveals a similarly all-embracing vision, a total response to the world. I am not suggesting direct influence here (although Peckinpah thinks *Los Olvidados*, the one Buñuel he has seen, a superb work); it is from Don Siegel, with whom he worked on a number of films starting with *Riot in Cell Block 11*, that Peckinpah originally learned most. However, Peckinpah's preoccupation with the existence of savage and destructive instincts, with the consequences of their repression or free play, and with the nightmarish struggle necessary before balance and identity can emerge, clearly anchors him in terrain that artists within the Surrealist movement have been traditionally concerned with.

The surrealist edge thus derives from Peckinpah's *realistic* world-view. In an increasingly liberal era, many American movies have underwritten the notion that evil resides not in our stars, nor ourselves, but in our environment. Peckinpah insists that men can be animals, that fate is inside us, that evil exists; that America's posture in the world, her power and menace, owe not a little to the existence of that evil. From the outset Peckinpah has resolutely demanded the material and conditions to make this personal statement. However, that he felt that he had been constrained from achieving his goal with *Major Dundee* is clear in his triumphant return to the cinema after nearly four years (given over to more television, as with the remarkable "Noon Wine," and to scriptwriting and planning) with what is a second and, on this occasion, completely realized *Major Dundee* in *The Wild Bunch*.

At the outset of this extraordinary work there is a shocking image which directly evokes the world that is to be explored. Scorpions struggle in a sea of killer ants, children gaily watching, as the Wild Bunch, disguised as U.S. soldiers, ride into Starbuck. While dramatically preparing us for the action that is to follow, the image also describes the relationship between Peckinpah's characters and the society through which they move. And we must not forget the children; above all, the moment introduces a network of detail that is crucial in the film, a structure in which innocence and cruelty, laughter and barbarity, idealism and blood lust, exist side by side. Like birds on a string, children are part of a violent world. Especially in Mapache's Agua Verde, Peckinpah insists on the point: a mother suckling her babe nestled between cartridge belts, children riding the tortured body of Angel round the courtyard. In the final, indescribably bloody massacre, a small boy is gleefully a participator, shooting Pike Bishop in the back. The action here balances the opening, the hail of fire between bounty hunters and Bunch tearing the innocent ranks of the Temperance Union literally to bloody bits; and Peckinpah returns time and again to the children who are the massacre's spectators. Peckinpah's own small boy, Matthew, stands in the middle of it all, his arms round a little girl.

Within this perspective it is wholly appropriate that the action of *The Wild Bunch* is played out—once again—with civil war in the background. For it is the fathers, sons and brothers (the women, too) of the same people who entertain the Bunch so gracefully in Angel's village, who eventually destroy Angel and his comrades. Man's twin capacities for love, joy and brotherhood, for destruction, lust and bestiality, is what *The Wild Bunch*—like all of Peckinpah's work—is finally about. And it is this central preoccupation that accounts for his abiding affinity for Mexico. Where Boetticher responds to Mexico as an arena in which individualism still flourishes, Peckinpah loves it for its special place below the American waistline. If the United States has been quick to deny death and violence by institutionalizing them, to rob love of meaning by romanticizing it, Mexico (like Buñuel's Spain) shows little inclination to do either. Hence, in Mexican history and culture, Peckinpah finds action and ritual that he sees as *universally* significant in its candor. One measure of this is Peckinpah's respect for John Huston's *The Treasure of the Sierra Madre*, from which *The Wild Bunch* borrows so freely for its structure and the important character of Sykes. Hence, too, the emphasis in the film on ceremonies (invariably accompanied by richly evocative Mexican music) which Peckinpah creates as tribal rites—most notably the generous farewell of Angel's villagers to the Bunch, the funeral procession for Teresa, and finally the march of the Bunch itself to the slaughter at the end. The range of Mexican character that Peckinpah achieves is also relevant. The birdlike grace of Pike Bishop's prostitute is balanced by the toothy, carnivorous accountant of the *federales*; the gentle wisdom of the village elder who tries to teach Angel discipline is matched by the grotesque honor of Mapache, who cuts his throat.

As Tector Gorch observes when the group are about to cross over: "Just more of Texas as far as I'm concerned." The world that Peckinpah creates is a continuous and morally complex one: Harrigan and the vulpine bounty hunters, the innocent U.S. Army recruits, the revolutionaries, the *federales*, the women and children, all have their roots in Peckinpah's metaphysical dialectic. However, as always, his vision forces a confrontation between what he feels to be essential drives in human nature, and the *social* costs of a failure to understand and control them. At the heart of the structure that I have been describing is the Wild Bunch itself; and Peckinpah's great achievement is to create these men both as a microcosm of the elements in conflict and as vividly particularized characters in time. The historical moment of the film is crucial: if *Ride the High Country* is an elegy on American individualism, if *Major Dundee* inquires into national identity, in *The Wild Bunch* it is the male *group* that is Peckinpah's subject. Properly understood, the film is criticism: of the American idea of the male elite, of the professionalism and incipient militarism of a Howard Hawks, of the slick evasions of a *Bridge on the River Kwai* or *The Professionals*. *The Wild Bunch* is set at a point in time when society is increasingly institutionalizing and rationalizing the function of the unsocialized group. In terms of the radical structure of the film, the criminal is being supplanted by a criminal society. What distinguishes Peckinpah's "heroes" from those who pursue them and those they traffic with is an extraordinary personal expertise and a fragile code of brotherhood, the two elements of their identity as the "Wild Bunch." If the Gorch boys are appetites and instincts, they are not vultures like the bounty hunters. Above all they are *brothers*, sharing a natural relationship rather than living out of principle. The threat their greed and violence pose to the unity—and hence the identity—of the Bunch is appropriately expressed through the constant friction between them and the two key characters, Sykes and Angel. Embodying the past and the conscience of the Wild Bunch, the old Sykes is created by Peckinpah as a mocking ("My, what a Bunch") liability, ever threatened by Tector, finally left to die in the mountains when wounded by the bounty hunters. Angel is similarly opposed to the Gorch boys by virtue of his impulse (as in the assistance he provides to his village) to *extend* the ideal by which the Bunch try to live. Outside law, society, politics—"We're not *associated* with anyone"—the Wild Bunch have but two choices for survival: they can give way to complete brutalization by serving a corrupt society, or can embrace the vision and future that Angel's simple communism offers. The tragedy is that the Bunch do neither, making the right choice for the wrong reasons.

At the center of the group are Pike and Dutch, both holding it together and, in the trust and affection of their relationship, embodying the spirit that allows both Angel and the Gorches to belong. Of course the Bunch are not moral men: Dutch's self-deception ("We don't *hang* nobody") should not obscure the evidence everywhere before our eyes. In particular, Peckinpah emphasizes that the Bunch attack women: Bishop trampling a young girl in his escape from San Rafael, the Gorches callously using them, Dutch shielding himself with a woman in the final massacre. Angel apart, the Bunch have no honor, only a way of life that is shared. Central to meaningful survival is *discipline*. *The Wild Bunch*, like *Major Dundee*, develops through a structure of divisive moments of impending violence alternating with rituals of celebration (especially drinking and shared laughter) which reunite. And what dooms the group finally is not only the fact that they cannot change; neither can they sustain their ideal of a disciplined unity.

It is Pike Bishop who is in every respect the leader of the Wild Bunch; and Bishop, like other Peckinpah heroes, is a crippled man burdened by his past. "When you side with a man you stay with him . . . if you can't do that, you're worse than some animal." Bishop asserts a value and an idea of himself that he is forced at every turn to compromise. "Why didn't you tell me he was your grandson?" That the slow-witted Crazy Lee, left behind to die in Starbuck, is of Sykes's blood ironically points to the issue of Bishop betraying the very history of the group. The execution of the blinded Buck, the acceptance of Angel's fate, the abandonment of Sykes himself: these acts develop the pattern of counterpoint between ideal and reality. The irony of the entrance of the Bunch, and their masquerade as a unit of soldiers, grows in this context. For Bishop this pattern has a special meaning, the vehemence of his commitment to the code informed by failure in the past ("Being sure is my business"), Deke Thornton left behind when a trap had been sprung on them in a bordello. Peckinpah's characters are always caught in the grip of their own instincts, the demands of man's law, the dictates of God's. The tragedy springs from the fact that we cannot serve them all. Hence the strange bondage of Thornton, Harrigan's "Judas goat," bound by his word to see his closest friend dead. At the end, Thornton marches straight to Bishop's body and silently takes his gun: both recording the end of an era and an act of love, the moment also marks Thornton's freedom.

"Angel dreams of love while Mapache eats the mango." Like Elsa of *Ride the High Country*, Angel is the spiritual center, the innocent vision, the imperiled values, of the world of *The Wild Bunch*. Angel's complete loyalty to himself and "family ties," his killing of Teresa in the lion's den, his commitment to "my people, my village, Mexico"—these cannot but describe a world of action for Bishop that his own life touched and departed from. The idea is sustained by another aspect of Pike's past, his love for the woman he hoped to marry blasted by her husband out of malice rather than jealousy, Bishop himself still limping from that wound of long ago. This delicate network of meaning is extended by the quiet moment Pike shares with a prostitute before the final battle, the scene carrying a bitter sense of what could have been and suggesting a capacity for love untapped. The scene also recalls Pike's escape from the bordello, the wounded Thornton left behind. In this light, Bishop's decision to return for Angel is classic Peckinpah action, the movement of a man into his past, a reassertion of identity, an honoring of the most important of contracts, that with one's self and with God's law.

The great force of *The Wild Bunch*, as with *Major Dundee*, flows from its attack on the audience through Peckinpah's brilliant orchestration of the romantic drive of the genre—the viewer both exalted and violated. With the march of Pike and Dutch, Lyle and Tector, back into Agua Verde to confront Mapache, the transcendentalism of *Ride the High Country* is left far behind. As the group step out past the drunken soldiers and the huddled family groups; as our whole world hangs in suspense after the death of Mapache; as the bloody slaughter begins and grows and grows; as Lyle howls out his joyful song of blood lust; as the Gorches die, their bodies endlessly dancing in the air; as Pike and Dutch finally expire after having "done it right this time"; as the bounty hunters sweep in to observe in hushed tones that history has been done ("T. C. — there he is . . . there's *Pike*"); as the film ends and Peckinpah, still unable to leave them, reprises the Wild Bunch to stop the picture with their ride out under the sunny trees of Angel's village — during and after all of this we cannot but experience the most painful confusion of feelings. *The Wild Bunch* succeeds in arousing in us precisely the world that it explores: an atavistic pleasure, a militant glee, a tragic sense of waste and failure. *The Wild Bunch* is a work of great audacity, a violent gauntlet at the feet of the liberal establishment of America. With this bleak and desperate film, the dialogue is now finished, the vision dead.

If the group honors its bond, if the spirit embodied in Sykes and Thornton is free to find what had always been its proper home ("even the worst of us . . . "), in the revolution, it is the unrelenting nihilism and despair, the absurd gratuitousness ("Why *not*?") of the action of the Wild Bunch itself that we are left with. For the Bunch it is too late, and history — their own way of life compromised rather than extended in a changing world — has gone too far. Finally, the group act not for Angel's values — the "dream of love" — but for the dead Angel, their own inadequate code, the *past*. More simply, they do what they do because there is nowhere to go. The Wild Bunch represent a way of life, a style of action, a *technology*, with no vision, no values, no goals. The quiet battle cry of the group is, ironically, "Let's *go*": but we can only ask *where*? In this context, although this great work is not the structured parable that *Major Dundee* is, we must see in it another chapter in Peckinpah's deeply troubled commentary on his country. *The Wild Bunch* is America.

6 ▶

The Wild Bunch and the Problem of Idealist Aesthetics, or, How Long Would Peckinpah Last in Plato's Republic?

Cordell Strug

I

1969. Nixon has just saddled up and the skies are dark over the republic. I drag my wife and a friend to a movie. A Western.

"A *cowboy* movie? You're putting me on."

When we arrive, we are jostled by two beefy males who caught the early showing. One of them says, "We need more movies like this one."

My friend balks when he hears that, his hand suspended over his right-rear pocket. "*Why* are we coming to this movie? Favorite actor?"

I tell him: Peckinpah.

Where has Peckinpah been? I hear the story later, but at the time all I know is that I have been waiting since *Major Dundee*, reading the small print in the movie ads or driving by the theaters, squinting at the posters, looking for "directed by . . . "

I am rewarded. " . . . Sam Peckinpah." My eyes move up for the title: *The Wild Bunch*. Incredibly enough, I have been living in an ivory tower: I have seen no reviews.

Why are we coming to this movie?

I had seen *Major Dundee* more times than I could remember. This was when what passed for film art among my friends was something like *Lord of the Flies*, and they would not be caught dead going

The Wild Bunch and the Problem of Idealist Aesthetics

to "another" Western. (I assume I have had the last laugh.) Years later, I saw an extraordinary film on the late show: entranced, I sat straight through the commercials. Following the strange logic of television, they ran the opening credit last: *Ride the High Country*, directed by Peckinpah. The connection was fused in my brain. And so I am dragging people to *The Wild Bunch*.

Like Steve Judd riding into the camel race, we come into the movie with no notion of what is happening. As the action freezes in the opening sequence like the beats of a funeral march, our minds generate hypotheses, expectations of what is to come, which are shattered as Pike says, "If anybody moves, kill him."

I have heard people in the theatre talk of Brecht's theories of alienating the audience . . . and then they would produce *Mother Courage* and *Galileo*. But I have never experienced that alienation until now. As the soldiers become outlaws and the lawmen turn out to be derelicts, I feel like shouting: Who are the good guys? Who should I cheer for?

No doubt about it: it's going to be a massacre. The Temperance Union is marching right into it. And never before this have I been without hopes or at least questions concerning the impending catastrophe: Will the heroine be saved? Will the hero make it across no-man's-land? Corny, obviously: but how many motion pictures, even very good ones, avoid raising those questions? Here, in *The Wild Bunch*, all the taps on my sympathy have been closed: I am paralyzed. There are no good guys. Gripped simply by the editing and the slow movement toward doom which began to build with the first shot of the horsemen, I have no sentimental interests at stake. This is pure contemplation.

And then the bank clerk is spinning into the street, the bounty hunters are slaughtering the Temperance Union, and the soldiers are running for their horses. The dance of death has begun.

It is a chorus number. Our attention is drawn to the major characters only sporadically, just enough to plant seeds of development in our heads: the one moment that sticks out at all being Thornton's hesitation at killing Pike, a memorable moment in this terrible sequence filled with blood and death, when we are only surprised the members of the gangs do not turn on each other.

It goes on and on. Incredibly, my interest is purely formal, my only concern being with more images, more graceful dying men filling the street. And when it ends I feel satisfied, almost physically, as if I had come through alive, had survived the slaughter that claimed so many.

I have never been pulled into a film so completely and not had my sympathies, my "identification" with causes or characters, engaged.

The Wild Bunch settles down. It becomes possible to be aware of the theater, to eat popcorn. Nevertheless, this film is experienced at the level of its images, something which is not always true, again, even of very good films.

When I saw *Citizen Kane* for the second time, I realized with some astonishment that it actually had a plot. I had the same experience with *The Wild Bunch*: the film advances along its plot line but is never obsessed with it, never hurries, never allows the audience to think out the plot alternatives, but rather fully realizes each of its scenes and keeps the viewer's attention on the values and images of that scene. The suicidal confrontation and mass killing of the climax follow with an almost chilling logic from the opening robbery, but like all of history as it is lived, that movement grows within the flesh of the concrete lives of the characters.

Some of the images are trite—such as the guitar-accompanied exit from the peasant village. And if it is true that we want to believe in scenes like that, it may be the sort of desire we would not like publicized. Some of the images walk a tightrope—the woman breast-feeding her child, her body crossed by bandoliers, is almost too explicit a symbol of the impact of war on life; like Gerald Crich digging his spurs into his horse in *Women in Love*, it says things too explicitly and almost demands translation into a conceptual point. The bridge collapsing under the bounty hunters as Pike doffs his hat is almost too theatrical. And yet—all of these are carried off with such flair that one is willing to forgive everything, just as one forgave the inspired clowning in John Ford's Westerns.

But beyond these images there are those which achieve real greatness, which in their originality and visual beauty hold the mind tightly within themselves, allowing no comparisons, no deciphering, no wandering. These have almost become too famous to need explicit mention: the bounty hunter kissing his rifle barrel; Pike's ride into the sun after he falls while mounting his horse; the whiskey bottle emptied by the gang; Lyle riding the engine after they steal the train; Mapache gleefully spraying his own troops with bullets as his machine gun jumps out of control.

And, finally, the silent decision to embrace fate and return for Angel. Like clerics donning their robes for a pontifical high mass, they put on their weapons—can they possibly *use* that many guns?—and take that incomparable, stylized walk through the

Mexican camp, their weapons, each one held carelessly, creating a pattern that suggests those stiff, twisted armies of Renaissance painting. As they walk by group after group of soldiers, we know they are walking into their grave. Again, we entertain no hopes. No cheering sections needed here. These doomed figures, moving into the heart of an army, were not fashioned for victory. Absurd combatants, they have their instant of repose on the very edge of chaos: enchanted, the army watches as they blast apart its general, then turn in defense, awaiting the mass riposte which the paralyzed audience cannot deliver, the silence cracked only by Dutch's laughter.

Then the inevitable slaughter—the Bunch absorbing bullet after bullet, taking their turns at the machine gun, their leader, Pike, dying with his hand frozen on the gun, as erect as a dead man can be, his body in a posture, if not of victory, at least of defiance.

The moans of the women. Thornton's escape from his debasing quest. The return of Sykes. The film lifts us from the slaughter and leaves us with the Bunch as they were before their dubious alliance with Mapache.

On the way home, we discuss the film in the dark, quiet streets but now no one asks why we came.

II

As I said, I had been living in an ivory tower. It took me some months to find out that *The Wild Bunch* was yet another film to become the focus of debates about violence, in film and otherwise.

Why do some films invite such discussion? The answer seems obvious, but as the movie detectives say, the answer may be too obvious. Films made with the express purpose of turning our stomachs—even behind a mask of piety, like *Soldier Blue*—or of selling a message along with the popcorn can almost be said literally to invite debates about violence. Even an almost purely commercial adventure film like *Bullitt*, with its closing image of the policeman's gun, asks us to ponder the issue of violence.

I am not condemning this sort of thing in itself (though both the hypocritical and sincere examples of violent-movies-condemning-violence are open to serious moral as well as aesthetic questions). What I want to get at here is that it really is obvious why the above movies should touch off debates about violence carried on at a conceptual level: they offer themselves to be used for philosophical and sociological debate. The same thing, I submit, is not true of films like *Bonnie and Clyde* and *The Wild Bunch*, which nevertheless touched off some of the most savage debates.

"Violence" is a word that makes the human brain turn to sawdust. Only a fraction of a brain wave separates "film violence" from "street violence" and images of gangs of dope fiends slicing up our neighborhoods with razor blades—as Aristotle tells us, the conclusion of some forms of reasoning is not another thought but an act. Once the mind is on this track, it is moving toward self-defense, not aesthetic analysis.

The questions I want to deal with, then, are (1) why is this so? For what reasons did *The Wild Bunch* make people want first to draw conclusions about violence and second to condemn the movie because of its violence? and (2) are those reasons relevant to a discussion of works of art? In particular, are they relevant to a discussion of *The Wild Bunch*?

The last are meant to be real, not rhetorical, questions. The problem, like most problems of this nature, is as old as Plato, and all I want to do here is throw some light on why it's going to remain a problem, especially for an aesthetic theory that doesn't wear blinders, and give my own conclusions about the moral and aesthetic balance of *The Wild Bunch*.

Beyond the particular nature of any given film, there is one general reason why any film is subjected to discussions essentially nonaesthetic in character; it is the reason that got Plato going on his diatribe against some forms of art in the *Republic*: the mind takes for itself the right to judge any and all forms of human activity because any and all of those forms have an effect on the general tone of human life. That is—and this is important if we are not to dispose of someone like Plato too quickly—Plato bases his judgment not so much on an organic theory of the state as on an organic theory of human experience. (This can be seen clearly, for example, in the discussion of the relation of sports and music to the development of character.) Though the *Republic* ultimately presents us with a form of totalitarian censorship, and Plato's theory of the state does have strong links to his theory of experience, they are at least separable notions, and I think we can be sympathetic to the latter without swallowing the former. Plato had great respect for artists and was not himself above carrying an argument by dramatic rather than logical weapons. Thus, it is not only "message" art with the wrong message that he condemns: this would make no sense, for example, as applied to the actors who do imitations of animals, a prime target for Plato's attack. It is any art

The Wild Bunch and the Problem of Idealist Aesthetics

that in any way might lower the tone of human life: poetry critical of the gods or the state; music with wild, over-exciting rhythms; plays that require actors to assume debasing parts and thus not only degrade themselves but furnish patterns of comportment that are degrading and might be copied on a wide scale. The Marx Brothers wouldn't last an hour in the Republic. How long would Peckinpah last?

Again, to be fair to Plato, one must realize that he acknowledges the power to charm and fascinate that the great artist possesses: it is precisely that power that makes the artist so dangerous. Thus, while acknowledging the beauty or aesthetic value of a work, Plato would condemn it on other grounds.

Are these grounds "proper"? Is it at all relevant to bring in political and moral issues when discussing art? I think it is fair to say that the dominant aesthetic tradition to come to us out of the nineteenth century would answer these questions with a fairly unqualified "no." While Plato operates with two judgments, linked by his organic theory of experience, the tradition I have in mind—taking for a slogan, just like MGM!, *ars gratia artis*—operates with only one, and reflects very little on the implications about man's nature implicit in the creation of such watertight compartments.

Of course, these are large issues which can in no sense be settled here. But I should like to suggest that there are two reasons, especially when applied to films, that ought to—I don't want to say "make us accept"—push us toward Plato's position.

First, watching a film is potentially a more "total" experience than, for example, strolling through a museum or reading a novel on the beach. When we put ourselves inside a dark room for two hours, we are giving ourselves to what we are about to see. Our bodies are given narrow limits; our attention is owned by the screen—by a physical contract. We do not, as in a picture gallery, determine how long we linger over an image. Nor can we determine their order, nor skip ahead, as in a novel, in case we get anxious. Without being dogmatic or making vicious distinctions, we can say that film is much less under our control than a painting or a novel: just as in music, time is in the hands of the artist, not the spectator. We cannot skim or hurry, we can only leave. But unlike music, a film engages more of us—not only visually (and some thinkers have claimed that the primary experience of the world for most of us is visual) but also emotionally (since the—admittedly fictional—destinies of other people are involved) and sometimes philosophically.

This leads me to the second point: the commercial film as we know it is no more a series of images than the traditional novel is a series of words. One could almost call them "impure" forms if that term did not have such dubious implications. "Realistic" theories may involve profound errors, but profound philosophical errors, as Hegel and Marx insisted, always contain partial truths. Both the novel and the film have given rise to theories of realism (Stanley Cavell in *The World Viewed* has argued that the motion picture is the direct descendant of nineteenth-century literary realism), and this is almost certainly because human action in the world and thought about the world have formed so much of their substance and structure and have found in the novel and film not only delightful forms but powerful weapons of propaganda.

These reasons ought to make us think twice, at any rate, about carrying on our discussion of these arts in a vacuum. Both the intimacy of the film experience and its "impurity" in the above sense make it almost inevitable—and in some sense justifiable— that any film which in any sense is above the ordinary will find itself the subject of discussion and arguments far removed from the realm of art. What I referred to in the title as "the problem of Idealist aesthetics" is simply this (and one can watch this struggle in the pages of all modern Idealists: Hegel, Croce, Collingwood, Dewey, Vivas): while retaining Plato's insistence that art be measured by how it affects a man's life as a whole, to retain as well some sense of the autonomy of the work of art, treating it as a thing to be respected in itself and not as something which does or does not fit political or moral categories.

This is a problem without a solution. The traditional answer has been to allow the artist his theme—so long as he preserves what Eliseo Vivas calls the "intransitivity" of the aesthetic experience: that is, so long as he merely holds up his theme for our contemplation and does not offer it as an object of worship or knowledge or as a directive for action. This clear theoretical distinction is almost never clear in practice. While obvious cases of propaganda can be rejected, what for one man can be an object of "contemplation"— say, the bombing of a city—for another man can only be an immoral spectacle which moves him to anger. Thus, the very notion of contemplation depends upon some degree of detachment in the spectator which for any given work simply may not exist. This leads to a further point: can we in fact "give" the artist his theme in all cases? Some works may be too disgusting, or even too trivial, to deserve our "contemplation." Words typically applied to "great" works of art imply a judgment of this sort, a judgment whose nature is difficult to state: "important," "significant," "powerful," even "great" itself. When we say these things, are we in the realm of aesthetics? Like Kant, do we assume some ideas are more "aesthetic" than others? Or is *any* theme fit for "art," these judgments being wholly "nonaesthetic" in nature? These are difficult questions and are so closely tied to the particular sensibility of the culture and even of the individual critic that it seems absurd to attempt a general answer. And this is why the problem of Idealist aesthetics remains a problem, something to be worked out with each work of art, especially those that present a challenge to our sensibilities.

Where does this leave *The Wild Bunch?*

As I said above, one of the most striking characteristics of the film was how difficult it was to "take sides" and how easy to leave one's emotions disengaged. This is true, I think, not only on the level of action but also with regard to the themes involved. Peckinpah is often taken as preaching one thing or another, and though Peckinpah may have some ideas he likes to argue, it is not Citizen Peckinpah that concerns us but the works of Peckinpah the director. And while it is a simple enough matter to identify his themes, or even to disentangle what is referred to as his "vision," I find it extremely difficult to extract a point in the sense of a "moral" which the films preach. (Perhaps in *Straw Dogs* or *Junior Bonner* we hear a message coming across the screen: but, for example, if one compares *Straw Dogs* with the novel on which it was based, it becomes clear that the film complicates matters immensely; the book is much more easily reduced to a kind of code which, deciphered, gives us a message. It may be the case that Peckinpah is not at all clear about his ideas: while this may pose a problem for him if he ever teaches a course in ethics, it is certainly an asset for him as an artist.) The films give the impression that "something is being said," but that is because they do not remain on the level of action films: the characters, even the primitives, have what Georg Lukács has called "an intellectual physiognomy," minds as well as bodies, thoughts as well as footsteps. Thus, in *The Wild Bunch*, many themes are stated explicitly: the end of the West, the narrowing possibilities of a violent life, the nature of loyalty, of patriotism, the moral value of the establishment—but these are simply part of the fabric of the film, whose characters and incidents are so particularized that it is folly to make of them instances of universal truths. The return for Angel and Pike's shot at the German officer

88

CORDELL STRUG

bring to a head the discussions of loyalty and the American identity of the gang, but in a dramatic, not an allegorical, sense. The final battle is a dramatic solution that makes sense in the lives of the characters themselves—not a conceptual solution that makes sense as an answer to an abstract problem. This is art, not philosophy, and such art that it cries out against being used as philosophy. If we are ever to contemplate such things, we can contemplate them in this film.

That, then, becomes the question. If Peckinpah's film is so fully realized that conceptual translation and moralistic interpretation of any sort only do violence to the film, then it is the images or themes themselves that elicit the condemnations, the moralizing, the abstract weighing of pros and cons concerning "film violence." And here we find ourselves in a real swamp of background and sensibility where theories help very little. On this point, then, two comments:

1. I suspect *The Wild Bunch* rubs some people the wrong way simply because it undercuts "establishment" violence so well. If we identify with anyone, we identify with the killers, and though they get theirs in the end, they are brought down by people even more mean and bloodthirsty than they are. This, it seems to me, makes it easier to contemplate violent action than films that glorify establishment violence: the brutal cops who always get their man, even the clean-cut, nonbrutal cops who always get their man. If *that* violence doesn't bother you, and *The Wild Bunch* does, then you are interested in propaganda (or what Collingwood in *The Principles of Art* describes as "magic"), not aesthetic contemplation.

2. In his best work, Peckinpah is absorbed not so much in violence or gore but in violent action. This may be a spurious distinction, but compare the lopped-off head and the sliced-off breast of *Soldier Blue* with anything in Peckinpah. The former are given to us as ends in themselves, they are stuffed down our throats, we are meant to be disgusted. Peckinpah absorbs the extremely explicit acts of violence into the rhythm of the action. Again, at this level, one's judgments become subjective, but I find myself remembering the sequence as a whole and many of the non-"bloodthirsty" images more than anything else: the outrageous death, the potentially revolting image, is firmly placed within an action sequence which draws all the aesthetic value to itself and doesn't allow itself to fall apart into outlandish fragments.

How long would Peckinpah last in Plato's Republic? Probably—like the Marx Brothers, Sophocles, and Shakespeare—not very

The Wild Bunch and the Problem of Idealist Aesthetics

long. And, even if we excise Plato's totalitarianism, our judgment on *The Wild Bunch* can certainly not be clear-cut. The images of the film, the film itself, are strong, disturbing. And if the film can be defended, as I have tried to do above, it is films such as this that raise a problem for aesthetic theories which have one eye on art and one eye on man, films which refuse to budge from the crossroads of ethics and aesthetics and prevent us from solving unequivocally the problem they raise.

7 ▶

The Tragedy of Love in *The Wild Bunch*

JOHN L. SIMONS

> Emotions are not expelled by reason, but only by stronger emotions.
>
> —Spinoza

Who are the Wild Bunch? From their incongruous name—"Wild" implying anarchic freedom, and "Bunch" a tenuous grouping—to their brutal deaths in which these bad men are ennobled, even elevated to the status of legendary heroes, Sam Peckinpah's strangely virtuous villains confound "safe" interpretation. In this essay I want to concentrate on an individual theme which effectively dramatizes the complex range of Peckinpah's moral and aesthetic imagination. I refer to the theme of male-female love, especially to the clash between archetypal male and female sensibilities. Peckinpah pours the full measure of his art into this most fundamental human confrontation, and in the process he demonstrates an acute sensitivity to women and to women's natures which critics too often refuse to grant him.

Near the beginning of *The Wild Bunch*, as the gang, disguised as government soldiers, ride into the starched southwest Texas town of Starbuck in order to rob the railroad bank, Pike Bishop, their outlaw leader, accidentally bumps into an older woman as he and his men cross the street to the bank. Within the amassing tensions of the moment—the anticipated robbery, a band of bounty hunters and railroad men waiting to ambush the Bunch when they make their escape—the scene functions as a suspenseful contretemps, delaying the imminent shootout. But there is more to the scene

"The Tragedy of Love in *The Wild Bunch*" by John L. Simons originally appeared in *Western Humanities Review* 39, no. 1 (Spring 1985): pp. 1–19. Reprinted by permission of John L. Simons.

than its dramatic function. It represents the first encounter between men and women in the film, and significantly, that encounter involves a violent collision. Thus, from the beginning of *The Wild Bunch*, even within its superb juxtaposition of credits against action sequences frozen into newsprint (the contrast—and yet continuity as well, for they are melded—between history and myth, temporality and timelessness, is thus established from the film's initial moments), director Peckinpah sets up the obvious difference between the world of the outlaw, dominated by coarse males, and the domesticated, civilized world of females. But the scene reverberates with other possibilities. After the surprised (one might say even shocked) Pike Bishop strikes the woman, knocking her load of packages to the ground, he immediately apologizes ("I beg your pardon, ma'am") and offers his arm to escort her across the street ("May I?"), while his lieutenant, Dutch Engstrom, politely volunteers to carry her packages ("Allow me, ma'am") to the other side of the street. Dutch's action is purely a stratagem, while Pike's is not. His courtliness may be better understood as both a strategic maneuver *and* a gentlemanly response, for he is, as we shall learn, a man whose tender solicitations toward women are too often opposed by the destructive consequences of his relationships with them.

This moment, coming so early in the film and so seemingly secondary, is important, for it allows us our first insight into the tragic doubleness which haunts and perplexes Pike Bishop. If he is a rather vicious outlaw, he is also a man dedicated, though haltingly, to an ideal notion of right conduct toward others and toward himself. In short, he is not like the feral Gorch brothers, who comprise the most disruptive element of the Wild Bunch. Forms interest Pike as much as actions. And it is those forms which lead to moments of introspective silence within the mad motion of Pike Bishop's life.

Although the scene with the woman and her packages lasts for only a moment, Sam Peckinpah weaves it into the unfolding male-female theme. As the gang leave the woman, who walks off to the right while they march in twos toward the bank, we hear first the voice of the bank's manager haranguing one of his tellers. In context with the film's mounting action, especially the imminent robbery, what he says makes no sense. But if we consider it in its relationship to Pike's collision with the woman on the street, the two separate events begin to reflect each other. The young teller has botched an important transaction with a woman customer, and what his manager tells him will reverberate throughout the film. "I don't care what you meant to do," rails the manager, "it's what you did I don't like." The director cuts from the banker's speech immediately to the crouched figure of Pike Bishop's estranged partner and friend, Deke Thornton, now waiting to ambush Pike from a rooftop. The action freezes to another newsprint credit, and when it resumes, we watch the Bunch approach the bank in a shot made from within the bank (they pass by its window), as the manager continues to berate his employee. We hear him in mid-sentence: " . . . to this lady, you made a fool of yourself and this railroad in the bargain. Now I want you to apologize to this . . . yes sir, can I help you?" Just as he is about to use the word "lady" once more, the gang enter the bank. Instead of invoking her, he speaks to Pike, who thus fills the ellipsis left by the omission of "lady." This is hardly an accidental conjunction of interrupted events in this superbly edited film. It is meant deliberately to state a connection between the "lady" standing there awaiting the teller's apology and Pike Bishop's first really planned utterance: "If they move, kill 'em!" Next comes another newsprint freeze-frame and the words "Directed by Sam Peckinpah." The fatal clash between the male outlaw and the civilized female is therefore propelled into even more emphatic motion.

It all happens so fast, and it is so soon nearly obliterated by the subsequent slaughter of Starbuck citizens, when the bounty hunters and railroad men open fire upon the Wild Bunch, that we tend to forget just what the bank manager has said, and why it is so significant. Only much later in the film do we realize that it is not just Pike Bishop's violent occupation which occasions his difficulties with women but also his personal nature, torn between principle and compromise, word and deed. Pike had always harbored dreams of love, of marriage, and of settling down to a peaceful, respectable life. But when Aurora, the woman he loved, was slain by her vengeful estranged husband, who also wounded Pike, he saw his hope defeated.

This brief description of Pike's putative true love belies the ambiguous psychological, even metaphysical, motivations which culminate in Aurora's death. As we learn from Pike's flashback narration much later in the film, he bears a heavy burden of responsibility for that death. Promising to meet Aurora at an appointed time, he callously, and for no apparent reason, delays their rendezvous for several days. He arrives at her door, clean-shaven (for this must have taken place some time back in Pike's

The Tragedy of Love in *The Wild Bunch*

more youthful past; we never see him in the film's other most important flashback without a moustache), his arms laden with groceries and conciliatory red roses, in a possibly self-conscious parody of a penitent guilty spouse's peace offering. A proud woman, insulted by Pike's casual indifference to her needs, Aurora slaps Pike hard across the face, knocking his groceries to the floor. It is Aurora's dignity versus Pike's buffoonery which gives the scene its dramatic edge, for she has far more at stake than Pike Bishop. She is, in addition, worried about her husband, who she fears will try to come back and do harm to both her and Pike. That night, as they prepare for bed, Pike and Aurora are interrupted by the gun-carrying husband's appearance in the bedroom doorway, where we see him first in Aurora's mirror; he then kills her and wounds Pike in the thigh.[1] The scene shatters whatever comfortable assumptions of conventional devotion we had made about Pike and this woman he purports to love. For when a man as good at his work as Pike Bishop says he is, when a careful, meticulous planner of jobs, whose life, and the lives of others, depends upon constant wariness and vigilance, neglects his responsibility to the woman he loves, we realize that he is expressing an unconscious conflict within his nature, a conflict between the outlaw's love of freedom and the would-be husband's desire for a civilized settled life. In addition, there is in Pike Bishop a fundamental, almost unappeasable sense of isolation, of aloneness which may, in spite of his yearnings toward love and friendship, be impossible to bridge, and which may bring us closer than anything to the true tragic core of Sam Peckinpah's world.

This crucial scene, omitted from all commercially released American prints of *The Wild Bunch* when it was released to a mass audience in 1969, is absolutely necessary to the line of argument which I am propounding in this essay. Without it we cannot possibly imagine Pike Bishop as a tragic hero, nor can we comprehend the small but significant details which support my thesis, which seem pointless outside the larger frame of the male-female theme.

Consider two key moments in Starbuck, during the melee precipitated by the Wild Bunch's attempted escape from the railroad's hired killers. In that bloody shootout, Pike Bishop's horse, crazed by gunfire, rears and tramples a defenseless woman to death. At the same time his boot hooks her shawl and pins it to the side of his horse. Later, after the gang has ridden to the town's outskirts away from the ambush, Pike discovers the white shawl and succeeds,

JOHN L. SIMONS

only after considerable effort, in shaking it loose from his boot. The subtle image of the clinging shawl reflects Pike Bishop's failure to free himself from his own inner conflicts over women as well as from the memory of Aurora, the woman he loved and betrayed.

Peckinpah stresses the poignancy of the shawl by foreshadowing its appearance in an action sequence with one of the gang members, shot, crashing on his horse through a dress shop window and toppling two clothed female mannequins. Exposed to the alien violence of men, women, symbolized by these mannequins, are powerless to avoid its brutal excesses. And by crosscutting the slow-motion scene of the rider falling into the dress shop with normal-motion scenes of the random devastation of the town of Starbuck, the director ties this specific violation to the larger destruction being inflicted on the town as a whole. Thus, within this elaborate sequence we witness first the relatively harmless collision between Pike and the older woman, then the trampled lady who falls under Pike's horse's hooves while he attempts to avoid crushing her, then the mannequins knocked down brutally by the falling horse and rider, and, finally, the subtlest image, that of the fallen woman's shawl. My point is that all of these images of violence are tied to the troubled identity of Pike Bishop.

Pike Bishop's failure to reconcile his outlaw's identity in the world with his need for female love leads inevitably to the terrible events I have described. Pike is, of course, a man divided against himself, but "division," as Robert Heilman has written, becomes the salutary "occasion of self-awareness or self-knowledge in the tragic protagonist." Out of "the inconsistent and the contradictory,"[2] continues Heilman, emerges the hero's desperate, ultimately failing attempt to render his life whole again. By the end of *The Wild Bunch*, Pike Bishop has made his journey to self-awareness, and he chooses to fight those divisions which so fill him with regret for his own existence. His moment of illumination comes in a woman's room, as it should. But before that can occur, Pike passes through those progressive stages of aloneness, community, and self-knowledge which will free him, paradoxically, to choose life and to die.

Pike Bishop resembles Odysseus—and all heroic adventurers, including the archetype of the male-female split in American literature, Cooper's Deerslayer—in his inability to resolve, except destructively, the warring male and female impulses which coexist within him. Only in the film's final moments will he attempt to reconcile the oppositions in his tragically divided self. We cannot

The Tragedy of Love in *The Wild Bunch*

begin to understand that calamitous finale unless we study its complementary opposite, the view of life presented in the village of Angel, the gang's youngest and only Mexican member. For there *The Wild Bunch's* feminine sensibility expresses itself most profoundly.

Like an earthly paradise, a green world of frame-filling trees, Angel's village, despite its recent pillaging by the army of the Huerista mercenary, General Mapache, thrives with abundant human and natural life. Although the first sight the Wild Bunch have of the town encompasses bleak, abandoned sunbaked adobes and a panting starving dog, these are, we soon learn, signs of Mapache's ravishment of the village and not reflective of the pueblo itself. Once they enter it, the gang are captivated by its festive vitality. Women and children abound, there is plentiful food and drink, and later in the evening a fiesta, with music and drink and dancing, is celebrated for the gang. Meanwhile, giggling girls draw water from a well with the aid of the amazingly courteous Gorches (Lyle is wanted for murder and rape!), as naked boys swim and dive happily in a pond, a moment of innocent youthful bliss straight out of one of Sam Peckinpah's favorite films, *The Treasure of the Sierra Madre*. Later on, the tamed Gorches play a children's game, cat's cradle, with the señoritas. Pike is dumfounded by all of this because he knows how brutal the Gorches can be. He is answered by a wise village elder, Don José, who remarks of the Gorches' play that it is "not so surprising. We all dream of being a child again. Even the worst of us. Perhaps the worst of us most of all."[3] And Pike Bishop, who longs "most of all" to forget his past and himself enter a time-negating pastoral world of childhood, nods in assent. It should be added that Peckinpah thwarts the potential sentimentality of this scene by portraying Don José as not just another benevolent Mexican peasant, but rather as a man whose insight is based on his own experience. "Then you know who we are?" Pike asks him, but he follows this with the laughing accusation, "And you too!"

Why does the village welcome the Wild Bunch so fulsomely into its midst? On a superficial level, it is because they ride with Angel, that because they are his "friends," they should be treated with hospitality. But the deeper reason, I suspect, lies with the village's ancient origins. Joseph Campbell, in examining the disappearance of myth and ritual in modern life, argues in *The Hero with a Thousand Faces* that, unlike ancient cultures, the modern "social unit is not a carrier of religious content, but an economic-political organization" from which the "dream-web of myth" has fallen away.[4] But this is untrue of Angel's village, where the myth of the hero, and the festive ritual that celebrates the hero's—and the guest's—life, is brought to full expression. The village seems classless as well, devoid of the strict hierarchies that over-determine one's place and status in Mapache's Agua Verde, where rank-obsessed German officers advise the general on the proper conduct of his murderous affairs. The village is then communal, not hierarchical, ritualistic rather than regimental, spontaneous rather than ordered, and its values symbolize also the fusion of male and female, paternal as well as maternal principles. This explains why the village is able to effect an almost miraculous transformation— and especially a feminization—on the ruthless gang. Because the village conjures myths of pastoral bliss, it cannot be seen as part of the strictly objective texture of *The Wild Bunch*. Instead, within the film it looms as a kind of romantic retreat, an island out of time, an oasis hovering somewhere between reality and dream (unnamed, it opens itself up to greater imaginative interpretation), a sort of actualized ideal, mediating between the arid, etiolated Protestantism of the American town Starbuck, its sin-crazed, alcohol-condemning citizens clothed in funereal black, and the lurid, too worldly cruelty and debauchery of Mapache's drunken, whore-filled Agua Verde. Between these falsely dichotomized versions of sacred and profane existence—for it is evident that Sam Peckinpah believes that the one cannot exist without the other—moves, through imagined space, Angel's village, synthesizing rather than separating spiritual and earthly values.

Although it has been damned by critics who score its apparent sentimentality, the Wild Bunch's overtly romanticized exodus from Angel's village seems perfectly apt, given both the village's character and the film's larger purpose. Photographed with slow forward- and side-tracking shots, from the point of view of both the Bunch (seen from low angles, against a background of trees) and the villagers who line and garland the gang's departure, the scene celebrates and memorializes a fate, a future of which the Bunch themselves are unaware: their subsequent destruction of Mapache's army.

While the brilliant morning sun riffles through the village's green trees, and families gather along the way, girls lavish flowers on these unlikely "heroes" (a bemused Dutch Engstrom holds a rose in his meaty hand). There is also music, "La Golondrina" ("The Swallow"), a lonely wanderer's song of love for and separation from his native land. Graciously Pike tips his hat to Don José, and Angel kisses his mother farewell. The scene swells with extravagant emotions, and so it should, because it elucidates a central paradox of the warrior's existence: in order to sustain (both in the world and in our imaginations) Edenic retreats (like the village), havens from history's nightmare, we must contrastingly fight for them, violate their underlying feminine or maternal principles of home, of family, of community so that, conversely, those principles may be preserved. Intuitively, without irony, the villagers seem to understand the Wild Bunch better than the Bunch understands itself.

We cannot begin to comprehend why the Wild Bunch rise to the fallen Angel's rescue in Mapache's stronghold, Agua Verde, unless we distill his roots, what those origins mean to the gang and to Pike Bishop in particular. When he chides Angel back in the latter's village for vowing revenge against Mapache for killing his father and "molesting" his sweetheart ("novia"), Teresa, Pike realizes, as Paul Seydor has observed,[5] that he can scarcely hold in check his own combustive emotions over the loss of Aurora. "Either you learn to live with it or we'll leave you here," he warns the head-strong youth, while at the same time we sense Pike's own impulse toward self-control. This appears in his altering expression during the fiesta, and especially during the dancing. Seated on the ground, bottle in hand, next to Don José and an attractive woman who seems to be with him, Pike declines to dance with her. This refusal is not just because of the hurt in his wounded leg but also because of the psychologically painful source of that wound. When Dutch Engstrom offers to dance with Pike's companion, and then is cut in upon by grimy, toothless old Freddy Sykes ("I'm gonna steal his girl!"), Pike laughs, but his expression quickly contracts to an ironic self-examining gaze, then to silent introspection. He is no longer quite present to the dancing, but rather he is transported back to the woman with whom he should be dancing, Aurora. This occurs as evening falls, a time of memory and inwardness.

There can be, of course, no certainty as to what Pike is think-ing—or feeling—but because of director Peckinpah's technique of dissolving from one scene to another, here from meditation to movement, from night to morning, we can deduce a close connec-tion between Pike's painful memories and the morning ride out of the pueblo. In this scene we begin to hear the initial strains of "La Golondrina" as Pike stares off into space that night, then we dissolve to departure the following morning. Utilizing this technique of what Richard Gentner and Diane Birdsall call "overlapping sound,"[6] Peckinpah is able to connect evening to morning, Pike's inner world of solitude and memory with the outer world of love and shared action.

While it is correct that Sam Peckinpah is, by his own admission, nothing if not romantic, it is equally true that his is a kind of very modern self-questioning romanticism. Pike's advice to Angel to learn to "live with" the loss of Teresa also underscores Peckinpah's implicit critique of romanticism's obsession with the Ideal, the Absolute, and the notion of Woman as only archetype and not flesh and blood. Angel lost Teresa because, as Don José tells Pike, he worshipped her from a celibate distance, treated her as if she were a virginal goddess. Mapache, on the other hand, won her over ("She went with him because she wanted to," says Don José) when he offered her the pleasures of food and wine and carnality. For Mapache, Teresa was no goddess but a fruit ripe for the picking. Angel's subsequent slaying of Teresa echoes Pike's own responsibility for Aurora's death, and in his half-comic, half-sardonic remark, "Angel dreams of love and Mapache eats a mango," he may be unwittingly commenting on his own inability to fuse idealistic commitments to Love and Friendship with his own less than perfect actions toward Aurora and toward Deke Thornton, as well as toward others whom he has had to shoot or abandon on the trail when the necessity of the moment led to imperfect responses. When Pike and the rest of the Wild Bunch march off to rescue Angel in Agua Verde, they do so not just for their maimed comrade but also for the values his village implicitly affirms, and especially for those communal, erotic feminine qualities from which Pike feels so tragically separated. For once at least they fuse idea to action, the warrior's destiny to die on the battlefield with his equal commitment to a life antithetical to war.

In Agua Verde, after the Wild Bunch have robbed an American arms train for Mapache, who offers them $10,000 for the job (though they personally revile the general), Angel is, as we know, taken prisoner and tortured when Mapache learns—from the mother of Teresa, whom Angel has killed—that Angel has saved a case of arms for his people. Reduced to four men against an entire army, the Bunch finds itself powerless to rescue Angel. For the first time in the film—other than in the bordello flashback which centers on Deke Thornton's capture—the noticeably chaste Pike Bishop, still in flight from the haunting memories of Thornton and Aurora (here, names partially rhyme with each other, suggest further relationships), chooses to vent his helplessness and disgust before Angel's torture in another brothel.

But the beautiful dark-skinned prostitute with whom Pike sleeps, though younger, resembles the equally striking Mexican woman Aurora more than the haggard whore whom the Gorches share. Pike had first seen her in one of the film's most extraordinary scenes, the shooting of Teresa. Wearing a softly colored blue-and-white-checked dress (blue is the color for the Virgin Mary in the Catholic Church), the young woman is first seen smiling at Pike. Enter Teresa, dressed in expensive (virginal) white satin. Then what Paul Seydor calls Peckinpah's "prodigious irony" goes to work. The young prostitute, as we learn, is really virginal in her authentic nature, while Teresa, once the symbol of uncorrupted purity to Angel, has become, in Don José's words, the true "whore of Mapache." In this role reversal, accomplished cinematically through a series of blinding crosscuts between Teresa's awful death, when seated on Mapache's lap, and the woman in blue's terrified reaction, we are asked ironically to identify the young woman with Teresa's fate, while simultaneously she begins to take Aurora's place in Pike's imagination by incarnating both the Teresa of Angel's dreams and the proud, sensual, loving Aurora of Pike's tortured memories.

This symbolic transposition of roles/selves becomes clearer in the subsequent scenes between Pike and the woman in her room. We first see her there photographed over Pike's right shoulder, as a cross glows over his other shoulder. Pike, dressing, turns and looks at her while she, wearing a clean white slip, quietly moistens her neck and her breasts with a cool cloth. (Water throughout *The Wild Bunch* is associated with the cleansing, regenerating process; even Angel's descent down a water chute during the railroad robbery embraces that theme, for the guns they take will rekindle the revolution.) Her breasts are here both erotic and maternal, linked to our conception of her as lover and mother, while the whiteness of her slip—ironic only if associated with her profession, prostitution—connotes a virginal purity, quite different from the flashy satin dress Teresa wore. The young woman never speaks. Nor should she, for silence within the roiling present of *The Wild Bunch* invariably provokes powerful retrospective emotions, echoes from the mourned world of Pike's past. Pike's own silence is then hardly exceptional either. Confronted by the tragedy of his life, of his lost love, he can only stare dumbly, immobilized, at the ruins of his ever-present past. For Pike keeps running into what he

loves, and has loved, and like most people—outlaw or intellectual—he cannot talk about that at all.

When the camera finally rounds to Pike's tired face, we see that it
limns the suffering, the rue and the loss he has known, all of them
elicited by the presence of the young woman, who, though she is
present in the same room with Pike, seems distant from him. She
then enters the expanded tableau of the cross, herself and her baby
stirring in its crib. Since we view each of them from Pike's perspective, his back turned to us and thus looking at them as we the
audience are, they assume a kind of stylized, triptych-looking
(Pike appears, back turned, in separate frames with all three),
frieze-like fixity. In essence Pike, like the audience of the film,
looks at cross, mother, and child as if they inhabit a plane of
reality—in part the dramatic plane of tragic art—in which he
cannot participate other than as a spectator.

This scene rouses and recapitulates, in synoptic fashion, Pike's
memories—though probably at an unconscious level—of Angel's
village, the young girls, their mothers with their babies, and the
naked boys swimming in the pond. It also brings to the surface
Pike's agonized remembrances of Aurora undressing in her bedroom, as well as the scene in the brothel when Deke was taken
prisoner and Pike escaped.

Numerous critics, in particular Mark Crispin Miller, have written intelligently on this critical scene. Miller rightly emphasizes
the "helpless sadness" etched on Pike's face as he gazes at the
woman and child, "at something that could have made him a
different person."[7] But I believe that Miller, though acutely sensitive to the mise-en-scène in the woman's room, misses the opportunity to shade his interpretation away from the sole rendering of
Pike's sorrow. Miller, nevertheless, keys us to possible larger implications of this scene when he draws our attention to a very
significant detail, i.e., that "[Pike] hears a baby cry, and turns to
see the infant lying on the other side of the cot. The camera zooms
in slightly, accentuating the infant in a sequence otherwise made
up of lingering stationary shots." I want to emphasize the difference between the static, motionless silence in the room and the
slight zoom inward toward the crying baby. For that subtle shot
activates, energizes the shadowy room, propels us, subjectively—
again, it is his vision we share in this scene—into Pike's dawning
awareness of the baby's existence—and promise. In a similar vein,
William Butler Yeats writes of tragic actions that in observing, as
Pike Bishop does, the specific "tragedy of love, we renew, it may be,

some loyalty of our youth, and go from the theatre with our eyes dim for an old love's sake."[8] When we "renew" our now tarnished youthful loyalties, by extension we become youthful—perhaps even like a baby—again. And that, I believe, is the process in which Pike slowly begins to participate.

If, initially, we find ourselves identifying with Pike Bishop as the would-be father of this child, at a deeper level I would argue that something broader, something more expansive, is also taking place. "We all dream of being a child again." Don José's profound and pregnant words prepare us for Pike Bishop's rebirth into heroic action. He does not just stare at the baby, but rather, in that slow zoom shot, he enters its new life, its pastlessness, its (therefore) guiltlessness, its freedom. Pike makes love with the young woman, recapitulates his physical and spiritual love for Aurora, and becomes at once a new man and the father of his reborn self. And because he has evolved into the hero, he can commit himself to vital action (the zoom shot), out of the lonely passivity of despair.

One way of describing what takes place in *The Wild Bunch* is to say that it embraces a process in which images, such as that of the woman and her child, are constantly enlarging toward the archetypal, then contracting toward the literal. At their best, these images should be felt simultaneously in their immediacy *and* in their larger dimension. And that is what is happening in the woman's room, where profoundly felt emotions, grounded in individual motives and personalities, expand beyond their immediate setting to absorb a larger area of experience and significance.

The subtle picture of the Madonna and Child (though she is also a woman, and the baby a baby) within a bordello (virgin and whore, spirit and flesh, united in one identity) embodies Sam Peckinpah's wish to unite within a single person the sacred and profane sides of Pike Bishop's once-divided nature. Unlike the austere, flesh-denying Puritanism of Starbuck (its very name an attempt to transcend earthly experience) and the soulless physical depravity of Mapache's Agua Verde (with its connotations of green, slimy water), the young woman (unlike Teresa), so representative of the authentic spirit of Angel's village, synthesizes warring polarities. No wonder Pike pines for what he feels in her presence, then realizes in some inchoate manner that it will be out of her being that his own transformation can take place. In a literal sense, it is clearly too late for this aging bandit to move forward, for he is already an anachronism in a new, modern, mechanized age, perched on the edge of world cataclysm. It is 1913, and if he is to begin again, it must be on a new ground, though paradoxically out of the old ground of this violent man's former existence. It is time, as his lover's/friend's/hero's code dictates, for him to affirm his ideals in action, fuse with his principles, even if he must die for those principles.

Angrily, disgustedly, Pike, holding an almost empty bottle in his hand, looks from the woman, the cross, and the child into the next room, where the seemingly unregenerate Gorches are haggling with a whore over her prices until, hurling the bottle down, he moves to the doorway and looks into their adjoining room. Pike rests his hands against the walls of the door and stares at the sordid Gorches. Those arms, partially stretched in an understated imitation of a weary Christ on the cross (we remember that directly behind Pike is that illuminated cross on the wall), create as well an image of Pike Bishop standing between two worlds. Finally he becomes those two worlds, the worlds of spirit and flesh, when he makes his single command, his only utterance here, through his call to action throughout the film, "Let's go." The Gorches, especially the mercuric and dangerous Lyle, stare back, not knowing what to make of Pike's look or his command. Tector Gorch lies on a makeshift bed, a bird, probably a sparrow, playing between his fingers but struggling as well against an entangling string which prevents it from flying away. The scene repeats the cat's cradle game the brothers played with the girl in Angel's village, but this time with a difference. The cat's cradle is a symbol of infinity, chiefly because it is capable of innumerable combinations. Here, though, the string, entwined within Tector's fingers, appears frayed, almost broken, the bird fluttering futilely to free itself. Finally the bird falls to the earthen floor as Tector rises to join Pike and his brother in battle. The men leave the room and we are left with a zoom close-up image of the panting bird, lying on its side, its life slowly ebbing away. Certainly this represents some kind of archaic omen, possibly Homeric (Penelope dreamt of an eagle ensnaring a serpent just prior to her husband's return), but it also conjures up the more immediate image of the warrior as the wanderer, far from home, who envies the migratory bird ("La Golondrina") in its homeward flight. Birds are so often identified with the spirit or soul that it barely requires mentioning that the tethered sparrow (swallow) is linked in its physical death to the higher destiny of those who will die and be reborn (out of that tattered cat's cradle?) through heroic actions in the battle of Agua Verde.

The Tragedy of Love in *The Wild Bunch*

In response to Pike's "Let's go!" Lyle Gorch gradually begins to comprehend the meaning of Pike's command. His "Why not!" seems to be less an interrogative than an imperative, as I have indicated, for he reverses Pike's same exhaustedly cynical "Why not?" uttered earlier when, helpless before the torture of Angel, Pike went off sullenly to the bordello. That both Gorches, one minute whoring and fighting over how much to pay the whore, can in the next moment go off and fight against a tyrannical dictator, for someone other than themselves, seems almost miraculous, and indeed it is, as is this whole scene in the brothel. As Pike says earlier in Angel's village, while he watches the Gorches play with the cat's cradle, "Now that I find hard to believe." But then as now, the Gorches' form of redemption is allied with Pike's rebirth and with the theme of the innocence and the freedom of childhood.

Before he goes to meet his lieutenant, Dutch, and the Gorches, now outside, Pike returns to the room, to the woman, her baby, and by extension, the softly illuminated cross. He gazes at her one more time, then reaches into his pocket and throws his last gold coins onto the table before her. She is disappointed, perhaps insulted, because her affections toward Pike obviously transcend those of a prostitute's normal financial transactions. But Pike does not throw the money down out of scorn for the woman; rather, he does so out of a complex of emotions. In part he feels a corrosive self-contempt, born of the tragic realization that the new life she proffers comes too late for an aging man so burdened by the mistakes of his past, and of his own nature, that he can no longer live with himself. But equally powerful in his dawning realization of new resolve is the equally tragic—for he must leave her and the world she and the child represent behind—but also heroic knowledge of what he must do, and why, and for whom.

As one man, equal in the purpose which unites them—they walk four abreast and not in military hierarchical twos as we saw them do at the beginning of the film—the Wild Bunch begin their slow progress through Agua Verde, indifferent to the heavily armed hordes of soldiers who surround but do not impede their march, to the square where the drunken Mapache waits with the hideously maimed Angel. Meanwhile, intensifying drumrolls punctuate the Bunch's movement toward certain death, but counterpointed to those martial drumbeats is "La Golondrina," the song Angel's people sang for the departing "heroes" as they rode out of the pueblo. Here, though, it is slurringly rendered by the drunken soldiers and their women, who are so stupefied by alcohol that they seem indifferent to the song's melancholy message. But the audience, by now sympathetic with the gang if the film is working for them, cannot miss the significance of that song. Nor can they ignore the tall, green tree of life—so out of place in this dusty town—talisman of Angel's village, toward which the Bunch move as they set out to rescue their doomed comrade.

That four men destroy an army of over two hundred men, a feat of fantastic, even legendary magnitude far exceeding any attempts to literally "understand" it, elevates the film's final cathartic action to a mythological dimension, a dimension for which we have been suitably prepared by the "reality past realism" (in Stanley Kauffmann's phrase) of the Bunch's exodus from Angel's village and Pike's emergence into heroic self-realization in the young woman's room.

The specifically female motif appears once more in *The Wild Bunch* when, after Angel's throat is cut, Mapache is slain and the fierce fighting begins, Pike Bishop veers into a whore's room off the plaza. We view the woman doubled, both standing before Pike and reflected in her wardrobe mirror. This is Pike Bishop's nightmare moment, for it recapitulates the scene in Aurora's bedroom when she was murdered and Pike was shot by her husband. Pike's hesitation before the whore, his rifle ready to fire, and his refusal finally to shoot her contrast with the massive carnage of the battle, a war in which soldiers are mowed down in machine gun fire like rows of wheat, and where the other members of the gang, particularly Dutch, indiscriminately use women as shields against the onrush of Mapache's *federales*. The scene repeats Aurora's death, it is true, but it also gives us one final indication of Pike Bishop's feelings about women, feelings fatally complicated, rent with ambivalences. Thus the doubled image of the woman, reflecting in its subjective—for Pike—context her virgin/whore, lover/betrayer nature, plus her presence in the room with another man, a half-clad soldier hidden behind the wardrobe, perplexes Pike, as he stalls for a moment within the battle's swirling action. Instead of killing her, he turns his gun on the wardrobe, shoots and shatters the mirror, perhaps killing the soldier, but, equally plausible, firing at his own image. It is never clear just what Pike sees or knows in this scene. For if he is instead firing at his own image, this may be another instance of this sad bad man's yearning for the peace of death. And if he is indeed reenacting the death of Aurora, it is he who takes the place of the murdering husband, a psychological displacement which can only increase the guilt of this already guilt-ridden man.

The Tragedy of Love in *The Wild Bunch*

Moments later that same prostitute, a cruel leer across her face, shoots Pike in the back, reflecting once again the agonizing doubleness he has always felt toward women. Furious, he turns toward her, cries "Bitch!" and shoots her dead in the breast. At the moment of his death, Pike is shot once more in the back, this time by a child, a little boy dressed in an ill-fitting simulacrum of the dead Mapache's uniform. Pike Bishop dies at the hands of a woman and child, representatives of the very world he longed for and yet fought against, a world symbolized first by Aurora, then later by the woman in the room with her cross and her baby. This then is a world Pike alternately desired and denied. Thus it is only appropriate, or just, that this doomed warrior-hero should die for what he loved—and feared.

Pike expires with his finger poised on the trigger of a machine gun, the gun's nose pointing proudly, arrogantly, into the air. It is a troubling image, one which we are not likely to forget. What can it mean? I would suggest that in a film filled with so many signs of entrapment—the walls and roofs of Starbuck and Agua Verde, canyon walls ringed with Mapache's double-crossing henchmen, a thatched enclosure for scorpions built by children who have learned evil only too well—that the gun arched upward toward the blue sky (toward perhaps the Virgin's maternal blue) implies a positive release, a romantic opening toward freedom—if even in death—and transcendence. On the other hand, I would stress the brutally insistent, perhaps even obvious, nature of a gun phallically pointed up, its defiant murderous energy contending with the other pole of its symbolic possibility. And finally, does not the gun, within its paradoxical capacity for both creation (Mapache's army destroyed, Angel's villagers taking arms and ammunition— even the machine gun itself—out of Agua Verde to feed the revolution) and destruction (so many dead, so many weeping wives and mothers, the line of refugees departing the ruined garrison a harbinger of wars and displacements to come in this bloodiest of centuries) underscore the general theme of relationship, made specific here through engendering violence of love which bonds both the spiritual and carnal capacities of humankind, forging a unity which Pike Bishop could act upon but which he perhaps only intuited, could never quite comprehend? Like the *Iliad*, and because it deals with warriors, adventurers, men of action, *The Wild Bunch* "lays claim to a form of understanding which it denies to those whose actions it describes."[9] But this does not mean that Pike Bishop understood nothing in his final moment

JOHN L. SIMONS

of glory. Otherwise, he would be neither tragic nor heroic. And he is both. Therefore, Pike's manner of dying helps us to understand, if not completely, why, out of frustrated but obdurate love, Pike merges his own self-annihilating but life-creating impulses in the shattering holocaust which concludes this wrenching film.

That spirit and flesh, myth and reality, potency and destruction should be so tenuously allied; that good and evil, female and male, should lodge so precariously in one man points explicitly, at film's end, to the terrible grandeur of human nature as it is conceived in *The Wild Bunch* of Sam Peckinpah.

Notes

1. That Peckinpah chooses to locate Pike's wound on his thigh marks that wound, and its subsequent scar, as a sexual symbol, a symbol of the confusion between sexuality and love, which are creative, and physical violence, which is destructive, in Pike's mind. Even Pike's name, which combines images of what is piercing and dangerous—a pike—with what is noble and spiritual—a bishop—reflects the duality which so torments him.

2. "Tragedy and Melodrama: Speculations on Generic Form," in Corrigan, Robert, ed., *Tragedy: Vision and Form*. San Francisco: Chandler Publishing Co. (1965), p. 248.

3. According to Paul Seydor, Peckinpah "considers the scene in which this line occurs the most important in the film and regards the Bunch's exit from Angel's village, which concludes the scene, as the turning point as far as the humanity of the Bunch is concerned. 'If you ride out with them there and feel it,' he says, 'you can die with them and feel it.'" *Peckinpah: The Western Films*. Urbana: University of Illinois Press (1980), p. 123. [See this book, chap. 8, p. 156 n.23. —Ed.]

4. Second edition, Princeton, New Jersey: Princeton University Press (Bollingen Series) (1968), p. 387.

5. *Peckinpah: The Western Films*, p. 94. [See this book, chap. 4, p. 65.—Ed.]

6. "Sam Peckinpah: Cutter," *Film Comment*, vol. 17 (Jan.-Feb. 1981), p. 36.

7. "In Defense of Sam Peckinpah," *Film Quarterly*, vol. 28, no. 3 (Spring 1975), p. 4.

8. From "The Tragic Theatre," in *Essays and Introductions*. New York: Collier Books (1961), p. 241.

9. Alasdair MacIntyre, *After Virtue*. South Bend: Notre Dame University Press (1981), p. 121.

Sam Peckinpah on location in "Angel's village"

The Starbuck massacre

The Bunch departing as heroes from the Edenic lushness of Angel's village

Angel and Pike planning the destruction of the bridge

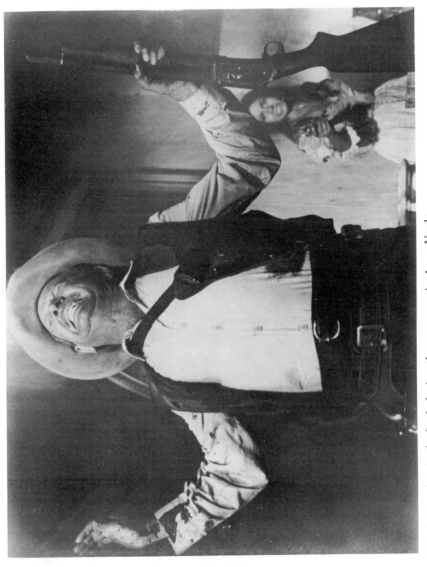

Pike being shot in the back during the massacre in Agua Verde

Lyle and Tector during the final shootout

8 ▶

The Wild Bunch as Epic

PAUL SEYDOR

I wasn't trying to make an epic. I was trying to tell a simple story about bad men in changing times. *The Wild Bunch* is simply what happens when killers go to Mexico. The strange thing is that you feel a great sense of loss when these killers reach the end of the line.

—Sam Peckinpah

I

The Wild Bunch has been criticized for its lack of ideas, but that tells us less about the intellectual depth or shallowness of the film than about the inability of most reviewers to comprehend how ideas really enter and operate in works of art. One reviewer claimed that for all the beauty of craft and image, never has so much virtuosity been made to serve so few ideas: "The moral idiocy of *The Wild Bunch* (it's all right to kill if you stay loyal to your buddies) was fairly obvious."[1] Fairly obvious to whom—people who go to the theatre or open novels as a substitute for reading philosophy? One of the things that distinguishes Peckinpah's treatment of the themes of friendship and loyalty is that he makes them unmistakably *felt* realities in his films, and he accomplishes this by staying close to the specific story he is telling. Cordell Strug, in a superb essay, put it this way:

[In] *The Wild Bunch*, many themes are stated explicitly: the end of the West, the narrowing possibilities of a violent life, the nature of loyalty, of patriotism, the moral value of the establishment—

"*The Wild Bunch* as Epic" by Paul Seydor is a revision of a portion of chapter 3 of *Peckinpah: The Western Films* by Paul Seydor (Champaign: University of Illinois Press, 1980). Reprinted by permission of Paul Seydor.

but these are simply part of the fabric of the film, whose characters and incidents are so particularized that it is folly to make of
them instances of universal truths. The return for Angel and
Pike's shot at the German officer bring to a head the discussions
of loyalty and the American identity of the gang, but in a dramatic, not an allegorical, sense. The final battle is a dramatic
solution that makes sense in the lives of the characters themselves—not a conceptual solution that makes sense as an answer
to an abstract problem. This is art, not philosophy, and such art
that it cries out against being used as philosophy. If we are ever
to contemplate such things, we can contemplate them in this film.[2]

If we must systematize Peckinpah's filmic visions into philosophical statements—which is, in a word, impossible—it would be
more accurate to say that what he is doing is showing us that one of
the consequences of loyalty may be bloodshed. What interests him
is the particular dramatic situation in which these men—these
limited, somewhat brutal, apparently "bad" men—make, once in
their lives, a decision that is, as Robert Culp put it, "neither Good
nor Bad . . . simply a *Right* decision, balanced on a hair" and
backed "with their lives."[3] All the rest is tragic consequence: and
although the fighting that follows "accomplishes" nothing (inasmuch as Angel is still killed) and although its moral implications
can be argued into perpetuity (much as can the moral implications
of any genuinely great artwork), the last thing that it can be said to
express is "Peckinpah's personal vision of the meaninglessness of
life" or his "conviction that humanity is worthless."[4] Even many of
the film's most enthusiastic critics subscribe more or less to these
notions, laying great stress upon Lyle's "Why not?" as evidence of
Peckinpah's nihilism. But Peckinpah doesn't provide an explicit
answer to Lyle's question because the answer is implicit throughout the film: in Pike's humiliating memories, in the torture of
Angel, in the degradation of Thornton by the corrupt Harrigan, in
the crass and degenerate bounty hunters. And also because
Peckinpah realizes that in this particular dramatic situation, the
Bunch's "no" contains an implicit "yes," like the "no" of Camus's
rebel, who by saying "no" means "that this has been going on too
long, up to this point yes, beyond it no, you are going too far, or,
again, there is a limit beyond which you shall not go. In other
words, his no affirms the existence of a borderline." Presumably,
most of these reviewers would have been happier had Peckinpah
altered the story so that when Pike offered half his share of the
gold for Angel, Mapache would have accepted, and that would

have been that. But then the film really would be meaningless, for it would assert that humanity has a price measurable in dollars and cents and would demonstrate that ten thousand in gold surely can cut an awful lot of family ties. It seems clear enough that what Peckinpah—who has been repeatedly betrayed by producers and moneymen whom he started out trusting—means by this theme of camaraderie is identical to what Whitman meant when he protested that the real import of the *Calamus* poems was not, as many critics felt, homoerotic but political: "It is to the development, identification, and general prevalence of that fervid comradeship (the adhesive love, at least rivalling the amative love hitherto possessing imaginative literature, if not going beyond it) that I look for the counterbalance and offset of our materialistic and vulgar American democracy, and for the spiritualization thereof." This is why both in *The Wild Bunch* and in *Ride the High Country* Peckinpah pits gold and greed against friendship and family.

However, even to say that much takes us in the direction of biographical criticism, a direction in which there is no real need to go except to satiate our curiosity. Pike's big speech about sticking together is thoroughly contained by the dramatic situation which gives rise to it. Sykes, Pike's oldest friend in the present membership of the Bunch, has just made a fool of himself, crossing the reins and sending horses and riders tumbling down a steep dune. In order to cover for his friend's mistake, Pike comes up with this speech. And since the first flashback has shown us that abandoning Thornton is eating at him, it is only right, natural, and logical that sticking together should be on his mind. The implications of his speech eventually entrap him, but that only strengthens its function in the dramatic structure. By the same token, there is no need to look for evidence of Peckinpah's cynicism in his extraordinary gift for grim comic relief, as critics have done with the aftermaths to the opening and closing gunfights, where Peckinpah has the bounty hunters descend upon and squabble over who killed whom and is therefore entitled to the loot. In another telling moment of equally black comic relief that occurs near the end of the film, T. C. and Coffer are so overcome with joy at the sight of all the bodies and the bounty they'll be collecting that they're speechless. Why should a touch like that be used, as it has, as evidence of Peckinpah's cynicism toward humanity in general, especially when it is not merely or even primarily intended as comic relief but as extension and further revelation of character? The posse, who have, without much success, been chasing the Bunch for the reward, finally catch up when the battle is raging in Agua Verde. Rather than enter right away, they wait, like the vultures they are, until the shooting stops and then converge upon their human prey, delighted that the job will now be so easy. As before, this is the work of a dramatist and a storyteller being true to the materials of his story, and here that truth involves the bounty hunters' responses to an appalling carnage in which they can see only material gain for themselves. Another critic, who once called Peckinpah's "ideas puerile as such," actually wrote: "The pronouncements about future Mexican democracy are so blatantly impasted that they don't even taint the film."[5] Of course they don't, they're *part* of the texture of the film. Pike's remark—"If [these people] ever get armed, with good leaders, this whole country'll go up in smoke"—functions primarily as a revelation of character. To use this and other overt pronouncements as indications of Peckinpah's thought not only reduces his thinking to the limited level of his characters' thinking, but it misses the point that he is *using* these limitations dramatically, that is, *as* limitations, thereby deepening our sense of these particular lives.

One regrets belaboring this point so, but some of the objections that have frequently been raised against Peckinpah and his films suggest a widespread misconception about the kind of artist he is and the kind of films he makes, and seem to be based on a critical fallacy. That fallacy consists in drawing a one-to-one relationship between the ideas that characters express and the artist's personal beliefs—as if an artwork were nothing more than a veiled sermon or confession. By this reasoning, an artist could never, say, tell a story about a character who has a racist mentality for fear that the character's attitudes would reflect on his own. (How often criticism has done precisely this in the case of a work like *The Merchant of Venice*.) There is no doubt some relationship between the overt ideas in an artwork and the artist himself, but if the artist is any good, the relationship is far from direct, and surely it can be established only—and then just tenuously, with severe qualification—by giving full weight to the totality of the artwork. Someone who knows Peckinpah calls him "one of the most histrionic men who have ever lived," adding, "I think Sam Peckinpah feels everything that he dramatizes—he allows himself to. He's a ham: he doesn't feel what he doesn't dramatize."[6] This is precisely why it is so foolish to try to yoke Peckinpah exclusively to this or that character as a way of getting at his own ideas. Peckinpah himself once said: "When I work, I become all the characters in the script, everything. . . . I'll be playing Jason Robards one second and the next second I'll be doing a McQueen number, and I act out. It's very dangerous. I act out for myself in real life for the illusion of what I'm going to shoot."[7] What he is really saying here is that he literally has no ideas but in things, which is not the same as saying that he has no ideas or that his ideas are puerile. It is rather to say that his imagination is such that it cannot coalesce except upon substance, whether that substance be character, event, story, detail, convention, structure, or so on. Peckinpah has frequently been called a visual poet, and what this means is that his mind is such that its terms are the terms of metaphor, simile, image, and symbol. Northrop Frye, in *A Natural Perspective*, his splendid critical study of Shakespeare's romances, described this kind of imagination and alluded to the aesthetic issues it raises:

> It is curious that we can think of impartiality only as detachment, of devotion to craftsmanship only as purism, an attitude which, as in Flaubert, turns all simple life into an enormously intricate still life, like the golden touch of Midas. We can hardly conceive of an imagination so concrete that for it the structure is prior to the attitude, and prescribes the attitude. Shakespeare's impartiality is a totally involved and committed impartiality; it expresses itself in bringing everything equally to life.[8]

Now Shakespeare is, as Frye points out, the supreme exemplar of this kind of artist, an artist who is virtually without ego because his ego is so thoroughly absorbed into his imagination. In American literature, Faulkner, Twain, and James are, at their best, examples of this kind of artist; and in films, Renoir, Kurosawa, Huston, and Peckinpah are similar examples. This is why Peckinpah has so frequently been drawn to the Western—much as Shakespeare was drawn to his "moldy tales," Faulkner to his mythical county, or Hawthorne to his Puritan heritage—because everything was there waiting for him: a repository of plots, characters, icons, conventions, settings, and themes—in short, a whole language of myth, symbol, and metaphor waiting to be exploited and capable of freeing his imagination for exclusive concentration on its most important task: giving form to its dictates.

In the case of Peckinpah's imagination, the paramount dictate originates in his discomfiture with all certainties and absolutes and finds expression in those polarized structural motifs we have already noted and in the antitheses, ironies, and ambivalences which mark his films and make them studies in ambiguity not unworthy of comparison to a James or a Conrad. (Peckinpah's discomfiture no doubt derives in part from all those dinner-table discussions of law and the Bible he participated in as a child, and it may help to account as well for his attraction to the Western, which of all popular genres has the most dialectical language.) Gil Dennis, a film student who once apprenticed with Peckinpah, said: "Sam is the one person in American films who has truly caught the idea of ambivalence. Sam respects his characters. He doesn't judge them, and that annoys people. They keep asking, 'Where does he stand?' Even in *Bonnie and Clyde*, you've got your villain in 'society.' Sam won't make it that easy, not ever."[9] Peckinpah himself is more laconic: "Things are always mixed." It is precisely his "mixtures" that reviewers distort when they try to harden this or that line of dialogue into a dogmatic statement that asserts, "This is what Sam Peckinpah believes."

Since Frye published his essay on Shakespeare's romances, our critical vocabulary has changed a bit, so that impartiality is now called cynicism and purism is now called nihilism. But neither gets the picture quite in focus. An artist's affirmation of life can find expression only in the vitality of his art, his commitment only in his devotion to craftsmanship. At roughly the same time as *The Wild Bunch* was first released, two other films, *Z* and *Midnight Cowboy*, were also released and greeted with great enthusiasm by the same reviewers who jumped on *The Wild Bunch*. However, what is morally ugly about both of these films is that the filmmakers diminish and even obliterate the humanity of several characters in order to score easy polemical points or buy cheap sympathy for the main characters. By contrast, what is so morally beautiful about *The Wild Bunch* is inseparable from what is so aesthetically beautiful about it; both are a function of the same imaginative impartiality which is so involved with and committed to its artistic materials that it cannot help granting even the vilest characters a full measure of the rich, pulsating vitality that animates every frame of the film and that leaves us with the unmistakable sense that each character, no matter how minor, exists in the fullness of his particular being. The extent to which this applies to all of Peckinpah's best films forces us to reevaluate the whole question of his so-called mindlessness and anti-intellectualism. When Dwight MacDonald defended Fellini's *8 1/2* against similar criticisms, he argued:

> Why "ignorance" is a fault in an artist I don't see, nor why he has to solve any problems except those of constructing a work of art,

which are difficult enough. Shakespeare was a bit of an igno-
ramus—"little Latin and less Greek"—nor do we expect *King Lear*
to "shed light" on geriatrics.

And don't the critics remind one of those all-too-serious students
who try to discover "Shakespeare's philosophy" and always fail
because Shakespeare hadn't any; his "ideas" were all *ad hoc*; their
function was to solve dramatic rather than philosophical problems.[10]

Sam Peckinpah is a first-rate storyteller and a great filmmaker. Is
it necessary that our appreciation of his artistry have as corollaries
attempts to make him into a second-rate thinker and a third-rate
philosopher, especially when it is so plainly obvious that he is
intellectual enough about what matters to him, which is manifestly
and by his own admission making storytelling films?

With its story of men as deadly companions, unified through
fighting and eventually through an ideal of personal loyalty, *The
Wild Bunch* takes up where aspects of *Ride the High Country, Major
Dundee,* and the aborted script for *Villa Rides!* left off, and it has
additional roots in films by others, in history, and in the epic
tradition of storytelling. Of the films by others, the most manifest
source is John Huston's *The Treasure of the Sierra Madre,* which
Peckinpah has on more than one occasion declared a favorite film.
Old Sykes is obviously patterned after Howard (right down to his
gale of laughter and his joining up with the mountain Indians at
the end of the film) and Mapache suggests the savage bandit leader,
Gold Hat. Furthermore, the two films share the same setting and
one thematic strain: gold and greed coming between friends.
Many filmgoers have also thought Kurosawa's *The Seven Samurai* a
precursor to *The Wild Bunch.* To be sure, it is, but this may owe less
to Peckinpah than to his script collaborator Walon Green, for
whom it is a favorite film.[11] And there are several thematic similarities—professional fighting men who have lived beyond their
time and been forced to become "whores" just to survive, uniting
for one last honorable cause, achieving both camaraderie and
nobility through fighting, dying, and self-sacrifice—and of course
there is the use of slow motion in the action sequences. But
Peckinpah's favorite Kurosawa film is *Rashomon,* which he once
pronounced "the finest picture ever made."[12] One can see why he
might think so with its links to myth and legend and with its theme
of perspectivism, shifting views of the same material, a method
which was to become—though in a radically different, more elabo-

PAUL SEYDOR

rate way—the informing principle of *The Wild Bunch*. And in the setting of the last scene, evocative of old ruins with a distinctly religious ambience, Peckinpah subtly fused allusions to both *Rashomon* and his beloved *Treasure*.

Peckinpah said that Emilio Fernandez, the famous Mexican director who plays Mapache, gave him the idea for the game the children play with ants and scorpions at the beginning of the film. However, another film Peckinpah greatly admires is the French director Henri-Georges Clouzot's fifties action film *The Wages of Fear*, which opens on an image of a child teasing several insects (they appear to be roaches of some sort); and there is a later scene in which a truck backs onto a rickety turn-platform built over a gorge only to have one of its wheels break through the rotted wood—not unlike the wagon wheel breaking through the bridge in *The Wild Bunch*. Peckinpah also specifically cited the influence of Clouzot's use of slow motion in this film. (Perhaps not uncoincidentally, *The Wages of Fear* was remade in 1976 as *Sorcerer* from a screenplay by Walon Green and directed by William Friedkin.)

Two other filmic influences on *The Wild Bunch* are Elia Kazan's film of *A Streetcar Named Desire* and David Lean's *Bridge on the River Kwai*. That of the Kazan—whom Peckinpah frequently named as one of his favorite directors, just as Tennessee Williams is his favorite American playwright—is quite specific and owes to the way the voices from Blanche's past are introduced as memory, echoing and reechoing in an artificially reverberant acoustic, exactly as the voices return to taunt Pike in the flashbacks from *The Wild Bunch*. As to Lean's film, which, like *The Wild Bunch*, stars William Holden, *The Bridge* is concerned with camaraderie among uneasy companions, though this is incidental to Lean's main story line. A major set piece in each film culminates in the explosion of a bridge (an incident not in the earlier drafts of the screenplay for *The Wild Bunch*). The films also share a couple of remarkably similar lines of dialogue. When the British officer played by Alec Guinness, at one point recollecting past hardships, remarks, "I wouldn't have had it any other way," the context is analogous to the moment when Pike tells Dutch, "I wouldn't have it any other way." And elsewhere the Holden character tells his wounded commander, "If we go on, we do it together," in a scene which suggests Pike telling Old Sykes, "We started it together, we'll end it together." The strongest link between the two films is, however, William Holden himself, a connection to which there is more than may at first be evident.

Peckinpah was once asked why he always feels the need to

revise and rewrite scripts, even scripts he likes or scripts he has written himself, and he replied, "No matter how good a script is, you have to adapt it to the needs of the actors."[13] In the early drafts of The Wild Bunch, before the cast was lined up, the characters ranged from slightly to considerably different from the way they are in the finished film. Dutch, for example, was a young man; and both he and Pike resembled the Gorch brothers to a far greater degree. Much of this would no doubt have been changed with subsequent drafts anyway, but there is equally little doubt that the casting profoundly influenced Peckinpah's later revisions and re-conceptions, particularly in the case of Pike, who, in the finished film, is a far richer and more complex character than he is in the earlier versions of the script. Peckinpah based him, in part, quite literally on Holden as both actor and star, in particular on a character-type which Holden had been playing, developing, and refining throughout his career, beginning with a 1941 film called Texas in which he and Glenn Ford played boyhood friends who wind up on opposite sides of the law, with Holden the hell-raiser and eventually the outlaw. Throughout the fifties—in films like The Horse Soldiers, The Bridge on the River Kwai, Picnic, Sunset Boulevard, and Stalag 17 (the last two directed by Billy Wilder, another director Peckinpah admires)—Holden played characters who are loners, outsiders, cynics, skeptics, misfits, compromised and compromising men who turn out at the very end of their lives to be reluctant, sometimes accidental, idealists, men who often wind up dying for that residue of integrity they are surprised to discover they still possess. Pike Bishop, as Peckinpah conceives him and as Holden plays him, can be thought of as an older version of this same composite character, which is what the director meant when he once described the film as being "about what Bill Holden is today— fifty, middle-aged, wrinkled, no longer the glamor boy."[14] The transformations in Pike throughout the several drafts of the screenplay to the completed film constitute a prime example of the way Peckinpah adapts a character to fit the emotional and psychological requirements of an actor, and also of the way he makes the personality and ambience of a star work for a role. He had already done much the same thing with Joel McCrea and Randolph Scott in Ride the High Country, and with Charlton Heston and Richard Harris in Major Dundee.

Of course, the most important sources for The Wild Bunch come from Peckinpah's personal interests and concerns. "The outlaws of the West have always fascinated me," he has said.

PAUL SEYDOR

They had a certain notoriety; they were supposed to have a Robin Hood quality about them, which was not really the truth, but
they were strong individuals; in a land for all intents and purposes without law, they made their own. . . . I've always wondered what happened to the outlaw leaders of the Old West
when it changed. . . . It's a very uncompromising film—the language, the action, the details, the lives of these people are as I
imagine they were. We tried to re-create an environment, an era,
and I think we were reasonably successful with it. . . . The
strange thing is that you feel a great sense of loss when these
killers reach the end of the line.

I'm exhausted when I see it, I'm literally exhausted for hours,
and all it is really is a simple adventure story.[15]

True enough, but then none of Peckinpah's films is elaborately
plotted. What he seems to need is a basic dramatic structure, the
simpler the better, for the complexity comes from the richness and
variety of texture, the elaboration from the way he dramatizes
character and visualizes incident and event. The story he told here
is a beauty, and it brought together the requisite ingredients—
outlaw men living beyond their time, bargaining for freedom,
compromising for gold, engaged in exploits that seem already the
stuff of romance and legend, all set within a historical framework
of violent social and political upheaval—for him to make the story
support the fullest, richest, and most comprehensive vision of life
he has given us before or since. Although he said he wasn't
deliberately trying to make an epic, The Wild Bunch became, and
remains, his epic all the same.

In Pericles on 31st Street, which he helped to write, he demonstrated some awareness of Greek history, in particular military
history; in The Wild Bunch he demonstrates an awareness of the
epic forms and conventions from which much of the film is
derived. Pike Bishop, the Bunch's leader, is different from other
men in degree but not in kind, a warrior-hero but not a god or
demigod; the immediate setting is large in scale (the United States
and Mexico of 1913, a time of cataclysmic social change and
conflict) and even larger by extension and implication (the imminent world war, the presence of German advisors on Mapache's
staff). The story begins in medias res; and Peckinpah's purpose is a
retelling of history not as documentary but as metaphor angled
toward recovering a mythology. About this last, he was more or less
explicit: "I don't make documentaries. The facts about the siege of
Troy, of the duel between Hector and Achilles and all the rest of it,

are a hell of a lot less interesting to me than what Homer makes of it all. And the mere facts tend to obscure the truth anyway. As I keep saying, I'm basically a storyteller."[16] As with Homer, however, Peckinpah's materials in this case are drawn from history and from legend, some of which he researched and some of which, given his Western background and his frequent trips to Mexico, he must have absorbed as a matter of course. For example, Pike, though completely a fictitious character, is obviously based in part on Butch Cassidy, who was notorious for robbing trains and whose Hole-in-the-Wall Gang was often referred to as the "Wild Bunch." E. H. Harriman, a tycoon whose railroad lines were often looted by Cassidy's bunch, hired a posse of gunmen to track the outlaws. When Cassidy realized that the posse was not about to give up their pursuit, he and his friend, the Sundance Kid, left the country for South America. Even the discussions in the film about keeping one's word of honor—which have, of course, their counterpart in the ancient epics—have a historical-legendary precedent. The story is told—and whether it's apocryphal hardly matters in view of its survival in folklore—of how Cassidy on the night before he was to leave for prison asked if he could be let out to say goodbye to a girlfriend. He promised the sheriff he would return by morning. The sheriff let him go, and sure enough come daybreak Cassidy was back at the jailhouse.

It is by now commonplace to call any long or sufficiently "big" story an epic, but the term connects to this film in enough illuminating ways (as it does not, say, to *Major Dundee*, where, among other things, the principal characters lack the requisite archetypal resonances of the principal characters here) to make its application far from factitious. The flashbacks, for example, reinforce the epic structure, because they are introduced as told or recollected material. And there are other formal devices that seem taken from the epic or at least are equivalents, like the fixed epithet, formulaic repetition, and the catalogue. The analogue to this last is to be found in the numerous slow-motion intercuts of violent details, which are also examples of formulaic repetition inasmuch as Peckinpah uses them both for rhythmic variation and accentuation and for comparison and contrast (as when he crosscuts between one outlaw falling from his horse to the street in normal speed and another outlaw falling from his horse in slow motion through a storefront window filled with mannequins, or the way the posse floating down to the water from the exploded bridge recalls the Bunch tumbling down the dune). Characters are also

given taglines which identify some important characteristic, sometimes straightforwardly (as "Old" Sykes or "Crazy" Lee), and
sometimes ironically ("C'mon, you lazy bastard," Pike tells Dutch
several times, or the appellation of "general" to Mapache, who is
also called a "killer"). In addition, there are countless musical,
visual, and verbal motifs whose function is not unlike that of fixed
epithets or formulaic repetitions: the clothing the various characters wear or the kind of weapons they carry; the deployment of
groups of children or of musicians at key moments in the drama;
the use of similar musical phrases at similar dramatic junctures (as
preludes, for example, to those lethally charged silences); the
charged silences themselves, impacted with energy that sometimes dissipates, sometimes bursts into violence; the flame racing
along the fuse; the rallying cry of "Let's go" or "Vamanos"; editing
together parallel actions or using the same setup to photograph
different groups of characters (especially well employed during the
chase following the train robbery, where the Bunch, the posse, and
the cavalry are each seen in identical compositions yet the point is
contrast); and the frequent use of laughter as a refrain to tie off
major sections of the story, thus giving the film a balladlike quality
that links it more closely to an oral tradition of storytelling. Three
instances are noteworthy: when the Bunch laugh off their mistake
after the opening ambush, celebrate their success after the middle
train robbery, and consecrate the (figurative) reintegration of
Thornton among their number at the end of the film. Juxtaposed
against these, in which laughter indicates solidarity, are several
other moments in which it takes on a grim, sinister coloration: the
giggling children surrounding the thatched cage full of ants and
scorpions, or their amusement when they contribute to Angel's
suffering at the end; the laughter that siphons off the tension after
Angel shoots Teresa; the laughter that ridicules Angel when he is
captured; and, most significant, the manic giddiness of Dutch and
Tector which breaks the silence just before the closing gunfight. In
addition to their immediate function in the dramatic contexts in
which they occur, these motifs also provide narrative ballast and
help to unify the narrative flow.

There also appear to be—especially in view of Peckinpah's
singling out, of all works, *The Iliad* as an example of a historically
based story that isn't a documentary—two deliberate allusions to
Homer's tale. The spectacle of Angel being dragged behind
Mapache's automobile is not unlike the spectacle of Hector being
dragged behind the chariot. And Angel himself, in his relationship

to Pike and in the function he serves in the plot, suggests Patroclus, Achilles' young friend whose death in battle inspires the older man to take up arms once again on behalf of his countrymen. In both cases — Achilles' and Pike's — the immediate impulse is for revenge, the long-term motivation an expiation for accumulated guilt born of pride.

While *The Wild Bunch* lacks an analogue to the opening invocation of and response to a muse, it does contain the equivalent to the machinery (gods and supernatural intervention) of the classical epic — the actual machinery like the automobile, the train, and all the advanced weaponry (rifles, grenades, and the machine gun). Peckinpah once said, "I detest machines," and while there is no reason to doubt his word, at the same time he has also said, "You're not going to tell me the camera is a machine; it is the most marvelous piece of divinity ever created."[17] The language here — the camera as divine, not invented but created — may indicate nothing more than an understandable chauvinism on the part of a filmmaker toward his medium, which, though an artistic one, relies more heavily than most upon technology. But it also suggests that Peckinpah's feelings toward technology are considerably more complex, even contradictory, than any simple expression of antipathy is able to contain. If, as Levi-Strauss has shown us, every age has its mythology, its religion as it were, then Peckinpah is especially attuned to the mythology of technological progress, which he often views cynically. Yet he also has an extraordinary sense — unparalleled in cinema since Keaton — of the absurdist possibilities for drama in the confrontation of living organisms with mechanical contraptions, and it is this sense more than anything else which prevents any pat moralizing or easy editorializing against the evils of progress in his depiction of machines. And that surrealistic element which creeps into his work from time to time is nowhere more apparent than in what he does with machines in his Western settings.

A good illustration is afforded by the first appearance of Mapache's automobile, for which a lesser director might have tried to prepare us. Peckinpah, by contrast, emphasizes its suddenness. With no warning at all, he has his composer, Jerry Fielding, strike up a mock-brass fanfare, and before we realize what has happened the village gates have swung open and the automobile is chugging straight at us.[18] The note struck is one of comic surprise. The automobile is not only a new element in this world, it is a completely different kind of element, which by its very distinctness looks by turns comic and grotesque, while the suddenness of its appearance, heralded with a fanfare, gives it a vaguely, and comically, miraculous air, making it seem like something created or descended rather than merely invented. Its bright, gleaming metallic-red contrasts baroquely, even violently, with the prevailing earth tones and the light-blue sky, constituting an intrusion not only upon the world in the film but also upon the visual texture of the film itself. To emphasize the car's comic-grotesque aspect, Peckinpah records its passage from far to near distance not in a single, unbroken shot but in a series of jump cuts, interspersed with reaction shots of the spectators, though at one point cut directly together with no intervening reaction shot. The effect is manifold. It confers upon the car a jerky, mechanical movement that emphasizes its comic, toylike quality and that contrasts with the smooth movement of horses and people, thus introducing a new motif—organic versus mechanical motion. The filmmaking itself is, moreover, made to convey what it must have felt like to see this strange thing for the first time. No one prepared the people in this village for the automobile—suddenly it was there, and suddenly life was different. The effect of the separate shots cut together is to force us to see the car as the spectators see it, still so amazed they can't follow its movements continuously, as if they were blinking their eyes, which is exactly what the editing is doing. Every time we open our eyes (that is, with each successive cut), the car has moved on only, owing to the jump cuts, we haven't seen it cover the intermediate space. Finally, in a typically subtle touch, Peckinpah has saddle holsters strapped to the sides of the automobile. It may be something new, but its owners are in no doubt as to the use to which it will be put. The holsters foreshadow the car's later lethal application—Mapache's using it to drag Angel through the streets of Agua Verde.

Most of the machines are eventually used for death and destruction, yet, ironically, they are given comic introductions. Our first sight of the train, for example, recalls our first sight of the automobile: chugging along jerkily in a succession of jump cuts. The first time we see a dramatic demonstration of the power of the machine gun is in a wild, slapstick episode in which the general tries to operate it without the tripod, sending the entire village scurrying for cover from the spraying bullets. Yet these comic introductions only heighten the sinister quality of the machines, which Peckinpah develops by making them appear as a different order of living thing in the landscape of the film. For example, when Pike gains control of the train and sends it back to its owners, it seems to acquire a life of its own, which is subtly reinforced by some camera setups that endow the train with its own point of view. Similarly, Pike eventually commands the machine gun, bringing it under his power as no one else can ("What I don't know about I sure as hell am going to learn," he said to Lyle who had asked, on first producing the gun, "Think you can handle this?"), but not before several others have tried only to be brought under *its* control. One of the film's most chilling images has Lyle, letting out a high-pitched animalistic scream, surrendering himself totally to the power of the gun as, wounded, he is yanked about by the force of its fire.

Owing to the transitional setting—from a primitive, agricultural society to a sophisticated, industrial society—and to the civil and international warfare with which the action is involved or to which it alludes, all of the advanced weaponry acquires an almost supernatural aura, which, as regards dramatic convention, makes the weaponry an equivalent to magic swords or sacred shields. Much of the conflict among the various forces involves their trying to gain the advantage of this superior form of knowledge because it will give them a superior form of power. Peckinpah introduces this motif quite early with the shot of T. C., tight with anticipation, kissing his rifle barrel, and in three parallel scenes he establishes the central preoccupation with the rifles. Don José, the village elder, tells Pike, "If we had rifles like these," the villagers could defend themselves against raiders; Angel tells Pike, "My people have no guns; but with guns, my people could fight"; and Zamorra tells Mapache after Villa has routed the *federales*, "*Mi generale*, with the new guns and ammunition this would never have happened."

Yet the rifles remain to some extent a discriminate and therefore a limited power, whereas the machine gun comes to represent something approaching omnipotence. Appositely, it acquires, in a succession of some of the film's subtlest imagery, a supernatural aura far beyond that of the other machines. When it is placed at last upon its tripod and positioned on a table in the *loggia*, it takes on the characteristic of a shrine or altar. And during the day and night of saturnalian revelry in which Mapache's court musicians serenade it, a whore does a dance around it, and the entire regiment celebrate their acquisition of it in drunken debauchery, the whole scene comes to suggest some kind of primitive rite. (As we see yet again, precious little of Peckinpah's biblical training, much of it from the Old Testament, was wasted on him.) The following day, after the battle is over, the most prominent figure is Pike's, now dead, sunk to his knees, his hat still on, his fist clenched tightly around the handle of the gun, the barrel cocked high in the air. It is a strange, disturbing image, with mystical reverberations and metaphysical overtones, the figure at once appealing and ominous, his posture both humble and defiant. It alludes to the wish of the Viking warrior to die with a sword in his hand, and it completes the theme of glory basic to this epic, as to all epics: the warrior's decision to live a brief but intense life of violent action in which his senses will be charged to the limits of physical endurance. No film, not even *The Seven Samurai*, has explored this terrain so completely as *The Wild Bunch*, or with so fine a regard for and balancing of all its attendant moods and states of feeling.

Probably one of the difficulties that some audiences have had with *The Wild Bunch* stems from Peckinpah's handling of the themes of glory and heroism, especially insofar as he internalizes them by making the very style and technique of his film embody the feelings and sensations his characters experience in action. He does not handle these themes as they have been handled in the Western, but as they have been handled in the epic tradition, where heroism and glory are inseparable from blood and gore, which is, of course, as it should be. It is in the very graphic depiction of the violence that these themes find their artistic validity, their complexity, and their irony. What Peckinpah shares with Homer, with the anonymous poet of *Beowulf*, with the Shakespeare of *Henry V* and the *Henry IV* plays, and with the Kurosawa of *The Seven Samurai* and *Yojimbo* is an ability at once to identify himself with a warrior-hero's sensibility and to stand apart from it. He is thus free to explore the nuances of feeling—the attractions, the excitement—of this kind of life and at the same time to leave us undeceived as to what it really involves—its limitations, its psychotic edge. As storytellers none of these poets is a preacher; and while they function as storytellers, they are neither for nor against violence, at least not in such a way that their poems are reducible to a polemic that will please simpleminded moralists. As poets, their point of view is not interested; it is sublimely, and rightly, disinterested. This is why it is a mistake to view *The Wild Bunch* as an antiviolence film or as an anti-Western, as if Sam Peckinpah had made nothing more than an exceptionally beautiful and exciting message movie. Attempting to appropriate such passionately charged images of slaughter and bloodshed and killing, such magnificent epiphanies of death and dying, on behalf of puny editorializing not only trivializes Peckinpah's achievement, but also, by reducing its grandeur, its terror, and its humanity to a *thesis*, constitutes a moral offense far in excess of anything that has been charged against film and filmmaker.

In a famous essay Robert Warshow called violence in the Western violence without cruelty,[19] which is accurate enough and which applies, as we shall see, even to *The Wild Bunch*. However, the conventional Western, for all its formulaic and ritualistic beauty, was always something of a fake with its combination of the excitement of violence, "clean" acts of violence, and an overlay of good versus evil that was somehow supposed to legitimate everything. What most conventional Westerns never dealt with is the trait of the Westerner which Warshow mentioned but did not himself deal much with when he observed that when the Westerner draws his gun, he does so not at all reluctantly. Heroes in the epic tradition like their way of life, they enjoy it, are fiercely, passionately committed to it; what limits their indulgence is not an external set of values, officially ratified, but an internal set which ensures some measure of restraint. What makes Peckinpah's violence so disturbing, ambiguous, and subversive is not that he removes the so-called countervailing values of law and order of the conventional Western or that he undercuts the excitement of violence by dwelling on its horror; rather, it is that he is able to render the violence so terrifyingly, so graphically, with such raw and unflinching power, yet *still* to respond, and make us respond, fully, even exultantly, to the joy, passion, and exhilaration these men experience when fighting, and, further, to display no misgivings about making his films embody these feelings.

It is nevertheless not uncommon to hear people object that, for all the similarities, *The Wild Bunch* is "somehow" different from the great epics of the past. This is both true and untrue, and for some of the same reasons. It is true to the extent that Peckinpah's heroes are outlaws rather than warriors as such. But the values of Pike as a fighting man are not fundamentally different from those of an Achilles or a Beowulf, neither of whose poets leaves us in any doubt as to where his hero really lives and finds his essential being. The real difference lies in the changes that history inevitably brings to artistic conventions. The closer we come to the modern world or, to put it more accurately, the deeper an action story is rooted in a period of transition characterized by increasing complexity of social organization and by increasing technological sophistication, the more ambiguous a hero's virtues are likely to appear and the more he will begin to assume the status of a buffoon or a maverick, until eventually he must be made either an actual clown or an actual outlaw, or at least a rebel with potentially criminal tendencies. This has been a concern of American literature since the time of Cooper (who, it will be recalled, introduced Natty Bumppo by having him get thrown in jail for violating game laws) and finds its most comprehensive intellectual statement in "The White Negro," where Norman Mailer resurrects the outlaw-hero in the form of the psychopathic Hipster, and its most comprehensive artistic statement in *The Wild Bunch*, where Sam Peckinpah resurrects the epic warrior in the form of the outlaw-hero. Peckinpah is absolutely aware of the changes time has wrought both upon the West and upon the heroic literary traditions to which he is drawn; indeed, these changes are informing themes of his films, and his prodigious sense of irony, which infuses all his work, expresses that awareness.

Still another, perhaps the central, difference between *The Wild Bunch* and past epics has to do with the intensity and vividness of the violence, and this relates to the different mediums in which they exist. Film has so radically altered our notions of just how much immediacy is either possible or desirable in art that it is questionable whether we can ever experience, say, Homer's descriptions of violence with the same impact that earlier generations of readers unfamiliar with film have experienced them. In a very real sense, what many people who object to Peckinpah's violence are objecting to is its power and immediacy, and they are thereby paying a lopsided tribute to his command, which is consummate, over the resources of his medium. Peckinpah's usual procedure for depicting violence (and also much action in general) is to film an event with cameras operating at standard speed and at higher speeds (the latter producing the slow-motion effect), then to take the standard footage and intercut it at a few points with very brief inserts from the slow-motion footage. This is a technique which rapidly shifts us from one perspective to another, forcing us to see from two different angles of vision and directing us toward two distinct modes of response, and it has, therefore, a curious, contradictory, even somewhat paradoxical effect. The slow-motion intercuts with their hypnotic allure distance us from the action by aestheticizing it, thus intensifying aesthetic feeling as such but ameliorating any vicarious experience we might have of the physical sensations the action produces. The normal-speed shots plunge us much more immediately into the action, making us almost participants by intensifying our vicarious experience of the physical sensations but vitiating any *purely* aesthetic feeling as such. We find here, then, yet another, though a more concentrated, manifestation of Peckinpah's favorite formal principle, polarized structural motifs. In a sense, what he is doing is referring us first to a romantic and then to a realistic view of the violence. In the one we are earthbound, right in the thick of bleeding, struggling, fighting humanity; in the other we have an almost Olympian detachment, the slow motion, with its sensuous, even erotic, attractiveness, lulling us into a purely aesthetic contemplation. By rapidly cutting these two perspectives together, Peckinpah has developed a technique which tends to divorce feeling from sensation (which is what makes his art so seductive, and hence disturbing) and which enables him to strike exactly the right balance between an emotional, indeed, an almost palpably physical, proximity to the action and an aesthetic distance from it.

Peckinpah has often been called a romantic (by himself, among others), which is usually taken to mean that his films express powerful feelings, that he is sympathetic to individuals as opposed to society, and so forth. But his aesthetics is, properly speaking, classical in at least one respect: he wants to maintain a dynamic relationship between the formal or decorative aspect of art and the substantive or material aspect. Those who condemn his violence as decadent or immoral are responding wholly to one or the other aspect, and they either will not or cannot allow themselves to see that with this director it is always the mixtures and combinations that count. Much of the moralistic cant that has been raised against his films can be seen for the obtuseness it is once we understand that what he makes us respond to is neither the matter—violence—nor the manner—aesthetic beauty—exclusively but both simultaneously. Just about the only critic who seemed to understand this when the film first came out was Stanley Kauffmann, who recognized that Peckinpah's "interest is in the ballet, not the bullet," and that the "slow-motion snatches are irritating in two ways: first, because they draw our attention to the film as such; second, because Peckinpah is right—right to remind us that more than one prism of vision is possible at every moment of life and that this prism at this moment magnifies the enjoyment of killing."[20] But, Peckinpah may be a bit more interested in the bullet than Kauffmann believes, as the slow-motion intercuts are almost always held to a particular, often subjective, point of view which is clearly, if implicitly, identified as such in and by the film. If it is necessary to

PAUL SEYDOR

make this explicit, we can say that the point is not that violence is beautiful, but that violence can sometimes appear beautiful depending upon the limitations and restrictions involved in the point of view, angle of vision, or perceiving eye. (For Peckinpah, even an Olympian view is limited.) In the largest possible terms, then, what Peckinpah does is alternate between a moral and an aesthetic view of the violence, which tends to divorce the moral from the aesthetic response (this is, of course, the analogue to the separation of sensation and feeling already noted and is another thing that makes his treatment of violence so disturbing) and which gives rise to one of his abiding themes: it is *only* by divorcing the physical sensations, the pain and suffering, from our apprehension of the violence that we can feel the violence as beautiful. This separation can occur in two ways: by our being totally removed from the physical or by our getting so caught up in the physical that we are overwhelmed by it—the bloodletting really coming to seem a ballet, we the dancers at last one with the dance.

When Peckinpah's violence is understood in this way, the whole issue of his so-called excesses is thrown into clearer relief. People who call *The Wild Bunch* excessive are referring to the protraction of the opening and, especially, the closing gun battles and to the number of bodies that pile up and the amount of blood that is spilled. However, in art excess is rarely a matter of quantity per se (it can be, of course, but it isn't in this film), but has rather to do with uniformity and intensity, or, perhaps more accurately, with uniformity *of* intensity. What keeps Peckinpah's depictions of violence from being uniform is that our slow-motion fascination is constantly being disrupted by the rapid cutting which introduces normal speed, thus jolting us back into reality, only to return us to the trancelike state when another slow-motion insert is cut in, which is then in turn disturbed once again. This technique was devised by Peckinpah—and despite dozens of imitators, no one has been able to use it as intelligently or as effectively as he does—precisely to ensure that the potential excesses of each device would be not so much neutralized as checked, balanced, and kept in suspension by each other; and so that his depictions of violence would remain securely within the purview of art, not extend to provocation, incitement, or mere sensationalism. This is exactly what he meant when he said, "If I'm so bloody that I drive people out of the theatres, then I've failed." In particular, what his imitators don't understand is that the greater effectiveness of his violence depends on two things: first, the brevity of his slow-motion inserts (his imitators drag these out so long that they no longer function as inserts); and second, the relative absence of gore, which keeps our eyes riveted to the screen even as the bloodshed makes a much more appalling effect subliminally. This is what he meant when he said that people want to walk out on his films "but they can't," "they watch, and that makes them mad." This is also why his method is to draw out the build up and the anticipation, extend the release and reaction, but get over the actual moment of bloodshed, collision, or contact almost in the blink of an eye (as a matter of literal fact, if the viewer *were* to blink his eyes at the wrong time—even during the notorious moment when Angel's throat is cut—he would miss all that Peckinpah usually shows of the gore, catching only the attendant action). Inasmuch as Peckinpah's films have always shown how difficult it is to kill people, how the life has to be beaten, bludgeoned, or blasted out of them, the slow-motion intercuts acquire a significance over and above the psychological, for their point is not, as is commonly assumed, to prolong the moment of death but to slow down the last few moments of life, thereby paying an almost elegiac tribute to the peculiar nobility Peckinpah finds in the reluctance of the human animal to give up life, tenaciously clinging to it right down to the last agonizing seconds before letting go. But these images are also infused with a savage irony, for the way the bodies twist and writhe in grotesque spasms suggests a parody of that very grace under pressure which the slow-motion technique appears to confer upon them by way of its aestheticizing function. As always with this director, then, the effect is profoundly ambiguous, the meanings deliberately paradoxical: whether parodies or elegies, these blood ballets are bacchanalias of death that express, tragically and ironically, a force and principle of life.

Once we realize the relationship between Peckinpah's artistry and his violent subject matter, we are able to see that he is not glorifying violence. He is instead telling a story about men who occasionally find themselves glorified in violence. To this end he makes the filmmaking style embody from time to time a sensibility that experiences great fulfillment in violence. However, this is a fulfillment that goes beyond violence as such, and at this point we might profitably return to the idea of Peckinpah's slow-motion intercuts as the analogue to Homer's catalogues. Both devices serve a similar function as regards the dynamics of experiencing the poems involved: they highlight physical detail yet keep it securely yoked to an overall arc of movement or pattern of dramatic action.

PAUL SEYDOR

Cordell Strug, in the essay cited earlier, explained this aspect of Peckinpah's violence better than anyone else has:

> In his best work, Peckinpah is absorbed not so much in violence or gore but in violent action. This may be a spurious distinction, but compare the lopped-off head and the sliced-off breast of *Soldier Blue* with anything in Peckinpah. The former are given to us as ends in themselves, they are stuffed down our throats, we are meant to be disgusted. Peckinpah absorbs the extremely explicit acts of violence into the rhythm of the action. Again, at this level, one's judgments become subjective, but I find myself remembering the sequence as a whole and many of the non-"bloodthirsty" images more than anything else: the outrageous death, the potentially revolting image, is firmly placed within an action sequence which draws all the aesthetic value to itself and doesn't allow itself to fall apart into outlandish fragments.[21]

This distinction between violence and violent action is not spurious at all but of the very essence, and it is ramified throughout the film. It is a distinction which makes it possible to say that, for all the ferocity of the Bunch's violence, remarkably little of it involves deliberate cruelty. When Dutch says that the Bunch are nothing like Mapache because they don't hang anybody, it is a meaningful distinction within the film's frame of reference. It also indicates why it is a mistake to view the film only as Peckinpah's attempt to exorcize his private fascist demons. There are fascist mentalities portrayed in the film, in particular those of Harrigan, Mapache, and the Germans, all of whom relish the power they wield over others and who take real pleasure in inflicting pain and ridicule. The Bunch, by contrast, experience as much joy and exhilaration robbing the train as they do fighting; they take as much satisfaction in doing a good job or confronting a powerful adversary (hence Pike's "I wouldn't have it any other way"); they appreciate similar displays of expertise and prowess in others (as when Dutch says of the Indians, "I'd say those fellows know how to handle themselves"); and their killings are tied more closely to necessity, given their line of work, than to sadism. Even the Gorch brothers, the most self-indulgent members of the Bunch as Pike is the most continent and restrained, lose their grip on their instincts only in the fury of the final bloodbath. In other words, the informing sensibility of the film is not fascist either manifestly or by implication. This is why Peckinpah includes all those shots of the Bunch riding across the desert or taking their wagon up and down the windswept, rocky terrain, and why he slows down so many images which are not of violence as such but simply of stirring action. These shots are, as we have seen, narrative ballast, but they also express, in the broadest possible terms, where the Bunch's real commitment lies, which is not centrally to killing but to a life of sensation, conflict, and collision—in a word, to kinesis at the most powerful and intense physical level where the alternatives are pushed to an extreme at once simple and profound: life and death.

Apropos of this, it is now possible to see that the best gloss, if one be needed, on *The Wild Bunch* is not Robert Ardrey's *African Genesis* (which, though touted by Peckinpah for a while in interviews, he discovered only *after* he had made the film), but Norman Mailer's "The White Negro." Some of the similarities are obvious enough—the Bunch, for example, as representatives of Mailer's psychopathic Hipster who refuses to conform to a stultifying commercial, mechanistic, and dehumanizing society and becomes thereby a rebel mostly by default and *sans* ideology. This is suggested with great economy in the opening sequence, where, on their way into town, the Bunch pass a man sweeping off the railroad tracks, another man in a ready-made suit that seems to squeeze his shoulders together, the mayor addressing the Temperance Union ("Five cents a glass. Does anyone really think that that is the price of a drink?"), and dozens of citizens in starched collars and tightly buttoned-up dresses. It is also suggested by a really spectacular irony that informs the closing scenes of the film, in which the Bunch's decision to reclaim Angel inadvertently has beneficial consequences for the revolution. The similarities extend to Peckinpah's conception of character, which, like Mailer's, views people not as fixed and limited but as fluid and dynamic, the determinant being the context in which action is taken and the available energy at the moment of decision. They extend further to include the drive one finds in both author and filmmaker to throw themselves and their characters into experience and, more disturbing, to their apparent belief in the creative and redemptive possibilities of violent action (which Mailer may have taken as much from Richard Wright as from Hemingway). Perhaps most significant, the similarities encompass even language. The single most important word that Mailer found in the vocabulary of Hip is the word "Go," and the most frequent refrain in *The Wild Bunch* is "Let's go." If this is mere coincidence, then it must have been tele-

PAUL SEYDOR

ologically ordained, for it includes even their fundamental dialectic, which is drawn not, as we might expect, between life and death, but between movement and death defined as stasis.

II

We can begin to get a clearer fix on what *The Wild Bunch* is about, its "ideas" as it were, when we realize that perhaps the most basic and unifying idea is that it is a vision in which concentrations of energy—primarily organic and mechanical or, alternately, human, animal, and technological—act, react, and collide within the same space. The theme is not of diminishing space, but of fixed and limited spaces becoming increasingly crowded, which then only multiplies the possibilities for conflict and violence. If, as Kenneth Burke has said, form is the setting up and fulfilling of expectation, then the opening scene of *The Wild Bunch* is practically a classic demonstration of his thesis. The first collision is minor: Pike and an old woman accidentally bump into each other, the moment so keenly shot and composed that when Peckinpah cuts in the reaction shots it is as if vectors have collided and splintered off in different directions. From this seemingly inconsequential accident, the sequence builds relentlessly to the moment of outburst when all hell breaks loose. The sense of mounting tension, of energy barely able to be contained, is conveyed by the increasing number, brevity, and intensity (e.g., closer close-ups, more setups off the level) of shots, edited together in accelerating tempo, which has the effect of concentrating and impacting the various dramatic forces—the Bunch, the posse, the temperance marchers, the band, the children, the citizens—as they converge in that single, restricted space where the street bends. The hymn "Shall We Gather at the River," which the marchers are singing and the band is playing, gets louder and louder, while, imperceptibly at first, then clearly, the sound of a heartbeat dislodges itself from the drone of the music and thumps a measured, then a racing beat. In a brilliant touch, barely two shots before Pike shoves the railroad official out into the street, Peckinpah inserts a zoom-out, as if the camera itself were trying to create more space in which to accommodate the accumulating energy. But it is too late, and the first volley of bullets prevents the zoom from completing itself.

This idea—of energy packed into limited space—is announced scant seconds into the film by the now-famous symbol of children huddled around a thatched cage filled with ants swarming over a few scorpions. Like most of the symbols in the film, this is too dense with allusions for its range of significance to be limited to one and only one meaning. Of all the symbols, however, this one has the characteristic of a true epic simile inasmuch as the symbolic component is detached from its immediate referent so that it may be ramified metaphorically throughout the rest of the dramatic structure. Initially, it refers primarily to the opening ambush, where the Bunch and the bounty hunters shoot at each other through the frantic townspeople—a connection Peckinpah makes almost explicit with that great lap dissolve which superimposes a long shot of the main street littered with bodies over a close-up of the ants and scorpions the children have burned. The symbol is later alluded to when the Bunch first enter the interior courtyard of Agua Verde, where the final battle will take place. Two sides of the courtyard are enclosed by high walls with barred windows in them; behind some of the lower windows several children sit aimlessly tossing pebbles at the passersby, among whom are the Bunch. The courtyard is filled with villagers crowded together, milling, teeming, pulsating with human energy. As the Bunch start to walk toward an available table, Peckinpah cuts in a shot from inside a window looking through the bars. The relationships are thus identical: the Bunch become the scorpions on the anthill of *federale* soldiers, the courtyard itself the cage containing them, presided over by the children. Within minutes, Angel will shoot Teresa and almost touch off a gunfight.

These relationships and their volatile capabilities are extended and developed dramatically in three later scenes. When the bridge explodes with Thornton and the posse on it, the event is witnessed by the Bunch on one side of the river and by the cavalry of "green recruits" (some of them only adolescents) positioned on the ridge that flanks the river on the other side. Shortly before the explosion, T. C., idiotically gun-happy, starts firing at the soldiers, killing one of the youngest boys, while the other members of the posse join in until Thornton shouts, "Don't shoot, it's the army, you idiots!" The motifs converge again in the scene where Herrera and a regiment of Mapache's soldiers try to take the rifles without paying for them. The setting—a deep canyon flanked by steep cliffs, the Bunch and their wagon load of rifles and ammunition near the middle at the bottom, Mexican soldiers positioned at both entrances and on the surrounding cliffs—recalls the cage filled with insects, the court-yard of Agua Verde, and the bridge nestled in the valley. When the Bunch uncover the machine gun, one of the soldiers panics and fires. Pike lights the fuse which will blow up both the wagon and themselves, the surrounding soldiers cock and aim their rifles, Lyle says, "Start the ball, Tector," and Tector readies the gun for action. As before, we have a restricted space existing within a much larger space, densely packed energies, a fuse racing against time, a world teetering on the edge of explosion. "Cut the fuse," pleads Herrera; the soldiers lower their weapons, Pike complies, and Herrera orders the miscreant soldier executed. This time disaster is averted, but the antagonistic forces converge at the end when the Bunch march through the crowded street, the soldiers moving aside to let them pass, to reclaim Angel. There is an electrifying moment of silence just after the Bunch have shot Mapache (for cutting Angel's throat) in which the very air crackles and bristles with immense energies charged for release yet momentarily suspended. Dutch's giggle, followed by Tector's, breaks the air; then Pike takes aim and fires and all hell breaks loose once more and for the last time. We can now see why Peckinpah felt it necessary to trim some of the violence from the opening gunfight: this closing one must resolve not only the energy accumulated in the immediate situation but all the energies accumulated in the rest of the film. It also resolves the symbol of the ants and the scorpions, as Pike is brought down by one of the children who, lifting a rifle with obvious effort, fires from behind one of the barred windows, bringing the "game" to an end as the children brought their game to an end at the beginning when they tossed straw into the cage and set fire to it.

It is interesting to note that this symbol was first presented to Peckinpah in the form of, quite literally, a simile. Emilio Fernandez, who plays Mapache, one day told Peckinpah, "You know, for me, the Wild Bunch is like a scorpion on an anthill." Peckinpah snapped to attention, saying, "Wait a minute, what's that?"[22] Fernandez told him about a game children play in Mexico, filling a cage with ants and dropping some scorpions into it. Peckinpah knew he had found what he needed for his film, and just how richly and complexly he has extended its implications throughout the film may be seen in what he does with children. Shortly after the lap dissolve from the burning insects to the massacred town, a group of children are seen running down the street and shouting, "Bang, bang! Bang, bang!" as Peckinpah cuts in a ground-level shot from the point of view of one of the dead bodies, with the children circling the camera and still firing their make-believe pistols. (This setup is parallel to the setups used for some of the close-ups of the children at the beginning, where it is as if we are looking up at them from inside the cage.) Their voices are momentarily carried over into the next scene, in which a wounded member of the Bunch falls from his horse because, shot in the face during the opening ambush, he can no longer see to ride. The effect is as if the children have dropped him with their innocent game, which Pike then joins and completes for real by executing the man (at his own request). Peckinpah repeatedly uses associative editing to link the Bunch, Pike in particular, to the children, as when he frames a tracking shot along several children's faces with close-ups of Pike, or, at the very beginning, when he cuts from close-ups of the children huddled around the cage to close-ups of Pike and Dutch as they ride by.

The association is made explicit at one point, when Don José, the leader of Angel's village, tells Pike, "We all dream of being a child again, even the worst of us. Perhaps the worst most of all."[23] This is a fine example of Peckinpah's writing skill, indicating how his sense of irony, ambiguity, and complexity extends to all facets of filmmaking (and thus undercutting a prevalent assessment of him as merely a talented image maker). For if the Bunch are among the worst of us, they are nevertheless recognizably *of* us. What Peckinpah means to express by associating Pike with the children is that Pike's capacities for moral growth and development are not yet completely closed off, that there is more to his character than may be apparent at any given moment. Of course this association only reinforces the parallels between the Bunch and Mailer's psychopathic Hipster, who in his rebellion "seeks to find those violent parallels to the violent and often hopeless contradictions he knew as an infant and as a child": by enacting the forbidden or, at the least, new impulse, the Hipster "can be aware actively . . . of what his habits are, and how he can change them." It is this childlike aspect of Pike's sensibility, free from habitual or learned response and conflicting with it, which makes any kind of redemption possible and is thus vital if his decision to reclaim Angel, which is a decision that breaks a pattern in his life up to that point, is to make any sense. By contrast, Peckinpah almost never symbolically associates children with the grown-up children, such as Crazy Lee (whose name tells us what we need to know about him) or the bounty hunters (who forever try to pass the buck for their mistakes) or even Mapache (who enjoys cruelty yet lacks the excuse of being a child). These characters are "children" with all the power and authority yet none of the sense of responsibility of adults.

PAUL SEYDOR

We can dispense—once and for all, it is hoped—with the banality that the children express Peckinpah's belief that all men are killers, that the children enjoying cruelty and torture and bloodshed indicate the innate evil of mankind. Peckinpah uses children to provide another perspective on the events; they become another sensibility upon which the action is registered, in their case a sensibility that has not yet developed resources for moral evaluation. What they appreciate is spectacle divorced from any evaluative context except the purely aesthetic. In this sense, then, Peckinpah's use of children recalls the Faulkner of the "Benjy" section of *The Sound and the Fury* and the Joyce of the opening section of *Portrait of the Artist as a Young Man*—children as prisms to record fact and sensation but not ethical judgment and evaluation. Peckinpah himself has said as much: "I believe in the complete innocence of children. They have no idea of good and evil. It's an acquired taste."[24] Not being a didactic artist, Peckinpah is not "saying" that one must become as a child to find violence beautiful. But he does weave a childlike *perspective* on the violence into the narrative texture of the film, and shifting, colliding perspectives are one of the main things *The Wild Bunch* is all about.

When one reviewer criticized Peckinpah for not being able to do more than one thing at a time in any given shot, he was apparently referring to the director's fragmented, mosaic editing style.[25] But surely it would be more productive to inquire whether the style functions positively within the film than to assume it is the result of deficient technique. What such an inquiry may lead us to first is something we have already noted: that Peckinpah almost never uses an establishing shot as such to open a scene. His method is usually to open out from some significant detail, occasionally with a reverse zoom in the manner of an iris effect (the starving dog at Angel's village; the woman suckling an infant, a bandolier slung over her shoulder). We may then notice that a good many of the establishing shots he does use after opening a scene are not "objective" but are tied instead to individual characters' points of view (as when the Bunch first enter the inner courtyard of Agua Verde). And next we may notice that several of the long or full shots are photographed with a telephoto lens. Lucien Ballard, the cinematographer, and Peckinpah pored over all the photographs and newsreels of the Mexican revolution they could lay their hands on.[26] What they noticed in all of them was a prevailing flatness of perspective, and they carefully chose a selection of telephoto lenses to replicate that flatness. The effect of the lenses is to compress the depth of field so that everything is pressed closer together. This is especially true in the Agua Verde setting, where we itch from the congestion of people and animals milling about. Often, when something moves laterally we fear a collision (watch, for example, as the camera follows a group of marching soldiers until Angel and Dutch appear in the frame). When they narrowly miss each other, the point has nevertheless been made subliminally: collision is at all times imminent and possible in this place. The telephoto lenses also have the effect, particularly when used for close-ups, of pressing us closer to the surface of the film and thus of subtly reinforcing our sense of congestion.

One significance of both the editing style and the compositions is thus psychological: Peckinpah wants to make us experience event and incident as vividly as possible, from the inside out as it were, more or less as participants, to which end the camera itself becomes less an observer than a participant in the action, a restless, shifting, wandering avatar which adopts numerous guises to investigate a seemingly limitless number of points of view. Peckinpah is a master of, among other things, that most problematic of all moving-camera devices, the handheld subjective shot, which he integrates fluidly into the ongoing narrative line by using it in ever-so-brief inserts that plunge us right into the thick of spectacle: for example, the rapid arc in which the camera spins topsy-turvy when a nameless member of the Bunch is shot off his horse during the ambush, or the momentary switch to the woman's point of view when Pike's horse rears above her. It would be tedious to analyze the whole film in shot-by-shot detail, but it should be noted that an incredible number of the film's shots are visualized in terms of the characters' impressions or are simply set up as they might logically see what is being shown. (For example, most of the exit from Angel's village is composed with two basic points of view in mind, that of the departing Bunch and that of the serenading villagers.) Except for when he wants to make a point of dramatic irony, Peckinpah is usually concerned with preserving the integrity of the sequence of the characters' sense impressions as long as he can, and this in turn indicates a larger concern of his: making the visual style approximate the way the characters experience the spaces they inhabit. Our sense of a world seen integrally is thus often illusory, because it has been built up piecemeal, from discrete fragments; and inasmuch as it is a function of the linear process of experiencing the film, it is continually in flux. The dramatic space itself is made to become a universe of emergents, and the jagged cutting is designed to register a war of sights and sounds continually vying for one's attention.

In the hands of a genuinely serious artist, style is never a mere extravagance used to decorate the material. It is determined by the material, has something of its own to say, and constitutes a kind of subtext that runs parallel to the main text. If the artist is any good, if he has mastered the resources of his craft, then it is not unusual to find that the style is telling us much the same thing as the manifest content of the artwork seems to be trying to tell us. We have seen that Peckinpah's fragmented editing and telephoto compositions have a psychological import. They also have a thematic import intimately related to the psychological import. They are the stylistic equivalent to and formal analogue of a world where, as in the cage of ants and scorpions crawling over each other, everything is so crowded together that it is impossible to concentrate one's attention on any single thing for longer than a few seconds, yet equally impossible to unify more than provisionally the multiplicity of fact and sensation that invades the senses. The compositions reveal a congested space, the editing records the massive implosion of data upon the receptor. Thus both the cutting and the cinematography grow out of and serve the opening simile; and as this simile is extended and ramified throughout the entire film, the visual style expands with it, embodying and expressing what it feels like to live and move and breathe in a space so crowded that it is like a cage full of insects. At the most concrete level the style demonstrates that if a dozen ants are biting us in a dozen different places at once, it is impossible to divide our attention equally among them. Moving up the scale toward abstraction, the style also has the effect, by way of the camera's restless exploration of new and increasing points of view, of piling perspective upon accumulating perspective until the density of conflicting points of view equals the density of conflicting energy within the film's space. The sense of being crowded eventually becomes so oppressive that implosion leads to explosion, the inevitable consequence of which is violence. Owing to that sense of pleasure we feel almost automatically when a great burden is lifted or an intense pressure is finally relieved, the violence becomes both exhilarating and horrifying, because both liberating and lethal. What the visual style is trying to tell us is what the film itself is trying to say; style becomes thus synonymous with and inseparable from meaning, and what it means is what it feels like to exist in this space from one moment to the next.

Just how subtly and surely Peckinpah can fuse style and substance, and ramify his symbolism, may be seen in the significance that dynamite comes to have in the course of the film's development. It is shown just a few times, three or four sticks wrapped in a tight bundle, caught in equally tight close-ups or, at one point, in a rapid zoom that completes itself in a tight close-up. If the caged insects symbolize the space within the film and its human, animal, and mechanical occupants, then the dynamite symbolizes the impacted energy in that space and leads us to consider how vital the basic structure of the film is to its overall effect. That structure is a chase structure, which is a race against time in which time runs out, space becomes more and more restricted, and protagonist and antagonist are brought into closer and closer proximity to one another until they cannot escape collision. It is a structure thus not unlike a flame speeding along a fuse, and it suggests a world in which things (vases, bridges, bodies and sensibilities, perspectives, points of view) explode, shatter, disintegrate on both the literal and the figurative, or the concrete and the abstract, planes. It is a world where things really do fall apart and the center does not hold for very long.

In this context, the slow-motion intercuts acquire another meaning. At the most intense moments of violence, which are a consequence of the densest concentrations of energy, space is at such a premium that time itself is forced to take up the slack, which it does by expanding to contain the violent energies released in collision. However, time in this sense is a matter not of measurement but of perception, so the slow-motion intercuts are usually located securely within a given character's point of view. In what is surely one of the film's great moments of architectonics, Peckinpah cuts together shots of a man getting riddled with bullets in normal speed, the man arcing to the ground in slow motion, children watching the spectacle, and bounty hunters aiming and firing their rifles at the man. With the utmost economy, Peckinpah pulls together and concentrates several ways of looking at the same thing and expresses the various states of feeling—the blow of the impact as metal hits flesh, the sensual beauty of the image when divorced from every evaluative context except that of the aesthetic, the thrill of the bounty hunters when their bullets find a mark, the pain of the victim as his body takes the slugs, and the reluctance with which the body gives up its life. Similarly, the dazzling shots of the bridge exploding, the horses and riders suspended in midair as the bottom drops out from under them, then floating gracefully

PAUL SEYDOR

to the water below, are held in Pike's and Dutch's line of sight. The slow-motion intercuts are thus not mere indulgent displays of pretty pictorialism that interrupt the continuity, as one reviewer charged:[27] they are part of an infinitely elastic continuity, and function as true epiphanies, gestalts realized out of the welter of conflicting sights and sounds. They are moments of equilibrium, dynamic rather than static (hence, *slowed-down* rather than stopped motion), always labile, subject to being shattered by the next sensation (hence, the rapid cut into each slow-motion gestalt almost as soon as it has been formed).

It is true, then, that Peckinpah does not do too much *in* any given shot—his general aims and purposes do not allow for that—but he makes all the shots count and so manages to do several things *with* each one. For example, we have already noticed how he extends the ants-and-scorpions simile to encompass Agua Verde; yet most of the Bunch's entrance into the courtyard is shot from Pike's point of view. At the same time, then, as Peckinpah is extending the range of his simile, he is establishing a new setting and developing his central character, making us see what Thornton meant when he called Pike the best and making us feel—through the fragmented cutting that forces us to pause and weigh the strategic implications of each detail just as Pike is doing—what it is like to be on guard every moment. Another example of how Peckinpah makes style and technique serve meaning is the Bunch's encounter with Herrera on the trail. Most of the scene is shot in long and medium shots until that terrifying moment when one of Herrera's men panics and fires at the Bunch, and Pike lights the fuse. At this point the action is seen in a proliferation of extreme close-ups (some of them the result of very fast zooms) of the Bunch and the soldiers rapidly cut against one another. The effect this has is to show us the characters' reactions, to pull us into the action, and to wind up the tension as tightly as possible. The paramount effect, however, is to obliterate our sense of the physical space separating the antagonists, which Peckinpah achieves by filling the cinematic space (that is, the space of the screen) with nothing but antagonistic energies—faces tight with anticipation, eyes narrowed and taking aim, weapons raised and triggers cocked. It is as if the filmmaking style had suddenly exploded. Then, as Herrera pleads for Pike to cut the fuse, the tempo of the editing slows down, but the shots remain tight close-ups. It is only when Pike finally does cut the fuse and the danger of explosion has passed that the filmmaking style completely "relaxes," the camera slowly zooming out from close-ups to medium shots of Pike and Herrera. It is obvious that if Peckinpah had wanted he could have filmed this moment with fewer cutaways, inserts, and reactions, but it would have been at the expense of feeling: using longer takes and a more distant camera, the film would have illustrated the tension of the moment but the style would not have embodied it, as a consequence of which the audience would have felt it less immediately, if at all. And, in the final analysis, the scene would then have meant something different, too: for with the camera farther from the action, the physical space in and around the characters preserved, we would have had less of a sense of a world always threatening to explode as conflicting energies exhaust the available space and more of a sense of those energies held in control.

Except in the most concentrated of art forms or in special cases, it probably isn't possible to document a one-to-one relationship between form and content. This is rarely what critics mean when they speak of the union of these two components in an artwork. Rather, what is meant is that there is a general correspondence between what is being said or shown and how it is being said or shown, and the correspondence is genuinely organic, usually functional, and mostly seamless. Having seen, then, how form follows function and manner mediates meaning in this film, we may wish to address ourselves for a moment to the question of whether the style can be said to represent the man, as we are often told an artist's style does or should. Until there is a full-scale biography of Peckinpah which would tell us more about his past and person, any answer we might propose must of course be provisional and subject to qualification or alteration in light of additional evidence. Still, we know something about him. We know that he is fond of saying that things are always mixed. We know also that he grew up in a family where one parent gave him pious certainties from a "Bible that was very big," while the other parent represented a figure of unquestioned authority. We know too that, as one reporter put it, the absolutes fed him of law and morality drove him nearly crazy; he started questioning them and, by his own admission, is still questioning them. This same reporter, who spent some time with Peckinpah, wrote, "Like the strained ground in earthquake country, slipping and shearing to adjust to an ever-shifting core, the ambivalences in Sam Peckinpah run deep," and she went on to report that at the same time the director was mocking his daughter's pacifism, he was handing out medallions which read, "War is not healthy for children and other living things."[28] Clearly this is a man who is quite unclear and very mixed up, and whose artistic style is designed to express his "mixtures." It is a style which shatters centers and makes things fall apart, and it indicates a person who is himself unsure of where he stands, what he believes, and how he knows. The multiple perspectives that are the organizing principle of his films suggest a mind dissatisfied with all absolutes, discontent with all certainties, disinclined to settle upon any single proposition. The style has been called, with considerable insight and accuracy, "prismatic," "kaleidoscopic," and "mosaic." It is prismatic because it tries to see from as many different points of view as possible; it is kaleidoscopic because it tries to illuminate its subject in as many different ways as possible; and it is mosaic because the unity of its effect is a function of quick glimpses, sidelong glances, and darting impressions caught by people who are often on the run, trying to avoid or avert collision. The style is expressive of a sensibility which is likewise restless, searching, and inquisitive and which reveals a man who is equally intense, alert, and uneasy. In this sense, the style is enough like the man, or at least like an important aspect of the man, that it can be said to *be* the man; and this is why analyzing the style of his films hastens us back to their meaning and why a discussion of meaning carried far enough turns into a discussion of style.

In general, Peckinpah may be said to have two basic styles: one, seen primarily in his Western films, that is open, somewhat lyrical, and expansive; the other, seen primarily in his films with contemporary settings, that is darker, tenser, and rather more jagged in its editing. However, there are elements of both styles in all of his films; and it can be seen that the contemporary-settings style is not so much an antithesis as an extension of the Western-setting style. When the setting gets more contemporary and space is at a greater premium, then the sense of being quite literally crowded intensifies, the flow of images is more punctuated by competing images, the glimpses of open space are more sporadic, and the expansions into lyricism—exemplified chiefly in the slow-motion intercuts, the deep-focus shot, or an image held for a long time—are of far briefer duration. Similarly, the camera moves closer to the action (in a crowded setting, even it has less space in which to maneuver), and as a consequence it sees less at any given moment, so the cutaways multiply. In *The Wild Bunch* the two styles are synthesized, because its setting is both savage and civilized, primitive and sophisticated—the most transitional of all his settings. His combination of deep focus, telephoto lenses, slow motion, and fast cutting is ideal for weaving the thick, pulsating, protean textures of life he is after and for expressing the psychological effects of living in a world of such density. The longest unbroken shot (nearly a minute in length) occurs in one scene where the Bunch seem to have the whole desert to themselves; strung along in file, giving each other ample space, and nestled in the seemingly infinite expanse of sand and sky, they can afford to relax, to drop their guard for a while. By contrast, the tempo of the editing increases as spaces become more crowded with antagonistic energies, and it reaches its peak during the moments of violent outburst in which everything disintegrates and in which, for self-preservation, we must be at our most alert and attentive. It is precisely at such moments, however, that it is most difficult to retain our wits sufficiently to see everything whole and unified, and the quickness of the cutting embodies the difficulty of being involved in something yet trying to remain detached from it. Peckinpah's visual style is thus not a function of any paucity of technical resources on his part; it is, instead, the logical consequence and expression of an insistent dialectic of forces in collision, which he pursues right down even to the smallest structural unit of his film, the shot-to-shot cut.

III

Peckinpah has an intuitive grasp not only of the most ancient archetypes and genres—the chase, the hunt, stories of revenge and honor and heroism—but also of the origins of drama in certain kinds of ritual and festival. His early training was in theatre, and he draws upon his theatrical background every bit as much as he uses his knowledge of the Bible. There is something, for example, almost Shakespearean about the way he builds his dramatic structures upon contrasting groups of characters. His materials do not, of course, permit the broad range of social types from the very highest to the very lowest that we find in Shakespeare, but this matters less than the amount of diversification he is able to draw from the materials. As in Faulkner, there is a rich and nearly exhaustive stratification within the terms which the materials do allow: the outlaw Bunch, the officials of the town, the Temperance Union, the middle-class citizens, the railroad men, the U.S. cavalry, and the gutter trash and dregs. This stratification is paralleled on the Mexican side of the border, where Peckinpah is able to expand the social scale by alluding to Europe in Mapache's German military advisors and spies and by immersing us in a peasant culture and then an Indian culture. Concentrated as it is into a single and restricted dramatic space, this diversification enables Peckinpah to reap rich dividends of irony and ambiguity and to incorporate yet another of his favorite dialectics, illusion versus reality. In the extraordinary opening, he deliberately upsets and confuses all our standard reference points, as soldiers turn out to be bandits, law and order are represented by mercenaries, and children engage in games of torture and cruelty. Similarly, in his scenes of comic relief, which involve mainly the bounty hunters, the cavalry, and the Mexican soldiers, he treats ironically, invertedly, or indirectly the themes of honor, courage, loyalty, discipline, restraint, and camaraderie which are handled more straightforwardly in the scenes involving the Bunch.

Peckinpah also likes to incorporate audiences within the dramatic fabric of his stories, and these audiences function somewhat in the manner of choruses as telltale signs or clues to the desired mode of response, again either straightforwardly or ironically. When Teresa presents Mapache with a horse as a gift from the village, the whole gathering bursts into applause. Elsewhere there is a moment in which Thornton asks Coffer what is in Agua Verde, to which Coffer replies, "Mexicans, what else?" and we join the rest of the posse in laughter. When Thornton glares at them, cutting their ridicule short, we too feel chastened for laughing at the stupid wisecrack. We are similarly chastened in an earlier scene. Crazy Lee drops three men; and when Peckinpah cuts in a shot of the bodies, which happen to have fallen into a neat row, it is as if he were daring us to laugh. If we do, the bounty hunters, gleefully shouting things like, "This is better than a hog killing!" remind us of just how obscene our laughter is. (In this Peckinpah is not unlike Buñuel.) There are also other kinds of internal audiences that proliferate his films and that recall for us elements of opera, song, dance, and festival used both dramatically and lyrically (occasionally at once, as when the Bunch leave Angel's village, where the peasants' song is both endemic to the drama and an accompaniment to the scene). This sort of thing also suggests how musical Peckinpah's dramatic constructions often are, with their recurring themes, motifs, patterns of action and movement, their contrasting sets of characters and locales, their verbal and visual reiterations and variations, and of course their musical materials. When Mapache gets the first load of rifles, he shouts, "*Musica!*" and his "court" orchestra of singers and guitarists breaks into song. These things are integral to Peckinpah's dramatic conception and have the effect of reinforcing the legendary quality of the story and of preparing us for the remarkable gradation of mood and tone in the last twenty minutes, during which the very language of the film is made to undergo a subtle transformation from the representational and symbolic to the iconic and imagistic, as Peckinpah pushes his drama to its final resting place.

The film opens with one kind of language: a silent, still image of the Bunch, deceptively dressed in army uniforms, riding toward us. Throughout the credit sequence, which is accompanied by ominous martial music, the color images are periodically frozen into black-and-white stills, the very alternation of the two kinds of shots "telling" us that the story we are about to see is going to move from fact to legend, from the world of history to the world of the imagination. The black-and-white stills, which suggest stylized lithographs, are Peckinpah's way of saying that here our avenue to the past is initially through material of record—old newspaper accounts and photographs, perhaps. This is one kind of truth, available through one kind of language: hard, decidedly fast, cut-and-dried. But there is another kind of language which yields another kind of truth: fluid, tenuous, ambiguous. This is the truth of the imagination, its language the language of art and originating in a mode of reportage quite different from that of the newspaper story. Perhaps nobody knows how legends really get started, but it is a respectable enough guess that the process has something to do with a spectator's being on the scene of some extraordinary event. He tells it to someone, who in turn tells it to someone else, perhaps embellishing it here, embroidering upon it there. Eventually someone may write a song about it, someone else a poem, until the story is well on its way to becoming part of folklore. This is why Peckinpah's films are so replete with songs, with balladeers and instrumentalists, with children, and with so many other kinds of internal audiences. These audiences are bearing witness to events of such stuff as legends are made on, and the import of the events is not lost upon them, but is being recorded in song even as they occur.

When the Bunch begin their march through the crowded streets of Agua Verde, they are enacting a pure ritual, and the film is already about to move beyond itself, as fact and legend are made to merge. The image, because of the morning heat, subtly shimmers, and the merger is heralded first in song, sung here by some drunken soldiers the Bunch pass along the way, and then, as the film comes full circle, in a reprise of the martial music that accompanied the Bunch's slow ride into San Rafael at the beginning. When the battle is over, the posse descend upon the village, while the vultures fly in over them and settle on the surrounding walls and rooftops, patiently awaiting their turn at the carnage below. In a quiet moment that seems to set a seal of benediction on all that has happened, Thornton walks up to Pike's body and takes his friend's pistol, a gesture that signals the fulfillment of his word to Harrigan and pays a tribute to his dead comrade, who was killed paying some old debts of his own. Moments later, Coffer comes upon Pike's body and says, in hushed tones, "T. C., it's *him* . . . it's *Pike*." T. C. is likewise momentarily awestruck, then regains himself and says, "You ain't so damn much now, are you, Mr. Pike?" — an irony, as Pike's stature will soon loom larger than ever. For the time being, however, it is not the meek or the courageous but the scavengers, human and animal, that will inherit this battle-torn piece of earth. The bounty hunters soon depart, taking with them the lifeless bodies of the Bunch to ensure getting the reward, and ride off into hostile country blithely singing, "I went to the river but I couldn't get across / Singing polly-wolly doodle all the day" — a prophesy that comes true as, a little later, victims at last of their own ineptitude, they are ambushed by the Indians of Angel's village, with whom Sykes has teamed up. After the bounty hunters have gone, the peasants enter the village to clear it of supplies for the revolution and to pick up the dead and assist the wounded. A woman dressed in black threads her way through the corpses, and the scene becomes appropriately dark, dusky, and windswept. The buzzards, impatient now, circle overhead, while the departing peasants seem to form a kind of processional which suggests a funeral march and file out the gates past Thornton, who sits leaning against the wall, squinting his eyes to keep out the dust, holding the reins of his horse. The last to leave is a man hobbling along on a crutch, and then Thornton is completely alone.

The mood is one of utter desolation. All the elements of the composition — the solitary man and his horse, the two vultures perched like sentinels on either side of the gates, the crumbling wall, the wind blowing up the dust, the darkening sky — seem to reveal the place in the characteristic of some ruined temple or monastery. Old Sykes appears, leading a band of revolutionary Indians (among whose number is the old man of Angel's village). Thornton joins up with them, and as they ride away, Peckinpah reprises the Bunch's exit from Angel's village. It is not difficult to see that here is a story if ever there was one—of the Battle of Agua Verde and the four strange *gringos* who returned for their friend and wound up liquidating an army of oppressors and liberating a village—which will be told for a thousand years around the campfires of these or any other people. Or, if not around the campfires, then in whatever form and format the storyteller's imagination dictates—song, dance, drama, novel, poem, or, of course, film.

In *Love and Death in the American Novel*, that massive reinterpretation of American fiction, Leslie Fiedler writes:

> The immense barrier of guilt between white man and dark man is no more mitigated in our classic fiction than is the gulf of color and culture itself; both, indeed, are emphasized to the point of melodrama, so that the final reconciliation may seem more tender and miraculous. The archetype makes no attempt to deny the facts of outrage and guilt; it is nurtured by them. It merely portrays them as meaningless in the face of a passion immune to what Melville calls "that climax so fatal to ordinary love." "It's too good for true, honey," Jim says to Huck. "It's too good for true."[29]

This is an insight that applies to all the dialectics and paradoxes, the polarities and contradictions, that animate and inform American literature: love and death, war and peace, savagery and civilization, the machine and the garden, light and dark, man and woman, the one and the many, the whole spiraling, expanding chain of *yin* and *yang* that gives our finest products of art and expression their power, their vitality, and their authenticity. "The fact is that many of the best American novels achieve their very being, their energy and their form, from the perception and acceptance not of unities but of radical disunities," Richard Chase has written. "The American novel tends to rest in contradictions and among extreme ranges of experience."[30] When it does reach the occasional moments of stasis and of peace, nothing is truly resolved or reconciled; what synthesis or mutual accord there is has been achieved at the expense of the fiercest, most intense and violent struggle, and is at best provisional, transitory, and equivocal.

It is no different in Peckinpah's work, and when it is understood that his work rests securely in this tradition, the whole matter of his so-called confusion, cynicism, and chaotic thinking is revealed in a different perspective. Peckinpah is not really calling into question our most time-honored conceptions of heroism; he is not really calling into question the whole symbolic notion of the West as a place where genuine liberation, free from society's constrictions, is possible; he is not really calling into question even the idea of regeneration through violence (however much he may ironize it). The ironies, the ambivalences, the ambiguities, the doubts, the fears, the angers that lace and lacerate his films serve the same purpose they have always served in our art and expression: they give depth and complexity to what might otherwise be complacent simplicities; they give dramatic form and order to feelings and desires so disruptive and instinctual they would otherwise be chaotic; they make rich and mature a radical diabolism that would otherwise be, in D. H. Lawrence's good phrase, "mere childishness."[31] If *The Wild Bunch* is seen as an anti-Western, then it is not seen at all. The whole point of its conflicting perspectives, its explosive polarities and dialectics, is not to "expose" the Western, much less to erode the basis of its heroic virtues, which Peckinpah carries all the way back to their first appearance in the epic tradition. These things are there rather to tighten the screws of the struggle, to make our assent more difficult, indeed, almost impossible, so that when the release comes and the heroic ideal is reclaimed in all its savage beauty and terror, it really is more miraculous than we had ever dreamed or imagined.

The dialectic here, a familiar one announced long ago by Hawthorne, is between the actual and the imaginary, which are but other faces for the tragic and the comic, the realistic and the romantic, the historic and the artistic. Peckinpah takes the actual as far as it can go: what is left in the world of time and circumstance, which is to say, the world of history, are two old men, survivors off to fight for a cause they don't believe in because it gives them another chance at something they do believe in, which is to stay on the run, on the move, on the *go*. "It ain't like it used to be," grins Old Sykes, "but it'll do." From this kind of realism, in which memory is already so mixed with desire that it borders on romance, Peckinpah can take his film in only one direction: the laughter of the two old men is swept up by the laughter of the other members of the Bunch, lately dead but now miraculously brought back to life again as one by one their laughing faces are faded in and out. Yet still this is not enough, for the device leaves each man isolated from his companions, and all isolated from the environment in which they find their ratification. So the laughter is dissolved into the song the peasants sang when the Bunch left their village, and the leave-taking itself is reprised. The landscape, mostly parched and barren throughout, is now green and lush, the color and mood of springtime; and the Bunch are no longer riding toward us in their false military uniforms, but are instead decked out in their true outlaw regalia and heading toward the eastern sun which shines through the trees, refracting off the morning mist and bathing everything in a nimbus that seems to transfigure and purify. Their destiny is complete and inscribes a wayward but inevitable odyssey that originated in wildest villainy and ended in heroic redemption.

Villains become heroes, yet another turn of the ironic screw? Perhaps, but just as extremes meet, so irony carried far enough turns in upon itself and becomes its opposite. When the Bunch attack a whole army on behalf of their fallen comrade, theirs is a sacrificial gesture of human solidarity not so very different in principle from the principles for which the revolutionaries are fighting. It may also be insane, but then this kind of insanity, when it instigates and occurs amid events of such splendor, magnitude, and complexity, has a way of masquerading as bravery, so that even sophisticates and cynics, to say nothing of these primitive peasants, might confuse these very bad men for heroes. Well, who wouldn't be confused? Perhaps heroism and villainy are for Peckinpah very much as love and hate are for Hawthorne: philosophically considered, the same at bottom, except that one happens to be seen in a celestial radiance, the other in a dusky and lurid glow. Peckinpah doesn't know; and if he thought he did, it would be only his opinion, which, ever the discreet storyteller, he would disdain to impose upon his film or force upon his audience. What he does know is that the perspective is everything, and the perspective to which he shifts in order to bring his turbulent film to rest is a peculiarly innocent angle of vision that takes the appearance of things for the reality and carries it all the way to celebration. The Bunch's villainy is left to perish in the dusky and lurid glow of the windswept desert when Pike, Dutch, and the Gorch brothers are carried off face down over a saddle as society's outlaws. When they are next seen, it is as heroes of some legendary adventure, illumined by a radiance if not celestial then at least transcendent, emanating from the faithful if factitious folk imagination, represented here by the people of Angel's village, who, childlike yet not childish, saw something in these men early on that we, less gullible, more prey to suspicion and cynicism, could not see, and that will ensure the Bunch are sent forth in glory whenever the story of the Battle of Agua Verde is told. The world at

PAUL SEYDOR

the end of *The Wild Bunch* is not the "real" world. Rich with laughter, song, and the great good feeling of brotherhood regained and community reintegrated, it is a festive world, that world of total human intelligibility which Northrop Frye has speculated it is the business of art to reclaim for us. By enclosing myth within ritual and festival and resolving his story therein, Peckinpah takes a dramatic structure that has been tragic for most of its length and at the last possible moment deflects it away from the tragic toward the comic. Order is reinstated, balance is restored, and paradox is resolved in the only way he knows how: through the language of image and metaphor, which is to say through the language of his art. This most volatile of films is thus made to close upon a chord of almost pastoral grace and tranquility, its actions and reactions in perfect harmony, its antitheses synthesized, its kinesis reaching in the end not so much stasis as an animated equilibrium. When horse and rider, leader and followers, liberators and liberated, and song of praise are revealed each in its ordered place, the image is frozen yet it doesn't cease moving. Instead, in a touch that subtly recalls the Quest myth, it is made to recede until it disappears into the redemptive blur of morning sunlight and springlike foliage that becomes the very last shot of the film. The mood is one of celebration and what it now seems to be celebrating is nothing so much as the return of the film itself to the world of romance that it appeared only minutes earlier to have forsaken when the vultures descended upon the ravaged village. This is not a world that we are asked to "believe" in. It is offered rather as a world seen through the eyes of some people who do believe in it, a world that the Bunch for one brief moment actually did occupy in fact by returning for Angel and so for these peasants may now occupy forever in folklore and fiction. In this world it still ain't like it used to be, but it'll do more than ever because it is like it never was though might and should have been, which is to say that it has become at last too good for true, too good for true.

Notes

1. David Denby, "Violence Enshrined," *Atlantic Monthly* 229, no. 4 (Apr. 1972), pp. 118, 122.

2. Cordell Strug, "*The Wild Bunch* and the Problem of Idealist Aesthetics, or, How Long Would Peckinpah Last in Plato's Republic?" *Film Heritage* 10, no. 2 (Winter 1974–75), p. 24. [See this book, chap. 6, pp. 87–88. —Ed.]

3. Robert Culp, "Sam Peckinpah, the Storyteller and *The Wild Bunch*,"

Entertainment World 2, no. 2 (Jan. 1970), p. 11. [See this book, chap. 1, p. 8. — Ed.]

4. See, for examples of this sort of criticism, Judith Crist, revs. of *The Wild Bunch, New York Magazine*, 30 June 1969, p. 43; and 14 July 1969, p. 57; and Arthur Knight, rev. of *The Wild Bunch, Saturday Review*, 5 July 1969, p. 21.

5. Stanley Kauffmann, rev. of *The Wild Bunch*, in *Figures of Light* (New York: Harper and Row, 1971), p. 181 (originally published in *New Republic*, 19 July 1969). Apart from this and a couple of other obtuse remarks, Kauffmann's is the most intelligent, sensitive, and perceptive of the first round of reviews the film received and is very much worth reading for his observations on perspectivism.

6. Pauline Kael, "Notes on the Nihilistic Poetry of Sam Peckinpah," *New Yorker*, 12 Jan. 1976, pp. 72–73.

7. Quoted in John Bryson, "The Wild Bunch in New York," *New York Magazine*, 19 Aug. 1974, p. 27.

8. Northrop Frye, *A Natural Perspective: The Development of Shakespearean Comedy and Romance* (New York: Columbia University Press, 1965), pp. 43–44.

9. This and the next quotation from Aljean Harmetz, "Man Was a Killer Long Before He Served a God," *New York Times*, sec. D, 31 Aug. 1969, p. 9. [See this book, chap. 10, p. 171.—Ed.]

10. Dwight MacDonald, *Dwight MacDonald on Movies* (Englewood Cliffs, N.J.: Prentice-Hall, 1969), pp. 28, 30.

11. Ernest Callenbach, "A Conversation with Sam Peckinpah," *Film Quarterly* 17, no. 2 (Winter 1963–64), p. 10.

12. Richard Whitehall, "Talking with Peckinpah," *Sight and Sound* 38, no. 4 (Autumn 1969), p. 175.

13. "Playboy Interview: Sam Peckinpah," *Playboy* 19, no. 8 (Aug. 1972), p. 74.

14. Quoted in Paul Schrader, "Sam Peckinpah Going to Mexico," *Cinema* 5, no. 3 (1969), p. 21. [See this book, chap. 2, p. 22.—Ed.]

15. Stephen Farber, "Peckinpah's Return," rev. of *The Wild Bunch* and interview with Sam Peckinpah, *Film Quarterly* 23, no. 1 (Fall 1969), pp. 9, 11. [See this book, chap. 3, pp. 42, 45.—Ed.]

16. *Playboy* interview, p. 72.

17. Quoted in Dan Yergin, "Peckinpah's Progress: From Blood and Killing in the Old West to Siege and Rape in Rural Cornwall," *New York Times Magazine*, 31 Oct. 1971, p. 92.

18. This is only one of several effects which depend in large part upon the extraordinary music score by Fielding, about whose contribution to the film a whole essay could be written. Notice, for example, how at the very beginning the ominous growl from the low strings sets the tone, literally *and* figuratively, for the entire film, signaling to us that all is not as it appears to be. Or take the moment near the end when Thornton pauses over Pike's body, then reaches down and takes his friend's revolver as a remembrance. The gesture is a symbolic farewell, but the way in which the music softly, almost imperceptibly, reprises the main lyrical theme reminds us that it is also a moment of reunion. Both Peckinpah and Fielding were in especially close accord on this effect: in one of their early conferences they discovered that each had independently come to feel that the entire film built to that moment. (This is the second of seven films on which Peckinpah and Fielding have worked together; and on

at least three of them—*The Wild Bunch, Straw Dogs,* and *Junior Bonner*—they produced marriages of image and music worthy of comparison with those of such celebrated director-composer collaborations of the past as Eisenstein and Prokofiev or Hitchcock and Herrmann.)

19. Robert Warshow, "The Westerner," *The Immediate Experience* (Garden City: Doubleday, 1962), pp. 89–106 (originally published in *Partisan Review,* Mar.–Apr. 1954).

20. Kauffmann, p. 181.

21. Strug, p. 26. [See this book, chap. 6, p. 88.—Ed.]

22. "Sam Peckinpah Lets It All Hang Out," interview with Sam Peckinpah, *Take One* 2, no. 3 (Jan.–Feb. 1969), p. 20.

23. Peckinpah considers the scene in which this line occurs the most important in the film, and regards the Bunch's exit from Angel's village, which concludes the scene, as the turning point as far as the humanity of the Bunch is concerned. "If you can ride out with them there and feel it," he says, "you can die with them and feel it."

This scene also contained in its original version the bit of associational editing linking Pike and the row of children; unfortunately, it was part of the footage that Feldman removed. It is precisely the loss of these kinds of things—subtleties and nuances—that Peckinpah fears when others tamper with his films, and it is what he means when he speaks of his films as being "intricately intertwined." When something is cut, the effect of the cut is never merely local or discrete but affects other things elsewhere.

24. Quoted in Joel Reisner and Bruce Kane, "Sam Peckinpah," *Action: Directors Guild of America* 2, no. 3 (May–June 1970), p. 27.

25. Andrew Sarris, rev. of *The Wild Bunch, Village Voice,* 31 July 1969, p. 39. Sarris has been criticizing Peckinpah's storytelling abilities since *Ride the High Country,* of which he has written, "Since Peckinpah obviously considers himself too intellectual to tell a story, it remains to be seen whether he will be forceful enough to develop a theme" (*The American Cinema: Directors and Directions, 1929–1968* [New York: E. P. Dutton, 1968], p. 219). In common with some other auteur critics in this country, Sarris has never forgiven Peckinpah for not being John Ford or for not making movies like John Ford's; nor does Sarris seem to believe that filmic narrative has developed or can develop beyond the likes of Ford, Hawks, and Hitchcock. What is ironic, not to mention a little sad, in all of this is that, in the review of *The Wild Bunch* just cited, when Sarris sets aside his prejudices he displays (in spite of his obtuse criticisms) insights into the workings of this film that are keener and more penetrating than those of any other reviewer of the time except Stanley Kauffmann and perhaps William S. Pechter—notably in his realization that Peckinpah's doubts and moral ambiguities exist (in part) as dramatic preparation for the Bunch's final redemption "by heroism on a Homeric scale of elemental commitments" and in such observations as "Peckinpah seems instinctively to affirm the power of the physical to express and transform the spiritual."

26. Lucien Ballard to P. S., 27 Feb. 1977.

27. Sarris, p. 39.

28. Harmetz, p. 9; see also Whitehall, p. 173. [See this book, chap. 10, p. 171.—Ed.]

29. Leslie A. Fiedler, *Love and Death in the American Novel*, rev. ed. (New York: Stein and Day, 1960, 1966), p. 390.

30. Richard Chase, *The American Novel and Its Traditions* (Garden City: Doubleday, 1957), pp. 7, 1.

31. D. H. Lawrence, *Studies in Classic American Literature* (1923; rpt. New York: Viking Press, 1964), p. 83.

9 ▶

The Conclusion of *The Wild Bunch*

MICHAEL BLISS

While there is no doubting its emotional impact, the end of Sam Peckinpah's *The Wild Bunch* so masterfully demonstrates Peckinpah's command of formal technique, especially with regard to the director's control over the fine points of narrative, that I believe this aspect of the film should be considered in detail.

By the time that Angel has been abandoned to Mapache by Dutch, the Bunch have hit a new low in morality, a situation exacerbated by the disunity that is reflected in the way that the men are spread out on the mountain overlooking the land on which Freddy Sykes (another of the many people left behind by Pike) has been seriously wounded. Nonetheless, Angel's loss weighs heavily on the Bunch.

It's important to keep in mind that the Bunch do not return to Agua Verde for Angel; they go there to ask Mapache to deal with Thornton and his gang. In other words, they intend to ask Mapache to do something that they should do themselves. However, although the men want to abdicate a responsibility, they nonetheless wind up taking on an even greater one: rescuing Angel. Yet before that point, the group is still reluctant to oppose morally objectionable acts. Even after witnessing the terrible treatment to which Angel is subjected, the Bunch do nothing. Despite the fact that they are all disturbed by what they see—with Pike and Dutch commenting to each other on their anger—the only statements made to Mapache are those by Pike: "I want to buy him back; I'll give you half my share for him." The statement is interesting for a

"The Conclusion of *The Wild Bunch*" by Michael Bliss is a slightly revised version of a portion of chapter 4 of *Justified Lives: Morality and Narrative in the Films of Sam Peckinpah* by Michael Bliss (Carbondale: Southern Illinois University Press, 1993). Reprinted by permission of the publisher.

number of reasons. There is the accent on selfish practicality (Pike offers only half of his money), a carryover from the discussions among the Bunch in the previous scenes. Additionally, Pike's offer implies that Angel has already been sold, which indeed he has. By virtue of Dutch's silence about the Bunch's complicity in the diversion of the rifles and ammunition, the men, to invoke the colloquial phrase, have "sold [Angel] out."

Mapache refuses Pike's offer, expressing himself, like Pike, in mercantile terms that, also like Pike's, are used to mask the emotional reason for his statement: "I need no gold, and I don't sell this one." Mapache will not sell Angel back to Pike because Angel betrayed him. The issue is now one of his honor, which Mapache intends to satisfy by publicly humiliating his betrayer. Moreover, even if Mapache had known of the other men's involvement in the theft of the rifles, Angel's act is probably more offensive to him since Angel is Mexican. In this sense, Mapache is undoubtedly very much like Angel. Angel cannot forget that it was Mapache who killed his father; Mapache cannot forget that it was a Mexican, one of his own people, who acted against him.

We might also surmise that since Mapache learns from the mother of Angel's ex-girlfriend, Teresa, that Angel stole the guns (this despite Mohr's aide's description of Mapache's "superb intelligence corps"), it is also possible that Mapache learned from the same woman that the man he killed in Don José's village was Angel's father; knowledge of this fact may suggest to Mapache that this Mexican youth has both personal and political grudges against him, thereby posing a double threat that should be dealt with as quickly as possible.

Pike's practical reply to Mapache's refusal to sell Angel ("Why not? You've had your fun with him") completely discounts the issue of honor, an intentional oversight considering that the return for Angel is prompted by a desire to do the honorable thing. Pike also overlooks that fact that Angel has embarrassed Mapache politically (a realm of which Pike, like the Gorches, is only vaguely aware) and that the "general" needs to have his political pride satisfied as well.

In the steam-bath and mountaintop sequences, a profusion of words is used, in the first instance to divert the emotional conflict in the Bunch between their ideals and their selfishness to the safer realm of a verbal debate between the moral and material realms, and in the second case to try to mask the sorrow over Angel's capture by expressing it through discontent and aggression. In

160

MICHAEL BLISS

both instances, though, words fail to hide the fact that the topics under discussion are really the most elemental matters concerning what is right and wrong. The sight in Agua Verde of Angel being tortured dismisses all abstract considerations, ultimately making it quite plain to the Bunch that what is needed is something at which they excel: action.

Dragged like a toy at the end of a rope behind Mapache's car, and thus a slave to a symbol of mechanistic progress (another example of which, the machine gun, will prove to be the entire village's undoing), Angel seems to be fulfilling the ambiguity implicit in Dutch's statement that "he played his string right out to the end." More importantly, though, the string that Angel is playing out is his keeping silent about the Bunch's involvement in the diversion of the guns, a gesture that ultimately plays on the sentimental strings of the Bunch's sensibilities, until at last they return their Mexican friend's grand gesture with an appropriately grand gesture of their own.

Before that point, though, an anxious and awkward emotional period must be passed through. The Agua Verde adobe sequence is notable not only for its tension but also for its virtual lack of speech and simultaneous richness of communication.

The guilt over Angel's abandonment, which in these sequences seems virtually palpable, first surfaces in Pike's awkwardness with his Mexican lover. Fortunately for Pike, the squabbling over money coming from the Gorches' room next door provides him with an excuse to leave his room temporarily. Pike has already gone through a series of gestures with the Mexican woman that exemplify his shame at trying to avoid being emotional with her, a shame that the liquor he has been drinking before and during the sequence has done nothing to diminish. Repeatedly, the woman's candid and direct looks at Pike cause him to avoid eye contact with her, something he can at this point only achieve with the members of the Bunch, which makes it quite clear how emotionally immature these men are.

After strapping on his gun, Pike stands up, walks across the room, and parts the curtain between his and the Gorches' room. As Pike stands in the doorway, we see that Tector is idly playing with a tiny baby bird. Thus, in another extension of the children/ants/scorpions image, human manipulation of animals occurs for a person's amusement. What follows are a series of "statements" conveyed through eye contact that signify what Pike, Lyle, and Tector are thinking; the direct way that these men meet each other's gazes shows that Pike and the Gorches are finally confronting the emotional issue that is bothering them all: Angel's capture and their abandonment of him.

First Tector and then Lyle look up at Pike, silently questioning his presence. Pike challenges the Gorches to ask more aggressively what he wants by looking at, and thereby confronting, each of his inquisitors in the order in which they first looked at him—first Tector, then Lyle. Lyle narrows his eyes in thought; he is trying to fully understand what Pike wants in the same way that he tried to divine Pike's reaction to Angel's mistreatment when the Bunch first rode into Agua Verde. Tector is still looking at Pike. Pike looks again at Tector, then at Lyle. Then, still keeping Lyle's gaze, Pike simply says, "Let's go." Lyle again narrows his eyes as if to divine the statement's true significance, then looks over at Tector. Tector meets his brother's gaze, understands his confusion, and looks over at Pike for an answer. Pike looks at Tector to reiterate the implications of his statement and, having "answered" Tector, looks once again at Lyle, ending this gesture by narrowing his eyes to indicate determination. As though to finally confirm what he has understood by this series of communications, Lyle looks one last time at Tector, then at Pike. Then, for the first time in the film, Lyle acts as the sole spokesman for himself and Tector, no longer invoking his brother in the reply (as in the "me and Tector figured" during the argument about the division of the Starbuck "gold") but simply and resolutely speaking for both of them. "Why not," he says. Unlike earlier in the film (as when Pike reluctantly agrees to join the post-robbery Agua Verde revelry), this statement is not an expression of despair but a direct affirmation of the fact that there is only one right thing to do in the current situation.

When Pike returns to his room and pays the Mexican woman, awkwardness and averted eye gestures again occur; Pike simply cannot express himself forthrightly to a woman (that is, except through violence, as he does when returning the fire of the woman who shoots him in the back). Pike's treatment of the Mexican woman here is so terribly materialistic and insulting that at one point the woman must avert her eyes from Pike out of embarrassment for the way that he is betraying his essential humanity. After tossing a few gold coins at the woman, Pike walks out.

After the men leave the Gorches' room, Peckinpah zooms in on the panting baby bird, a poor plaything worn out by the kind of moral indifference that the Gorches and Pike have finally repudiated.[1] As they emerge from the adobe, the men all look in turn at

Dutch, who is dispiritedly whittling and who, like Thornton at the film's beginning and end (the connection signaling affinity between two of the film's most moral member), is forlornly sitting with his back to a wall. In response, Dutch directly meets Pike, Tector, and Lyle's gazes in a replay of the eye-contact order from the adobe sequence. Then, Dutch looks again at Pike.

The communication between Pike and Dutch outside the adobe is nonverbal, a quality we might very well expect given the great understanding that always exists between the two men. Moreover, we are given an interchange of gestures and reactions that not only mirrors those that Pike and Dutch exchanged when they were watching Angel being tortured but which also will be repeated at the film's end when Sykes and Thornton face each other. The relative physical positioning will be repeated as well, with the superior, authoritative member (Pike/Sykes) looking down at his second in command (Dutch here; Thornton will assume the role with Sykes), who is seated on the ground with his back to a wall, the secondary member's dual physical position (the low vantage point and the fact of being backed against a wall) indicating an impasse that somehow must be overcome.

Pike and Dutch engage in a communication even more perfect than the one just achieved among Pike, Tector, and Lyle, since here, no words are used. Dutch looks at Pike, "reads" him, and just barely begins to smile; Pike not only looks back but for one of the few times in the film he also smiles. Dutch smiles broadly and then laughs (the same triad of gestures that Thornton and Sykes will exhibit at the film's end). Only Dutch responds to the men's unspoken common intentions with laughter, thus indicating that he realizes more clearly, a bit more consciously, the true purpose behind their return to the center of town: not just to redeem Angel but to redeem themselves as well through a final acting in concert that will surpass all of their other endeavors. Dutch's laughter demonstrates his ability to intuit and anticipate the joy to which such a pure act can give rise, and signals the fact that the compact, begun inside the adobe, has been sealed through good humor (a reinvocation of the bonding through laughter we've previously seen). Everything is now in readiness. This time the Bunch will, in Pike's words from an earlier scene, "do it right."

The four men prepare their guns; once ready, they pause for a fraction of a second to line up, thereby asserting in physical terms the unanimity that they have already reached emotionally and psychologically. As the Bunch move into formation, they thus repeat the response to Pike's "fall in" from the Starbuck scene and echo the clockwork precision of the train heist, with the difference that in the present case, we see the Bunch displaying the kind of "stick[ing] together" that Pike has always really wanted them to have, a unity deriving from fidelity to a common cause that has compassion, not greed, as its basis.

The regimentation of this march befits the essentially military mission that these men are on, right down to the military-sounding snare-drum accompaniment. There are further parallels with the Bunch's first "military" march. In both scenes, a counterpoint to the Bunch's precision is provided by an essentially buffoonish collection of people: the Temperance Union marching band in the first scene (whose music, although it comes later than the Bunch's march, nonetheless contrasts with it) and the drunken Mexicans in the Agua Verde scene. Additionally, whereas in the first scene the Bunch, drunk with desire for money, had their actions contrasted with an accompaniment associated with sobriety (in the form of the Starbuck residents' seriousness of purpose), here music is played and a song is sung by a literally drunken group of people whose inebriation contrasts with the important sobriety of the Bunch's mission, which nonetheless turns to a kind of joyous drunkenness after the shooting begins.

The initial scenes in Agua Verde provide an important contrast to the departure scene from Angel's village. When the Bunch left the village, after a life-affirming fiesta, they were a unified group being serenaded out as benefactors and heroes. In Agua Verde, after a series of situations connoting death—the abandonment of Angel, the failed attempt at diversion with prostitutes, the terrible emotional estrangements of Pike and the Gorches in the adobe scenes (a continuation of the negative ambience from the mountaintop scene, with both the mountaintop and adobe scenes' discrepancy from the fiesta being painfully obvious)—the Bunch are once again alienated.

Physical separation as a sign of alienation, used with success in the mountaintop scene, reappears in the adobe sequences. Pike and the Gorches are in separate rooms. Dutch is even further removed; he is outside the building in which the other men are located. The manner in which the Bunch, when leaving the adobe, are piece by piece reassembled—first Pike, then the inseparable Gorches, then Dutch, with all then proceeding toward Angel—signals a rebuilding of the united Bunch, and suggests a return to the type of fidelity and life we felt when they left Angel's village.

164

MICHAEL BLISS

Moreover, the men leave the adobe in the same order used in the eye-contact sequence in the Gorches' room—first Pike, then Tector, then Lyle—a note of directorial precision that ranks these men according to the strength of their influence. (As usual, Lyle is the minor member.) Yet in opposition to the positive connotations created by this orderliness, that insistent snare drumming, and the trivialization of the Mexican song created by its being drunkenly rendered, cast an apprehensive gloom over the proceedings. What we are being prepared for is the contradictory nature of the scene of Angel's reclamation, with Angel seemingly recovered by the Bunch, then abruptly stolen away when Mapache kills him, then (figuratively) recovered again as the Bunch make all of Agua Verde pay for Mapache's brutality. Finally, Peckinpah will end the film with two more recoveries, first by resurrecting the Bunch in the flesh through their successors—Thornton and the Sykes gang—then by resurrecting them in spirit through the memory images that, spiritlike, seem to hover over Thornton and Don José's men as they ride away.

It's significant that at *The Wild Bunch*'s end, the Bunch's newfound unity of purpose and action doesn't occur in the United States but in Mexico. In other words, we're on the other side of the mirror, in that special Peckinpah region where anything can happen. The film has been leading us here all along. We have to wait for that final moment, though. By photographing the first part of the Bunch's march through Agua Verde's heat-shimmering, dust-filled air, Peckinpah lends a dreamlike unreality to the image. Additionally, the telephoto lens's flattening of the perspective prolongs the drama of the moment, giving the sequence the quality of that kind of nightmare in which one is moving but making no progress, and collapses the foreground Mexicans (who are walking back and forth) against the Bunch, so that the Mexicans seem at every moment to be threatening the Bunch with their (apparent) proximity.[2]

However, this anxious part of the scene lasts only a short time. When the Bunch round a corner, Peckinpah photographs them with a lens of more normal perspective. Having turned the corner, Pike, Dutch, and the Gorches can now be seen by Mapache and his retinue. Once again, the men pause. The nightmare is finally over; a fantastic reality, full of a different kind of horror, one made up not of compromise and abandonments but of forthright explosions of revenge, is about to take place.

Immediately before Angel shot Teresa, Dutch, anticipating what was about to happen, cried out "No!" Here, just after Mapache starts to bring his knife near Angel's throat and before he actually cuts it (like Mapache's bravery during the train assault sequence, this act demonstrates the "general's" consistency of behavior), Dutch once again opens his mouth to cry out. But he cannot speak; this is one of his own being killed. Dutch can only look and stare.

After Mapache is shot (first by Pike, then by Dutch and Lyle), the whole village freezes. Herrera, Zamorra, Mohr—everyone is struck immobile by the act's swiftness and daring. Seeing this reaction, and knowing that despite the odds the Bunch have once again achieved an effect quite out of proportion to their strength in numbers (as they twice did: when they managed to escape from Starbuck and when they successfully robbed the munitions train), Dutch—who laughed before the Starbuck escape when contemplating Pike's plan to use the Temperance Union marchers as a diversion, and who smiled during the train heist when, after getting the drop on some soldiers, he knew that the plan was going to succeed—laughs once again. Then, Pike makes his final decision for the Bunch.

It's possible that having so outrageously stunned Agua Verde, the Bunch might conceivably be able to move beyond this exaggerated Mexican standoff and safely ride out of town. However, it's more likely that Pike reasons at this point that there's simply nowhere for them to go from here. In Pike's words from an earlier scene, the Bunch are about to complete their "last go-round." Pike turns and shoots Mohr, who is clearly the second most objectionable man in the village. After Mohr's death, Mapache's two seconds-in-command—Herrera and Zamorra—are shot, followed by Mohr's aide, thereby killing off everyone with any degree of military authority in the town. Having rid the village of its leaders, the Bunch now turn on its troops.

The chaos that breaks loose in Agua Verde is similar to that in Starbuck, in that the Bunch initiate it and best their opponents. The men are in full control, right up to the end, when a young boy delivers the first of three *coup de grace* shots to Pike (since the child uses one of the weapons the Bunch stole against Pike, the act replays the manner in which the Bunch turn Mapache's machine gun against him).[3] Except for Dutch, who has never seemed as capable of overt brutality as the rest, each Bunch member takes his turn at the machine gun, first Tector, then Lyle, then Pike. As we might expect, Pike exceeds everyone else's efforts. Dutch uses grenades; Pike does him one better by using machine gun fire to detonate boxes of dynamite. With one last (unanswered) call to Dutch to "Come on, you lazy bastard," Pike and Dutch go out in a blaze of protesting gunfire.

After the massacre, the vultures arrive, first as animals, then in the form of their human counterparts: T. C., Coffer, and the rest of Thornton's gang, who are preceded by glimpses of mourning villagers, women in black, and grim funeral processions—images that create a sensation of depression and despair that contrasts with the feelings of transcendence and hope that Peckinpah will soon create. There follows the looting of the bodies, a replay of the Starbuck slaughter aftermath. Then, Deke Thornton moves forward and tenderly removes Pike's gun from its holster. For Thornton, the gun has obviously assumed talismanic significance; his taking of it presages his assumption of Pike's late-realized political mission. This gesture also marks the beginning of reverence and acts as an affirmation of tradition, effects that are undercut somewhat by Thornton's forlornly sitting down outside the village walls (although this despondent reaction is compromised to a degree when Thornton smiles slightly after hearing the shots signaling the deaths of his men). Finally, after Thornton acknowledges the truth of Coffer's observation that he "ain't coming," the gang leaves.

T. C., Coffer, and the other members of Thornton's gang, with the Bunch hanging over saddles as Harrigan wanted them, ride off to their doom. After a few moments, whose desolation is underscored by the sound of the whistling wind and the sight of blowing dust (a nondialogue interlude that Peckinpah uses to build up our expectations for the film's finale), Sykes, Don José, and the mountain Indians come riding up.

> SYKES: I didn't expect to find you here.
> THORNTON: Why not? [The last "why not" in the film, here a signal not of resignation but of affirmation, of Thornton's determination to be where he is, knowing as he must that, given those shots in the distance, Sykes and the rest will soon be along.] I sent 'em back; that's all I said I'd do.

Thornton's comment demonstrates how closely allied the film's three leaders—Pike, Thornton, and Mapache—are. Each of them makes a statement whose literal meaning is intentionally at variance with what the speaker really feels. Pike's earlier comment, "We share very few sentiments with our government," and Mapache's "I . . . give [Angel] to you," are both intentionally duplicitous

The Conclusion of *The Wild Bunch*

statements. In the present sequence, Thornton lives up to the letter of his pledge to Harrigan when he sends his gang back to the United States but retains what he obviously regards as the spirit of his deal by his remaining behind.

SYKES: They didn't get very far.
THORNTON: I figured.
SYKES: What are your plans?
THORNTON: Drift around down here. Try to stay out of jail.

Thornton undoubtedly has no real plans, although it's safe to say that in his reply he intentionally omits his hope that he can join up with Sykes. Then, the great offer: to fight with purpose, for idealism, for social change, to fight back against the oppression that we've seen throughout the film.

SYKES: Well, me and the boys here, we got some work to do. You wanna come along? It ain't like it used to be, but it'll do.

And yet, for one last time recalling Pike's "stick together" speech, we realize that in an important sense, it *is* (to use both Pike and Sykes's words) "like it used to be." The Bunch, in a new incarnation, are spiritually and physically together again, a fact affirmed by the action that next takes place: the repetition of bond-creating gestures that occurred between Pike and Dutch outside the Agua Verde adobe (which tells us that Sykes now equals Pike, and that Thornton is now his sidekick). Thornton looks up and begins to smile: Sykes laughs; Thornton laughs. Finally, the men, laughing, ride off together. As they do, the old Bunch come back to life, reappearing in images, and *they* all laugh,[4] which tells us more successfully than words that because fidelity is now linked to political purpose, it's not only like it used to be, it's better, and that eventually all of them—Pike, Thornton, Angel, Dutch, the Gorches, and Sykes—will finally be united—in legend, in memory, forever.[5]

Notes

1. Interestingly, Tector's bird is tied with a piece of string so that it cannot fly away. The image of the tied bird recalls Angel, who is tethered at the end of Mapache's rope and, like the bird, is being used as a toy, a notion that reinvokes the ideas associated with the ants-and-scorpions image in another example of the film's thematic richness.
2. At one point, contact is made between the Bunch and the Mexicans when Tector angrily shoulders a Mexican out of his way.

3. Ironically, just as the continuation of the Bunch's tradition is symbolized after the massacre through Thornton's appropriation of Pike's gun, so too does Mapache, through the child's rifle, (briefly) exert influence after death. Both pieces of armament were stolen from the U.S. government, a fact which goes to prove that regardless of their source, the end to which weapons are put is determined by the person wielding them. Another piece of American issue, the machine gun, first passes to the Bunch, then to Mapache—who, fortunately, never has the chance to use it in battle—then back to the Bunch, who turn it against Mapache, and finally to Sykes, Thornton, and Don José, who will use it in furtherance of the cause that the Bunch, through the Agua Verde massacre, have unwittingly assisted.

4. The fact that this ending, which reinvokes the feelings of reverence associated with the Bunch's departure from Angel's village, was not in the original script (indeed, the Bunch's touching departure from the village was not in the script either) but was later added by Peckinpah, shows what a romantic Peckinpah really was.

5. Through a device whose self-reflexivity recalls the black-and-white still frames used intermittently at the film's opening (which have deadly connotations almost identical to those resulting from the freeze-frames at the beginning of the long version of *Pat Garrett and Billy the Kid*), Peckinpah reminds us at the film's end (when our sentimentality concerning the Bunch is at its height) that *The Wild Bunch* is a crafted, storytelling vehicle that creates, and fosters the continuation of, the Bunch's myth. The director accomplishes this effect by having the final anamorphic Panavision image (a freeze-frame of the Bunch riding out of Angel's village) recede within the original frame after the final credits and just before "The End" appears on the screen. Like the song that is used to serenade the Bunch out of Angel's village, the film is a mnemonic device that in the future will be used to evoke feelings and ideas, in the same manner as the stories about Major Dundee (to which Sam Potts refers in the earlier film) will be used.

10 ▶

Man Was a Killer Long Before He Served a God

ALJEAN HARMETZ

"The noble savage?"

The voice is a stream bed eroded by rivers of whiskey. The face is a road map of the high country—nights cold enough to freeze your butt off, chunks of venison tossed in the fire while the dead buck hangs high, covered with a web of snow.

"The myth of the noble savage is horseshit, lady. Law and order and grace and understanding are things that have to be taught."

Sam Peckinpah sits in his Warner Bros.-7 Arts office dreaming of Hawaii. His four children, the salvage of his first marriage, are on the beach at Kuhio waiting for him. He will join them tomorrow, when a pause in the editing of his new film allows him to flee Los Angeles. After Hawaii, there is a woman, somewhere in Mexico. He wears around his neck the gold Spanish cross with its tortured Christ that she gave to him. For added insurance he wears a less agonized cross of Mexican silver. Occasionally, the gold and silver chains get tangled in his patriarchal beard.

In white Levi's and gray tennis shoes, he sits stiffly, as though to move would jar his bones. He has directed two pictures back to back—*The Wild Bunch* and *The Ballad of Cable Hogue*—and he is exhausted from twenty-two months of hacking at his guts and pasting them artistically on celluloid. Although the outer office is littered with empty bottles of club soda from some gargantuan revel, Peckinpah sips spartanly at a vodka. He is on the wagon—somewhat—"until I hit Shipwreck Kelly's tomorrow afternoon."

Forty-four-year-old Sam Peckinpah made his reputation—as a "genius" and a "bastard"—on just four motion pictures spaced out over seven years: *The Deadly Companions*, *Ride the High Country*, *Major Dundee*, and *The Wild Bunch*. There is no question that the last three films are his, even *Major Dundee*, which was sewn together with a meathook by a producer who wanted to make it commercial and only succeeded in making it grotesque. Peckinpah's spurs are dug into every frame, twisting the films toward the moral ambivalences that make them so annoying and so powerful.

In a Peckinpah film, a good man is incapable of doing good, and a noble action ends by destroying its maker. Yet it is not a question of being "beyond good and evil," as one critic said of *The Wild Bunch*, but of being *before* good and evil. Peckinpah hands out copies of Robert Ardrey's *African Genesis* by the dozens. He came across the book after he had finished *The Wild Bunch*, and he is "astounded" that Ardrey's theories are a scientific statement of his own theme.

"I have a twenty-year-old daughter who is a very strong pacifist and who believes that people are born without sin and without anger, which is not necessarily the same, and without violence. I totally disagree with her. People are born to survive. They have instincts that go back millions of years. Unfortunately, some of those instincts are based on violence. There is a great streak of violence in every human being. If it is not channeled and understood, it will break out in war or in madness."

In *The Wild Bunch*, judgments of good and evil are irrelevant. Morality is irrelevant. Children play "an ugly game" with scorpions and ants, "but it's a game children play—unless they're taught different." The children were not taught to play the torturer's game by the brutality around them. "They would have had to be taught *not* to play that game. And man was a killer millions of years before he served a God."

"The point of the film," says Peckinpah, "is to take this facade of movie violence, open it up, get people involved in it so that they are starting to go in the Hollywood-television predictable reaction syndrome, and then twist it so that it's not fun any more, just a wave of sickness in the gut."

"The kids who came up to us at our first preview, in Kansas City, understood," says *The Wild Bunch*'s film editor, Lou Lombardo. "There was one nineteen-year-old kid on his way to Vietnam. He told Sam, 'I found myself shouting for more when William Holden was on the machine gun and saying *Go baby, get them all*, and now I feel ashamed of myself for having felt that way.' Then he said, very politely, 'Thank you, Mr. Peckinpah.'"

At least twenty minutes of that Kansas City version are lying on various Hollywood cutting-room floors because middle-aged members of the audience were so revulsed by the violence that they bolted from the theater, one or two of them to vomit in the alley.

Peckinpah, an uncompromising man, accepts that judgment with surprising equanimity. He is less polite about more recent cuts that drained ten minutes of humanity from the film while leaving all the finger-licking violence. He is particularly angry about the elimination of a human moment between the Mexican general Mapache and a young Mexican boy. "Possibly one of the best moments in the entire film. It made the point that I tried to make with the entire film, that the Mexicans were no worse than William Holden's Bunch. Removing that scene was an absolute disgrace." It is this boy who kills Holden at the end of the film. Without the earlier scene, the later one seems just an added senseless piece of violence.

One searches *The Wild Bunch*, as one does all of Peckinpah's films, desperately, for innocence. A few people escape the massacre at the end of the film, but Peckinpah denies their claim to being higher on the moral scale than those who have died. Of the least violent character, the head man of the Mexican village, Peckinpah says softly, "Instead of fighting, that old man ran away when the general's army raided his village. We are all guilty to some extent."

"Sam is the one person in American films who has truly caught the idea of ambivalence," says Gil Dennis, an open-faced, young American Film Institute intern who chose to work with Peckinpah when he was allowed to apprentice himself to any American director. "Sam respects his characters. He doesn't judge them, and that annoys people. They keep asking, 'Where does he stand?' Even in *Bonnie and Clyde*, you've got your villain in 'society.' Sam won't make it that easy, not ever."

Perhaps he *can't* make it that easy. Like the strained ground in earthquake country, slipping and shearing to adjust to an ever-shifting core, the ambivalences in Sam Peckinpah run deep.

Although he mocks his daughter's pacifism, he carries a pocketful of Another Mother for Peace medallions bearing the legend "War is not healthy for children and other living things." He hands them out as casually as he does Robert Ardrey's book. He skins the deer he kills and proudly boasts that "I've fed my family," but he is contemptuous of men who kill for sport. He is a Catholic convert who prays only at his own convenience, a booted Westerner in a two-hundred-and-fifty-dollar custom-tailored suit.

He has a favorite Nevada bordello and a favorite Parisian restaurant where dinner for two costs seventy-five dollars. On his ninety-thousand-dollar lot at Malibu, he is planning to rebuild a 108-year-old mountain cabin that he bought for five hundred dollars in the high Sierras and took to Nevada for *The Ballad of Cable Hogue*. During the filming of *Cable Hogue*, he slept in the cabin, alone in the desert, "sometimes, just to get out of the motel."

Since the end of his brief second marriage, he considers himself unencumbered, but he clings to his past. He still wears the signet ring given to him by his father on his graduation from grammar school, and he has in storage a pair of torn blue denim pants that he could not bear to give away because "I had some good times in Nevada in these pants." His tastes are simple: eggs drowned in chili sauce, liquor—any kind, straight from the bottle—but his fantasies are complex.

He revels in having two hundred crew members and actors under his thumb, but he hates it with equal passion. People who care too little about his film are "put on the bus" and sent back to Hollywood. Those who are cashiered from his sets speak of him as "a dictatorial bastard," "a weird son of a bitch." Those who stay become a family that travels together from picture to picture. He has formed a stock company that echoes the early John Ford. R. G. Armstrong, Strother Martin, Warren Oates, L. Q. Jones have appeared in all or almost all of his films. "They're all crazy, dedicated, lascivious bastards," Peckinpah says. "Basically they're all country people, like me."

Yet those who stay in his rough, masculine world with its sweat-stained long johns and unprintable nicknames, also speak of him as "weird." He is, says Gary Weis, a barefoot young photographer whose buccaneer-length hair is tied back with a black ribbon, "a charming, strange, kind, weird man with a deep and primitive kind of insight." (The "weirdness" that both friends and enemies refer to is partly a strange intensity that seems to eat him up from the inside while he is making a film.) "He is a generous, gentle, and very angry man," says Gil Dennis. "It's a childlike anger. As a child, you're told the world is one way and you believe it. Then you grow up and it isn't that way at all and you still believe it should be and you hate the people who fooled you."

The world that Sam Peckinpah believes in has not existed during his own lifetime except for a few wilting fragments, stalks of dry wheat in a long unplowed field. ("That tent city of Coarse Gold in *Ride the High Country*, that was what the gold-mining camp Fine

Gold looked like in 1930 when I was five years old, riding down from the mountains on my father's horse.") It is a world of tin hammered on salvaged wood to make a house where there was nothing but desert in *Cable Hogue*; of a country moving into the twentieth century ("They're going to use flying machines in the war, they say," William Holden tells his gang in *The Wild Bunch*) without moving out of savagery; of old men with frayed cuffs and clean pistols selling their memories for ten cents a chance in *Ride the High Country* or not selling them, it doesn't much matter.

When he ended *The Ballad of Cable Hogue*, Peckinpah felt he had ended for a while his obsession with the moment of change when the West turned in a man's hand like a key in a lock and the horseless carriage collided with the man on horseback. The last, most beautiful evocation of that moment is in the final frame of *Cable Hogue*. A yellow motorcar and a stagecoach move together for a moment, then turn and take their separate paths across the desert.

"I can't live it," Peckinpah says. "So I remake it."

His great-grandparents came to central California in covered wagons—the Churches in 1848, the Peckinpahs in 1851. At fourteen, his grandfather, Denver S. Church, was a professional deer slayer and a tent master for the Seventh-Day Adventists. His father was born on Peckinpah Mountain. His grandmother came down from the high mountains to meet Calamity Jane.

The complexities started when they rode down from the high country into the valley. In 1917, Denver Church was one of three congressmen to vote against America's entrance into the First World War. His grandfather, father, uncle, and brother became superior court judges. The dinner-table conversation balanced between two worlds. "It was about the meaning of law and the price of cotton cake." Peckinpah describes cotton cake as "a winter food for cattle."

Sam Peckinpah's moral training was crude but effective. When he was in high school, his father forced him to sit through the trial of a seventeen-year-old boy arrested for statutory rape. At home and at military school, things were right or wrong, guilty or innocent, true or false—and so were people. The absolutes drove him crazy. "Things are always mixed. We're all guilty to some extent." His films, and his life, would become, in some part, a denial of the absolutes of his childhood.

He became a Republican in a family of Democrats (a phase which lasted "until I saw the Goldwater campaign on television"). A storyteller in a family of men who were solely concerned with truth. A year as a private on the fringes of World War II ("I was shot at in China, and it meant nothing, absolutely nothing, just a sound heard through the window of a train") was followed by Fresno State College and an M.A. in drama from the University of Southern California. He became a screenwriter with *Invasion of the Body Snatchers* in 1956. He created "The Rifleman" and "The Westerner" on television, directed half a dozen notable television plays including an adaptation of Katherine Anne Porter's *Noon Wine*. In 1962, his fifteen-year first marriage broke up after the birth of his fourth child and only son, Matthew, and he got a chance to direct a movie.

After five movies, he sat in his office, bone tired and bewildered. He is, as one friend says, "confused by this sudden recognition as a genius." He derides those who call him an intellectual. His strength as a director is both simpler and more complicated than that. His statements come from the guts of his heroes, who are obsessed in their own ways with morality, each "seeking a way to enter his house justified."

Will he make another movie as violent as *The Wild Bunch*? "Never. If I didn't say it in that one, then I'll never be able to say it." His next movie, *The Ballad of Cable Hogue*, starring Jason Robards, Stella Stevens, and David Warner, was a surprisingly gentle Western in which only two men were shot.

Ironically, he has never come very close to the death that he shows so graphically in his films. There was, of course, one fight in a Mexican bar, but he was not aware of his dangerously smashed kidney until after it had been mended. He shrugs at the thought of death. "I suspect it's inevitable. I'm not afraid of it. What I am afraid of is stupid, useless, horrible death. An automobile accident. A violent death for no purpose." For a moment the room is silent, and he leans forward wearily.

Twenty-four hours later, the office is empty except for remnants. A pair of skis and a tennis racket are left and a rosary hung across the desk lamp, but the skin-diving equipment has gone with Peckinpah to Hawaii. There are enormous photographs of Pancho Villa and Zapata and a smaller—yet more real—one of his father, taken at the end of a brilliant trial. Smaller still, there is one photograph of himself, holding the horns of the first eight-point buck he ever killed. In the photograph, his white pants are splattered with blood.

But the man in the photograph is elsewhere, twenty years and 2,500 miles away, his white beard buried in the warm sand, far, far from the high country.

PART 3

Epilogue

11 ▶

Sam Peckinpah, 1925–1984

MICHAEL SRAGOW

We are gathered here in the sight of God and all his glory to lay to rest Cable Hogue. Now, most funeral orations, Lord, lie about a man, compare him to the angels, whitewash him with a really wide brush. But you know, Lord, and I know that it is just not true. Now a man is made out of bad as well as good, all of them. Cable Hogue was born into this world—nobody knows when or where. He came stumbling out of the wilderness like a prophet of old. Out of the barren wastes he carved himself a one-man kingdom. Some said he was ruthless, but you could do worse, Lord, than to take to your bosom Cable Hogue. He wasn't really a good man, he wasn't a bad man. But, Lord, he was a man! When Cable Hogue died, there wasn't an animal in the desert he didn't know, there wasn't a star in the firmament he hadn't named, there wasn't a man he was afraid of. Now the sand he fought and loved so long has covered him at last. Now he has gone into the whole torrent of the years, of the souls that pass and never stop. In some ways he was your dim reflection, Lord; and right or wrong I feel he is worth consideration. Take him, Lord, but knowing Cable, I suggest you do not take him lightly.

—From *The Ballad of Cable Hogue* (1970)

Just as there were an unusual number of deaths in the films of Sam Peckinpah, there were also an unusual number of funerals— not only for the dead but for the living. In *The Ballad of Cable Hogue*, the hero is so curious to know what people will say of him when he's gone that he demands to hear his funeral oration while he's still

"Sam Peckinpah, 1925–1984" by Michael Sragow originally appeared in the *Boston Phoenix*, 8 January 1985, pp. 3–5, 9–10. Reprinted by permission of the *Boston Phoenix* and Michael Sragow.

177

(barely) alive. In *Convoy*, the Rubber Duck, presumed dead but hiding in a bus within earshot of his mourners, is eulogized in a comical racetrack funeral celebration by some of the same people who've hounded him to his coffin. Peckinpah believed that there were so few individualists left in this world that they deserved all the stroking they could get.

When his heroes died, it was often in circumstances too violent to permit a formal commemoration, but Peckinpah marked their passing in some of the most eloquent, piercing imagery ever committed to celluloid. I know of no more haunting sequence in all of cinema than the final ten minutes of *The Wild Bunch*. After the gang led by Pike Bishop (William Holden) is killed while annihilating a Mexican army, bounty hunters led by Pike's former partner, Deke Thornton (Robert Ryan), arrive to gather up their booty. The old rider walks over to where his friend lies fallen, pauses, and in a gesture full of significance draws Pike's pistol from its holster. Sobered by the sight of the slaughter, Thornton refuses to return to Texas with his men, instead staying on in town. He watches his pack of "gutter trash" leave, Pike's men slung like meal sacks across their saddles. The mass evacuation of the town becomes a funeral procession for the Bunch. The legend has begun. Minutes pass. Shots are heard in the faint distance. Thornton, slouched against the town gate, smiles. The bounty hunters, too, have met their fate. Even in death, Pike's Bunch are not caught; their bodies are retrieved by a former member who has taken up with Mexican freedom fighters. He invites Thornton to join him, and the two old comrades laugh, perhaps for what they consider Pike's bitter folly, or perhaps for the new bitterness of their own lives. As they ride off, the screen fills with images of the Bunch as they once were.

Peckinpah was attracted to eulogies and funerals because they permitted him, in the right old phrase, to take the full measure of a man. That's what his best movies were all about: defining heroes not by psychological profiles or sociological explanations but by the way they attacked the world. His aesthetic pioneering included the poetic use of slow motion, the use of color as a dramatic force, the extensive use of long lenses to give his frames a teeming, impacted look, and, most of all, the creation of (in William S. Pechter's words) "a profusely edited style in which, despite the shimmering mosaic effect, there's no sense of narrative fragmentation, but rather, as much as in the long-take cinema of Renoir, the sense of an integral world seen wholly and of a wealth of detail available to the uncoerced eye." Peckinpah used his techniques to see men whole, to capture their personalities in everything—from the way they drank whiskey to the way they faced death. And women, too. One indelible scene in *Ride the High Country*, of a new bride (Mariette Hartley) nearly raped by her groom's white-trash family, marked Peckinpah as the rare Western director who could sympathize with women as deeply as with men: he caught the subtlest shifts of expression crossing over Hartley's face as she grasped what the men intended. Even during the middle period of Peckinpah's career, when his lead female characters were apt to be untrustworthy minxes, he displayed an empathy that knew no sexual bounds. He gave Ida Lupino one of the fullest roles of her career as the mother in *Junior Bonner*, and there is interplay between her and her estranged husband, Ace (Robert Preston), that says more about male-female relationships (and with the slightest means) than people thought him capable of imagining. "All you are is dreams and sweet talk," says the woman. "And I sweetened the dreams as well, if you remember," says Ace. Her look hardens, despite her tears, and she slaps his face. "I sure as hell deserved that," he says. "You surely did," she replies.

The greatest lesson that Peckinpah imparted to his best students, Walter Hill (who wrote *The Getaway* and went on to direct *The Long Riders* and *48 HRS.*) and Roger Spottiswoode (who edited several Peckinpah films, including *Straw Dogs*, and went on to direct *The Pursuit of D. B. Cooper* and *Under Fire*), was that "action, if it's to work, must be rooted ruthlessly in character." In his pursuit of that goal, he galvanized some of the leading actors in the business into taking chances. "*The Wild Bunch* really started something new for me," William Holden told a *Village Voice* writer in 1971; "it was the film in which I decided not to take it anymore—to use, or try to use, my liabilities as advantages: the lines around the eyes, the beer belly." On *Major Dundee*, Peckinpah marshaled Charlton Heston through the rugged Mexican locations until he began to feel—and more importantly, to act—like a maverick cavalry officer on the run, setting his shoulders square against destiny.

Yet even more crucial to Peckinpah were his perennial supporting players (especially the late Warren Oates and Strother Martin), who seemed to embody much of his own rage and irony and sense of the absurd. They were his illiterate Greek chorus, commenting on his pilgrims' progress with the barbed glee of men who have no ambition beyond their appetites—and no sympathy for those who reach for more. That he could get these urchins to rise to humanity, and occasionally heroism, reflects the extent of his sympathetic imagination. If all his action was rooted in character, all his movies were rooted in his own. But when he said (as he did frequently) that everything he did came out of anger, he was oversimplifying. His anger came out of his reverence for the natural beauty and nobility that war or greed or simple daily commerce inevitably defiled.

Sam Peckinpah is the man who made me want to write about movies. When *The Wild Bunch* opened sixteen years ago, I saw it six times in two weeks; I can't count the number of times I've seen it since. To this day, I can't think of another film that's had such a near-hypnotic holding power. It puts you in touch with the spirit of a man who's tearing himself apart on screen, expressing whatever is in him. After seeing that film I had to write and persuade others that it isn't just an essay in violence or even a magnificent Western. It is a great original work of art.

Peckinpah was part of the first generation of directors (including John Frankenheimer, Franklin Schaffner, and Martin Ritt) who graduated from television into movies. Most of the other prominent names worked in live dramatic television, and the experience they got there was in tactical dramatics—getting the job done quickly and efficiently. Peckinpah cut his teeth writing filmed Western television shows like "Gunsmoke" before creating "The Rifleman" and then the classic "The Westerner," with Brian Keith— a series that he directed as if it were made for the movies, with a visual fluency that's rarely been paralleled on television and a feeling for atmosphere and character that heralded the emergence of an heir to Howard Hawks and John Ford. By the time he'd made his second feature, *Ride the High Country*, in 1963, he was already displaying the intuitive command over the expressive powers of filmmaking that should earn him a place in movie history not as a maker of shoot-'em-ups or thrillers but as the bravest, most gifted, and most troubling poet of the American screen.

Peckinpah was a mere thirty-six years old when he made *Ride the High Country*, yet this elegy for an aging Western lawman was so complete in its evocation of fading frontier values and so mature in its classical storytelling and firm, understated lyricism that it seemed the work of a much older man. It was as if he, like Cable Hogue, had come stumbling out of the wilderness like a prophet of old. Throughout his career, Peckinpah's ambivalence was the keynote of his art, and that ambivalence included his vision of the Old West and Old Westerners. He was torn between love for the romance of sweeping landscapes and abhorrence of the ruthless machinations of rail barons, the corruption of land and stage officers, the Puritan harshness of the religion that sustained the settlers. He knew that frontiersmen could be the most honorable and joyous of people, living life intensely, with untarnished purpose and without pretense; he also knew that they could be even more status-conscious and materialistic than their Eastern cousins, moving West only to gain wealth and respectability more quickly. The men Peckinpah celebrated held onto their pioneer idealism after it went out of fashion. In his gentler films, like *Ride the High Country, Cable Hogue,* and the contemporary *Junior Bonner,* he crystallized his ambivalence into tributes to men who refuse the "benefits" of middle-class American civilization: whether lawman Steve Judd, who's willing to take a job as a bank guard so long as he can continue to do good work and "enter my house justified"; or the desert rat, Cable, who finds a waterhole in the desert, builds it into a thriving business, and finds such love and pride along the way that he nearly forgets his revenge on the friends who left him there to die; or Ace Bonner, the ex-rodeo champ, who wants to raise sheep in Australia; or his rodeo-riding son, Junior Bonner, who has to "go down my own road." These are by no means "soft" movies; their poignance cuts right through you. Steve Judd "going it alone" to his death, staring back to the high country as he sinks to the bottom of the frame, is a mournful image so filled with love it's ennobling. Yet it isn't only the extreme moments in Peckinpah's work that are this vivid and unshakable. There's an unsentimental bittersweetness to such scenes as the one in *Junior Bonner* when Ace persuades his estranged wife to join him in one last afternoon of love before he leaves and the rickety wooden back steps of a seedy hotel become the stairway to a perishable paradise. Peckinpah was a master of the long goodbye.

And as that partial accounting suggests, throughout his career he was far more than "Bloody Sam." Still, there's no question that his films increasingly reflected the fierce, embittered temperament which emerged in his third movie, *Major Dundee.* It looked like a coup for a comparatively unknown director, who'd achieved only a succès d'estime with *Ride the High Country* (which played out on the second half of double bills), to direct an epic Civil War-era Western starring Charlton Heston as a Northern officer who's determined to punish a bloodthirsty Apache even if it means crossing the border into Mexico and using some of his Confederate prisoners as soldiers. But two days before filming started, fifteen days were cut from the shooting schedule. Studio executives

MICHAEL SRAGOW

hounded Peckinpah throughout filming, and eventually they barred him from the editing room. As Heston noted in his book, *The Actor's Life*, "Sam has a spectacular gift for making enemies, and he's already succeeded in arousing a good deal of suspicion and hostility on the part of the producer and the high Columbia brass. They suspected, accurately enough, that he was likely to prove difficult to manage."

According to Peckinpah, the final cut removed nothing less than the title character's motivation. But even in its butchered form, you can see that in *Major Dundee* he was trying to bring his ambivalence to the fore, to make a hero out of a monomaniacal son of a bitch. Perhaps it was this ambivalence that confounded the Columbia magnates who commissioned the film. *Major Dundee* is still a stirring movie, with suggestions of the glancing vignette style that was to explode in *The Wild Bunch*. There was never a public screening of Sam's version, but maybe we can guess at what the studio cut by comparing the studio's "complete" version with the version usually shown on television. Some of the most striking episodes tend to go because, however brief, they zero in on character and don't appear to advance the plot. For example, in a characteristic Peckinpah aside, Major Dundee, leaning over a parapet as he studies the expanse of Confederate prisoners, throws a cigar butt in their midst. To Dundee's sadistic pleasure, the men converge on it like jackals—until one of them calmly grinds it out with his bare heel.

Peckinpah had displayed enough incendiary ability to win another assignment, *The Cincinnati Kid*, but he was fired from that film after four days of shooting, for reasons that to this day remain obscure. The incident cost him five years out of his career. Then a television adaptation of Katherine Anne Porter's *Noon Wine* that he wrote and directed for ABC's "Stage 67" put him back on the map. "Noon Wine" was itself a major accomplishment, a harrowing critique of male pride and patriarchal bluster. And it earned him the chance to make one of the most controversial movies of all time: *The Wild Bunch*.

To discover *The Wild Bunch* in the summer of '69 was to be shocked, riveted, moved, pummeled, and finally reduced to awe. It was as if for two hours and twenty-three minutes (or two hours and fifteen minutes, if you saw the studio's cut version two weeks later) Peckinpah had managed to juggle and tap-dance over a minefield. The Western landscape beloved by directors as a "pure" canvas for morality plays has been transformed: Peckinpah's south Texas and

Mexico still have a parched visual grandeur, but they are filled with impurities. The Wild Bunch, an outlaw gang operating on both sides of the Rio Grande right before the First World War, are unrepentant thieves and killers looking for one last big score. The "law" is just as bad or worse. The bounty hunters pursuing them are ragged mercenaries working for the railroad. The Mexican overlord Mapache, who ropes the Bunch into stealing guns for his troops, is the worst of all, ravaging his country as he rules it. And society is no more responsible or cultivated than its sleazy citizenry: the south Texas civilians are unable to fight for their own interests, and the soldiers in their army (which ends up pursuing both the bounty hunters and the Bunch) are shown as peach-fuzzed bumblers. You feel that even if the Bunch were on the "right" side of the law, they would choose not to remain there, because their hunger is insatiable. The only community toward which they feel any sympathy is a group of Mexican revolutionaries fighting for freedom.

The most innocent member of the Bunch is a Mexican named Angel. It is Angel who appreciates the wild beauty of his Mexican homeland; it is Angel who serenades the children and weeps for their rape and destruction. When he steals guns for his embattled revolutionaries, he goes beyond the pagan self-interest of the Bunch. When Mapache seizes Angel, Pike and his three remaining followers redeem their entire misspent existence by avenging him. By the end of the film we see these men as heroes.

Technically, the movie is superb. The gunfights are among the most amazing action sequences ever filmed. By combining slow-motion photography with rapid cutting, Peckinpah achieved powerful physical imagery while furthering the narrative's developing tensions. When a townsman is caught in the opening battle's crossfire, he punctuates the scene by framing two young children hiding by the side of a building, their initial horror at the bloodshed turning to overwhelming fascination. The conventional wisdom says that the grisliness of these scenes makes voyeurs of us all: as the camera records its subject, a man is shot full in the face, or a throat is slit. But Peckinpah's techniques *objectify* the violence by first catching us up in its surging emotions and then impelling us to grasp the viciousness of slaughter.

In any case, *The Wild Bunch* has a power that goes beyond its technical brilliance and impassioned ambivalence. Part of this has to do with our seeing a piece of history told straight out for the first time. According to Jay Robert Nash's *Bloodletters and Bad Men*, in the last decade of their existence the real Wild Bunch "left hundreds killed, wounded, and crippled." The response of proper citizens matched the Bunch's savagery. When a sheriff killed Bunch member George L. "Flat Nose" Curry, Nash recounts, the townspeople "took out hunting knives and stripped away his flesh from his chest. One ambitious townsman made a pair of shoes from the flesh. Another swatch wound up as a good-luck charm and was carried from vest to vest through generations of outlaw *aficionados*."

Peckinpah's emotional commitment to his work prompted Dan Yergin, in a 1971 profile, to quote Saul Bellow on those people "who take on themselves to represent or interpret the old savagery, tribalism, the primal fierceness of the fierce, lest we forget prehistory, savagery, animal origins." Yet that primordialism doesn't fully encompass his power either; this director's art is more than a mere volcanic outburst. When an instinctive artist like Peckinpah works all out, he touches on eternal mysteries. He brings us such a full understanding of tragedy that we feel both purged by pity and terror and haunted by the question, "What was it all for?" *The Wild Bunch* is Peckinpah's answer.

After this milestone he made a small-scale, seriocomic companion piece, *The Ballad of Cable Hogue*, a summation of his Old West obsession, and then *Straw Dogs*, which examined the violence not in professional killers but in present-day Cornish villagers and an American mathematics professor who with his Cornish wife takes a sabbatical among them. Both these movies are acutely observed portraits of opposite sorts of men: Cable is the classical Westerner, with all the virtues celebrated by Frederick Jackson Turner: "That coarseness and strength combined with acuteness and inquisitiveness; that practical, inventive turn of mind . . . that masterful grasp of material things . . . ; that dominant individualism, working for good and for evil, and withal that buoyancy and exuberance which comes from freedom." David Sumner, on the other hand, is a portrait of the modern American male as an arrested adolescent, and the violence in *Straw Dogs* bursts from this antihero's repressed soul—and from Peckinpah's painful sense of the psychic mess in people whom marriage has horrendously entwined. Both films got their share of critical approval (indeed, reviewers relieved by *Hogue*'s gentleness gave Peckinpah his all-time-best notices), and *Straw Dogs* had some commercial success as well. But thereafter Peckinpah gradually fell into disrepute. He was blamed for all the hack imitators he inspired, and his single return to the lyrical mode, in *Junior Bonner*, went unnoticed. His continued fights with producers and studio executives fueled the harshest aspects of his own personality; he was unable to do some of his most coveted projects, even when his reputation and clout were at their height. These projects include *Play It As It Lays* (he was Joan Didion's and John Gregory Dunne's first pick to direct the project); James Gould Cozzens's *Castaway*, a story of a man trapped in a department store that encapsulates the constriction of the modern world and contemporary man's paranoid retreat from instinct; Max Evans's *The Hi-Lo Country*, which depicts the twentieth-century West in transition, and his *One-Eyed Sky*, a story of survival among an old coyote, an old cow, and an old cowboy; and William Gass's "The Pedersen Kid," a chilling poetic thriller about a search for a killer through a Midwestern blizzard, and a story known for its "visual purity."

Typecast as an action director and prevented from realizing his richest action dreams, Peckinpah had to try to pull off magic acts on limited or substandard material. The alchemy never again worked on the scale of *The Wild Bunch*. Too often, his ordered visions of chaos degenerated into chaos themselves. But if we didn't have those earlier films to measure against the later ones, movies like *The Killer Elite* might have been hailed by cultural avatars other than Pauline Kael as the creation of an archetypal auteur working his vision into every available nook and cranny of a crude or trashy script. Indeed, with the exception of the studio-mutilated *Pat Garrett and Billy the Kid* (brilliantly explicated by Paul Seydor in *Peckinpah: The Western Films*) and Peckinpah's craziest private fantasy, *Bring Me the Head of Alfredo Garcia* (which also has its defenders, notably Mark Crispin Miller), I can't think of a single Peckinpah film I couldn't see again and again just to revel in the moviemaking. The opening credit sequence of *The Getaway* expresses more of the tension of penitentiary life than *Brubaker* and *On the Yard* put together; it makes you wish that Peckinpah had been picked to direct *The Executioner's Song*. The section of *Cross of Iron* in which the sergeant recuperates in a hospital and keeps seeing his own men in place of the patients says more about the insidious residue of war than any tame pacifist statement. And in *The Killer Elite* and the more unjustly maligned *Convoy*, Peckinpah managed to create glorious hybrids. As Kael was the first to note, in *The Killer Elite* he expanded his hatred for corporate Hollywood into a condemnation of the white-collar viciousness that dominates most business today; he came up with the *Goodbye to All That* of espionage films. And in *Convoy*, Peckinpah turned a trucking movie into a comic ode to American individualism. He transformed trucks and drivers into mammoth dinosaurs who've lived beyond their eons and have somehow resurfaced in the American Southwest. Here the desert is like a blank slate that people of huge appetite can write their names on and make their own.

Convoy made money in 1978, but its production was the scene of so many bitter fights, the industry reaction to it was so dismissive, and the reviews were so pitying or scathing, that it looked as if Peckinpah would never work again. He tried, in vain to form a production company in Mexico; he had a heart attack; he wrote a script from Elmore Leonard's *City Primeval*, and another based on a John Milius original, *The Texans*, which was an update of one of his favorite Westerns, *Red River*. But the only projects he could have launched were, he said, filled with the sort of *gratuitous* violence he detested. One of his old mentors, Don Siegel, put him back in business by having him work second unit on *Jinxed*. Then came the offer to direct a Robert Ludlum thriller, *The Osterman Weekend*. Although Peckinpah hated the book, he thought the Alan Sharp script was at least a minor improvement. Most of all, he felt he had to reestablish himself as a working director. So he took the job. And even though he was prevented from reshaping the script as he desired, even though he was barred from the final cut, he did remarkable things with the material.

When a man I know first got cable television, he signed on for the Playboy Channel; when his wife canceled it, he continued to turn to the station anyway, trying to make out the nude bodies through the squiggly lines. When he saw *The Osterman Weekend*, he told me it reminded him of this viewing habit. I think he got Peckinpah's point. For even though *The Osterman Weekend* had a convoluted espionage plot, Peckinpah turned it into a horrific black-comic jeremiad against the everyday pornography of a global village flattened out by the media. This combination of *The Big Chill*, *The Killer Elite*, and *Straw Dogs*, about a reunion of upper-middle-class friends that turns into a terrorist *Walpurgisnacht*, is punctuated by dozens of video monitors. Peckinpah's television sets leer and smirk the way his eighteen-wheelers brawl and dance in *Convoy*. Seizing on what could have been just another gimmick in Alan Sharp's script—that every dubious government manipulation can be given credence by television—Peckinpah sharpened Ludlum's pulp to a derisive, satirical edge, and with the help of his craftsmen and performers, he conjured up a creepy, nightmarish aura. *The Osterman Weekend* isn't *Touch of Evil*—with Peckinpah handcuffed to Ludlum's material, how could it be? But after a dreadful opening fifteen minutes, he dispensed with the plot and brought the film to vital, lunatic life. The movie is an intriguing collection of kinky bits of carnage, dank visual coups (with John Coquillon shooting in a "rum-to-cocoa" palette), and daring actors' turns (notably by John Hurt, Helen Shaver, and Craig T. Nelson). And when, in the penultimate shot, we see a pet dog gagged and chained, this visual sick joke registers as Peckinpah's signature on the movie. Even his muffled bark is stronger than most directors' bites.

Although Peckinpah deliberately made a hash of the narrative, *The Osterman Weekend* was his most successful attempt at creating a sort of Halloween satire. He said he was attempting the same thing in *The Getaway* and *The Killer Elite*, but in the event his ferocious emotionality kept exploding his parodistic "cool." In *The Osterman Weekend*, the glares of the television sets seem to coat the action in a membrane, providing Peckinpah with the Brechtian distance that he often had to struggle to attain.

His last work was for television; with it, his career came full circle. I've seen only the first of his two collaborations with Julian Lennon, yet it must rank as one of the simplest and most subtle rock videos ever made. It shows a man alone in a recording studio, singing a melancholy song, with only one other person in view—probably a producer—watching him obsessively, maybe worriedly, behind a glass booth. This is one producer who lets the song go on, who doesn't hype it up or obscure its lyricism. Lennon looks at his own reflection, presses on the piano keys, stops and paces, and returns, while the camera shifts discreetly, sometimes retreating. Like all of Peckinpah's work, this video speaks of the loneliness, the passion, the desperation—and ultimately the salvation—of artistic creation.

If, unlike Cable Hogue's eulogist, I've emphasized the man's heroic qualities rather than his feral, self-destructive ones, maybe that's because they were all so intertwined; if he partly provoked his fights and made his own power plays, he channeled all the energies he aroused into his work. The one extended correspondence I had with Peckinpah came in 1974, after I panned *Bring Me the Head of Alfredo Garcia* in *New York Magazine* while Judith Crist was on summer vacation. I received the following letter:

"Dear Michael Sragow: Thank you very much for your review, particularly the mention of *Straw Dogs*, because you captured the essence of that picture. Where did you read it? You are doing a magnificent job filling Judith Christ's [*sic*] boots. What else do you fill? If you consider it necessary to reply to this letter please reply to James Aubrey or Doug Netter somewhere in Nevada. Yours sincerely, Sam Peckinpah." I wrote back to Sam care of his production company, saying simply, "When you make good movies, I back them," and enclosing my reviews of *The Wild Bunch* and *The Ballad of Cable Hogue*. I received the following reply: "Dear Mr. Sragow: I can be wrong. That is my saving grace, I was reaching maybe too far with *Alfredo*. But if you don't reach, how do you learn? I'd like to do better, I don't know if I can. Kindest regards, Sam Peckinpah."

Appendix
Selected Bibliography

Appendix

The Wild Bunch Credits

DIRECTION: Sam Peckinpah
SCREENPLAY: Walon Green, Sam Peckinpah, based on a story by
Walon Green, Roy N. Sickner
CINEMATOGRAPHY: Lucien Ballard
EDITING: Louis Lombardo
ASSOCIATE EDITOR: Robert L. Wolfe
MUSIC: Jerry Fielding
MUSIC SUPERVISION: Sonny Burke
SOUND: Robert J. Miller
ART DIRECTION: Edward Carrere
SPECIAL EFFECTS: Bud Hulburd
MAKEUP: Al Greenway
WARDROBE: Gordon Dawson
SCRIPT SUPERVISION: Crayton Smith
SECOND UNIT DIRECTION: Buzz Henry
ASSISTANT DIRECTORS: Cliff Coleman, Fred Gammon
PRODUCTION MANAGER: William Faralla
ASSOCIATE PRODUCER: Roy N. Sickner
PRODUCER: Phil Feldman
RELEASED BY: Warner Bros.-Seven Arts
YEAR OF RELEASE: 1969
RUNNING TIME: 145 minutes (European version), 143 minutes
(original domestic version), 135 minutes (final
domestic version)
CAST: William Holden (Pike Bishop), Ernest Borgnine (Dutch
Engstrom), Robert Ryan (Deke Thornton), Edmond O'Brien
(Freddy Sykes), Warren Oates (Lyle Gorch), Jaime Sanchez
(Angel), Ben Johnson (Tector Gorch), Emilio Fernandez
(Mapache), Strother Martin (Coffer), L. Q. Jones (T. C.),
Albert Dekker (Harrigan), Bo Hopkins (Crazy Lee), Dub
Taylor (Wainscoat), Jorge Russek (Zamorra), Alfonso Arau
(Herrera), Chano Urueta (Don José), Sonia Amelio (Teresa),
Aurora Clavel (Aurora), Elsa Cardenas (Elsa), Fernando
Wagner (German army officer), Paul Harper (Ross), Bill Hart

(Jess), Rayford Barnes (Buck), Steve Ferry (Sergeant McHale), Enrique Lucero (Ignacio), Elizabeth Dupeyron (Rocio), Yolande Ponce (Yolo), José Chavez (Juan José), Rene Dupeyron (Juan), Pedro Galvan (Benson), Graciela Doring (Emma), Major Perez (Perez), Fernando Wagner (Mohr), Jorge Rado (Ernst), Ivan Scott (paymaster), Sra. Madero (Margaret), Margarito Luna (Luna), Chalo Gonzalez (Gonzalez), Lilia Castillo (Lilia), Elizabeth Unda (Carmen), Julio Corona (Julio), Matthew Peckinpah (child in Starbuck)

Selected Bibliography

The reader should note that this bibliography does not include works that appear in this casebook.

Armes, Roy. "Peckinpah and the Changing West." *London Magazine* 9 (March 1970): pp. 101–6.

Blevins, Winfred. "The Artistic Vision of Director Sam Peckinpah." *Show* 2, no. 1 (March 1972): pp. 37–40.

Blum, William. "Toward a Cinema of Cruelty." *Cinema Journal* 10, no. 2 (Spring 1970): pp. 19–33.

Brown, Kenneth. Review of *The Wild Bunch*. *Cineaste* 3, no. 3 (Winter 1969–70): pp. 18–20, 28.

Butler, Terence. *Crucified Heroes: The Films of Sam Peckinpah*. London: Gordon Fraser, 1979.

Canby, Vincent. Response to letter by Tracy Hotchner. *New York Times*, 20 July 1969, sec. D, p. 21.

———. Review of *The Wild Bunch*. *New York Times*, 26 June 1969, p. 45.

———. "Which Version Did *You* See?" *New York Times*, 20 July 1969, sec. D., pp. 1, 7.

Cook, David A. "*The Wild Bunch* Fifteen Years After." *North Dakota Quarterly* 51, no. 3 (Summer 1983): pp 123–30.

Cutts, John. "Shoot! Sam Peckinpah Talks to John Cutts." *Films and Filmmaking* 16, no. 1 (October 1969): pp. 4–8.

DeNotto, Dennis. *Film: Form and Feeling*. New York: Harper and Row, 1985.

Desser, David. *The Samurai Films of Akira Kurosawa*. Ann Arbor: UMI Research Press, 1983.

Galperin, William. "History into Allegory: *The Wild Bunch* as Vietnam Movie." *Western Humanities Review* (Spring 1985): pp. 1–19.

Gilliatt, Penelope. Review of *The Wild Bunch*. *The New Yorker*, 5 July 1969, p. 74.

Hedges, Charles. *Film: Magazine of the British Federation of Film Societies* (Autumn 1969): pp. 31–32.

Humphries, Reynold. "The Function of Mexico in Peckinpah's Films." *Jump Cut*, no. 18 (August 1978): pp. 17–20.

Kauffmann, Stanley. "*The Wild Bunch*." *New Republic*, 19 July 1969, pp. 24 and 35; reprinted in *Figures of Light*. New York: Harper and Row, 1971.

SELECTED BIBLIOGRAPHY

Knight, Arthur. Review of *The Wild Bunch*. *Saturday Review*, 5 July 1969, p. 21.

McCarty, John. "Sam Peckinpah and *The Wild Bunch*." *Film Heritage* 5, no. 2 (Winter 1969–70): pp. 1–10, 32.

McKinney, Doug. *Sam Peckinpah*. Boston: Twayne Publishers, 1979.

Miller, Mark Crispin. "In Defense of Sam Peckinpah." *Film Quarterly* 28, no. 3 (Spring 1975): pp. 2–17.

Milne, Tom. Review of *The Wild Bunch*. *Sight and Sound* 38, no. 4 (Autumn 1969): pp. 208–9.

Morgenstern, Joseph. Review of *The Wild Bunch*. *Newsweek*, 14 July 1969, p. 85.

Pechter, William. "Anti-Western." In *24 Times a Second*. New York: Harper and Row, 1971.

"Peckinpah Hits 'Butchery.'" *Variety*, 4 March 1970, pp. 5, 26.

Pettit, Arthur. *Images of the Mexican American in Fiction and Film*. College Station: Texas A&M University Press, 1980.

————. "Nightmare and Nostalgia: The Cinema West of Sam Peckinpah." *Western Humanities Review* 29 (Spring 1975): pp. 105–22.

————. "The Polluted Garden: Sam Peckinpah's Double Vision of Mexico." *Southwest Review* (Summer 1977): pp. 280–94.

Pilkington, William, and Don Graham, eds. *Western Movies*. Albuquerque: University of New Mexico Press, 1979.

"Press Violent about Film's Violence; Prod. Sam Peckinpah Following 'Bunch,'" *Variety*, 2 July 1969, p. 15.

"Sam Peckinpah Lets It All Hang Out." *Take One* 2, no. 3 (January–February 1969): pp. 18–20.

Sarris, Andrew. Review of *The Wild Bunch*. *The Village Voice*, 31 July 1969, p. 39.

Schickel, Richard. "Mastery of the 'Dirty Western.'" *Film 69/70: An Anthology by the National Society of Film Critics*. Edited by Joseph Morgenstern and Stefan Kanfer. New York: Simon and Schuster, 1970.

Shaffer, Lawrence. "*The Wild Bunch* versus *Straw Dogs*." *Sight and Sound* 41, no. 3 (Summer 1972): pp. 132–33.

Simmons, Garner. *Peckinpah: A Portrait in Montage*. Austin: University of Texas Press, 1982.

Simon, John. "Violent Idyll." In *Movies into Film*. New York: Dial Press, 1971.

Solomon, Stanley J. *Beyond Formula: American Film Genres*. New York: Harcourt Brace Jovanovich, 1976.

Sragow, Michael. "*The Wild Bunch*." *Film Society Review* 5, no. 3 (November 1969): pp 31–37.

Sturham, Lawrence. "It's a Long Way from Your Heart and on the Wrong Side . . . " *North American Review* 260 (Spring 1975): pp. 74–80.

Time. Review of *The Wild Bunch*. 20 June 1969, pp. 85, 87.
Whitehall, Richard. "Talking with Peckinpah." *Sight and Sound* 38,
no. 4 (Autumn 1969): pp. 172–75.
Wright, Will. *Sixguns and Society*. Berkeley: University of California
Press, 1975.

A Ph.D. in English from the University of Minnesota, Michael Bliss teaches English and film at Virginia Polytechnic Institute and State University. His previous books include *Brian De Palma*, *Martin Scorsese and Michael Cimino*, and, from Southern Illinois University Press, *Justified Lives: Morality and Narrative in the Films of Sam Peckinpah*. Bliss's updated study of the films of Martin Scorsese, *The Word Made Flesh*, will be published in 1995. Having just coauthored *What Goes Around Comes Around: The Films of Jonathan Demme*, which is forthcoming from Southern Illinois University Press, Bliss is now writing a book about the work of director Peter Weir.